MW00527108

"We have waited too long for exactly this without question, the most profound litu century. Yet, though his writings are en. general, up to this point they have been seriously engaged almost exclusively by fellow members of his Orthodox tradition and by members of one of the other 'higher' liturgical traditions. Here, at last, we have a truly ecumenical engagement with Schmemann's thought. Top scholars from a variety of ecclesiastical traditions offer illuminating interpretations of Schmemann's texts, subject his thought to critique when that seems relevant, and then use his ideas in their own theological reflections on liturgy. Altogether, a superb contribution to the cause of liturgical theology."

—Nicholas Wolterstorff, Yale University

"In this collection, Orthodox, Catholic, Anglican, Methodist, Reformed, and Evangelical essayists consider the life, work, and thought of Alexander Schmemann, whose contributions to sacramental theology, liturgical and pastoral reflection, and ecumenical engagement remain pertinent today. Readers familiar with Fr. Alexander will find here new interpretations by authors of different generations, while those not yet acquainted will come to understand the Orthodox theologian's connections between theology, liturgy, life, Church, and world."

—Karen B. Westerfield Tucker, Boston University

"Porter Taylor assembles an expansive ecumenical group of authors, often from unexpected corners of Christianity, to connect, challenge, and extend Schmemann's work into encounters with new research and questions. What better way to honor such a foundational figure in the field of liturgical theology?"

—Lizette Larson-Miller, Huron University

"For over fifty years, serious students of Christian worship have been stirred by the writings of the late Orthodox theologian Alexander Schmemann. This volume of equally outstanding essays not only pays tribute to his intellectual legacy, but also advances exciting new lines of inquiry for the next generation of ecumenical liturgical theologians who seek to follow in his footsteps."

—Melanie C. Ross, Yale Divinity School

"*We Give Our Thanks Unto Thee,* edited by Porter C. Taylor, brings together essays that honor Fr. Alexander Schmemann, both with its title, most apt for a eucharistic man, but also by means of its rich content. Roman Catholic, Reformed, Anglican, various evangelicals, and, of course, Orthodox join in offering perspectives by which we can better appreciate the light that continues to radiate to diverse places from this remarkable thinker and pastor, since his falling asleep in the Lord thirty-five years ago. The essays vary from a practical supplying of historical details for the purposes of contextualization, to an appreciative engagement with bracing points of disagreement, to a demonstration of how Fr. Alexander's sacramental understanding may become a means of transformation in surprising places. In all this, the joy and grand vision of Fr. Alexander emerges, encouraging readers to re-read his most well-known book, and to go beyond to those writings that are more demanding!"

—**Edith M. Humphrey**, Pittsburgh Theological Seminary

We Give Our Thanks Unto Thee

We Give Our Thanks Unto Thee

Essays in Memory of Fr. Alexander Schmemann

Edited by
PORTER C. TAYLOR

Foreword by
SERGE SCHMEMANN

PICKWICK *Publications* · Eugene, Oregon

WE GIVE OUR THANKS UNTO THEE
Essays In Honor of Fr. Alexander Schmemann

Copyright © 2019 Wipf and Stock Publishers. All rights reserved. Except for brief quotations in critical publications or reviews, no part of this book may be reproduced in any manner without prior written permission from the publisher. Write: Permissions, Wipf and Stock Publishers, 199 W. 8th Ave., Suite 3, Eugene, OR 97401.

Pickwick Publications
An Imprint of Wipf and Stock Publishers
199 W. 8th Ave., Suite 3
Eugene, OR 97401

www.wipfandstock.com

PAPERBACK ISBN: 978-1-5326-3270-9
HARDCOVER ISBN: 978-1-5326-3272-3
EBOOK ISBN: 978-1-5326-3271-6

Cataloguing-in-Publication data:

Names: Taylor, Porter C., editor. | Schmemann, Serge, foreword.

Title: We give our thanks unto thee : essays in honor of Fr. Alexander Schmemann / edited by Porter C.v Taylor; foreword by Serge Schmemann.

Description: Eugene, OR: Pickwick Publications, 2019 | Includes bibliographical references.

Identifiers: ISBN 978-1-5326-3270-9 (paperback) | ISBN 978-1-5326-3272-3 (hardcover) | ISBN 978-1-5326-3271-6 (ebook)

Subjects: LCSH: Schmeman, Aleksandr, 1921–1983. | Liturgics. | Ecumenism. | Sacraments.

Classification: LCC BX350 W35 2019 (print) | LCC BX350 (ebook)

Manufactured in the U.S.A.   04/12/19

The contributors give this volume in loving and grateful memory of Father Alexander Schmemann, without whom much of our work would not be possible.

This book is also dedicated to those readers who are engaging with liturgical theology for the very first time. We hope that Fr. Alexander will be as powerful a guide for you as he has been for each of us.

Contents

Contributors

Kimberly Belcher, Assistant Professor, Notre Dame, IN.

David W. Fagerberg, Professor, Notre Dame, IN.

Steve Guthrie, Professor, Belmont University, Nashville, TN.

Todd E. Johnson, William K. and Delores S. Brehm Associate Professor of Worship, Theology, and the Arts, Fuller Theological Seminary, Pasadena, CA.

Paul Meyendorff, Editor, *St. Vladimir's Theological Quarterly*, St. Vladimir's Orthodox Theological Seminary, Yonkers, NY.

William C. Mills, Rector, Nativity of the Holy Virgin Orthodox Church, Charlotte, NC.

Bruce T. Morrill, SJ, Edward A. Malloy Professor of Roman Catholic Studies, Vanderbilt University, Nashville, TN.

Timothy P. O'Malley, Director of Education; Academic Director, Notre Dame Center for Liturgy; Editor, Church Life Journal, Notre Dame, IN.

Don E. Saliers, Theologian-in-Residence, Candler School of Theology, Atlanta, GA.

Eugene R. Schlesinger, Lecturer, Santa Clara University, Santa Clara, CA.

Porter C. Taylor, PhD student, University of Aberdeen, Scotland.

Dwight W. Vogel, Professor *emeritus*, Garrett-Evangelical Theological Seminary, Evanston, IL.

John D. Witvliet, Director & Professor of Worship, Theology, and Congregational and Ministry Studies, Calvin College, Grand Rapids, MI.

Joyce Ann Zimmerman, CPPS, Director, Institute for Liturgical Ministry, Dayton, OH.

Presenters of the Father Alexander Schmemann Memorial Lectures[1]

1984 Father Boris Bobrinskoy
The Holy Spirit in the Thought of the Cappadocian Fathers

1985 Metropolitan George (Khodr)
St. Basil the Great as Bishop and Pastor

1986 Sir Dimitri Obolensky
The Cyrillo-Methodian Mission: Scriptural Foundations

1987 Professor Nicolas V. Lossky
Traces of Orthodoxy in the West after the Schism

1988 Father Aidan Kavanaugh
Confirmation: From Missa to Chrismation

1989 Father Sergei Hackel
The Orthodox Church of Russia in the Millennium Year

1990 Metropolitan Theodosius (Lazor)
Canonical Unity in America

1991 Professor Dimitry Pospielovsky
Orthodox Christianity and the Crisis in Soviet Society

1992 Father Thomas Julian Talley
Memory and Hope in the Eucharistic Prayer

---

1. This list was compiled with the help of Fr. Chad Hatfield and it can be accessed online as well: https://www.svots.edu/presenters-father-alexander-schmemann-memorial-lecture

2007 Father Paul Lazor
Father Alexander Schmemann: A Personal Memoir

2008 Bishop Basil (Essey)
Father Schmemann as Teacher and Liturgist

2009 Archimandrite Robert F. Taft, SJ
The Liturgical Enterprise Twenty-five Years after Alexander
Schmemann (1921–1983): The Man and His Heritage

2010 Rowan Williams, 104th Archbishop of Canterbury
Theology and Contemplative Calling: The Image of Humanity
in the Philokalia

2011 Metropolitan Hilarion (Alfeyev)
The Meaning of "Icon" in the Orthodox Church

2012 Margaret Barker
Our Great High Priest: The Church as the New Temple

2013 Professor Peter Brown
Constantine, Eusebius, and the Future of Christianity

2014 Father John McGuckin
On the Mystical Theology of the Eastern Church

2015 Bishop Nicholas (Ozone)
The Life and Ministry of St. Raphael of Brooklyn

2016 Father Deacon John Chryssavgis
Toward the Great and Holy Council: Retrieving a Culture
of Conciliarity and Consensus

2017 Professor Lewis Patsavos
Reflections of a Canonist: Account of a Teaching Ministry
Spanning Four Decades

2018 Associate Professor Scott Kenworthy
St. Tikhon of Moscow (1865–1925) and the Orthodox Church
in North America and Revolutionary Russia

2019 Professor David W. Fagerberg
The Anchor of Schmemann's Liturgical Theology

Books by Alexander Schmemann

Celebration of Faith, Volume I: I Believe

Celebration of Faith, Volume II: The Church Year

Celebration of Faith, Volume III: The Virgin Mary

Church, World, Mission

The Eucharist—Sacrament of the Kingdom

For The Life of the World

Great Lent

The Historical Road of Eastern Orthodoxy

Introduction to Liturgical Theology

The Journals of Father Alexander Schmemann

Liturgy and Life

The Liturgy of Death

Liturgy and Tradition (edited by Thomas Fisch)

O Death, Where is Thy Sting?

Of Water and the Spirit

Our Father

Ultimate Questions

Foreword

Serge Schmemann

When I first learned from Father Porter Taylor about the project for this book, I was glad. I am not a theologian, but my father continues to play a major part in my own life thirty-five years after his death, and I never cease to be amazed and elated at the continuing impact of his life and work on so many different people and in so many different ways. I, too, often find my eyes opened in new ways in conversation with people who have been touched by Father Alexander. The scholars from different traditions gathered in this volume offer new perspectives and a new affirmation of the truth of his vision and work.

That is good not only for the spirit of ecumenism it reflects, though of course that too, but also because Father Alexander's life and faith were manifested in an engagement with the world, with life as a wondrous gift to be joyously embraced and cherished, and with the Eucharist as the ultimate act of thanksgiving. The last words of his last sermon were, "Lord, it is good to be here!" "Here" was in the many places I so vividly remember him: in the parishes he visited in every corner of the country; in Harlem, stopping to talk to an African-American on his way to the train station; in the Norman chapel of the Episcopalian school I attended, which was always his first stop; on the streets of New York, relishing a hot dog from a steaming street cart. And "here" was the Eucharist, for which and through which he was forever giving thanks.

For Father Alexander, Orthodoxy was never ethnic identity, though he was deeply committed to assisting Russians in their suffering through weekly radio broadcasts; theology was never a "science," though he dedicated much of his life to study and teaching; his faith was never a catalogue of rules or proscriptions, though he was a stern disciplinarian in his priestly duties. There were no contradictions here; there was a rejection of "reductions," a word he used often and always in sadness. It grieved him when the liturgy was reduced to an ethnic duty, when "religion" was reduced to the opposite of "life," and when life was turned into the opposite of the Kingdom. The Church, the faith, and the liturgy were his life, a life he celebrated to the last minute. I was there with him when he received his last Communion, suddenly emerging from apparent oblivion to loudly proclaim, "Amen, Amen, Amen."

He shared his vision not only from the pulpit, but also from the lectern. As a graduate student at Columbia University, I took my father's course on "Religious Themes in Russian Literature." Father Alexander ardently devoured literature and poetry—Russian, French, and English— and the course consisted of reading and discussing his favorite Russian works. "But where are the religious themes?" a student asked. My father was incredulous: Literary genius is a divine gift, a miracle; it is by definition religious. So it was with the most trivial of daily pursuits. Up by the lake in Quebec where we spent our summers and where the chapel became the center of a sizeable community, the daily walk became a noble ritual, and our full cycle of church services included an annual procession to the lake to bless the waters.

It was wonderful to have had him as father, priest, teacher, and friend, and it is wonderful to see on these pages that his life and work continue to bear fruit.

Serge Schmemann

February 2018

Acknowledgments

WRITING THESE ACKNOWLEDGMENTS HAS been the hardest part of this project for me. I find it hard to put into words the depth of gratitude I feel to each of these people, but this is my whole-hearted attempt to do so.

To each of the contributors in this volume, "Thank you" feels insufficient. Your books have lined my bookshelves for years and your thoughts have helped to shape my own as a novice in our field. You took a chance on me when you signed up to participate in this volume, and provided not only remarkable essays, but invaluable advice, support, and guidance to me personally. Working with each of you has been a joy and a privilege. To your family, friends, and colleagues who provide you daily inspiration and encouragement, I extend my thanks. I know without them you could not do the work that you do.

While each of the contributors has been shaped by the work of Father Alexander Schmemann, one person knew him in a way none of us ever could: as a son. Serge Schmemann, thank you for your support and involvement in this volume. Your father's work has shaped the foundation of my theological work, and while I did not meet him, "meeting" you through this work has been an honor. I hope one day to meet you in person and share a meal.

To the whole team at Pickwick, thank you for providing a home for this project, especially to our editor, Chris Spinks. From our first conversation to publication, thank you for your support. Thank you also to Matthew Wimer, Joshua Little, and James Stock whose inboxes and voicemails have been flooded by this first-timer.

It was during a directed study of the Eucharist during my studies at Fuller Theological Seminary that I first encountered Schmemann. Mike McNichols, your guidance and leadership during that course changed the trajectory of my life and career, and I am forever grateful to you.

xvii

Andrew Eaker, thank you for responding to a random message from your childhood friend's husband and graciously making the introduction that started this whole process.

Thank you to Bruce Morrill for being the first contributor on board with this project. You gave me permission to use your name when inviting other contributors and I believe it was due to your participation that the ball started rolling. I have been blessed by your insight every time I have asked you a question about academia, publishing, liturgical theology, but more blessed by your friendship over the last several years.

It was not until I became a parent that I was able to fully appreciate that role. Mom, you gave me a love of books, and Dad, you gave me a love of theology and waking up before the sun, which is when this volume was edited. Please consider this book a result of your "encouragement" to try harder in school. I may have delayed listening for two decades, but I finally did.

I have been fortunate to work under two doctoral supervisors who have been supportive of this venture. Chris Brittain and Tom Greggs, thank you for reading my essays, encouraging me in my craft, sharpening my ability to communicate effectively, and for providing me the space to see this through to completion. Tom, a special thanks to you for understanding when my material due to you was late (on more than one occasion) because of this project.

Kevin, thank you for helping me "right size" my problems, encouraging me to do the next right thing, and being there for me when I don't. You help me live life one day at a time. I'll call you tonight and I might even remember to ask how you are.

To Church of the Apostles, Kansas City, your loving support and genuine interest in my work has meant the world to me. I wish I could thank each of you by name here, but since I cannot, let me say this: thank you for being family. I'll see you on Sunday.

Cynthia and Ellis, there are countless jokes about in-laws but none of them apply to you. Thank you for your love, your patience, your friendship, and for showing me what authentic leadership looks like. You are an example of the "feet-on-the-ground" work that makes academic work have meaning. You have taught me more than you know.

To my sons, Jet, Case, and Ellis: being your father is one of the greatest joys of my life. Thank you for the mornings you slept long enough to let me work on this book, but thank you especially for the mornings you woke up early. Those are the mornings that writing didn't happen, but story books were read and block towers were built, and memories were made. Those are the mornings that really matter. I love you.

Finally, to my wife, Rebecca. Truly, this volume would not exist without you and the love and support you have always given me. The beautiful life we have built together continues to be my single greatest joy and honor. Thank you for being my courage, confidant, and companion, for teaching me what it means to be and to belong, and for being the embodiment of unrelenting and unconditional love. Of all that I have ever done or accomplished, I am most proud of being your husband. I love you!

Introduction

PORTER C. TAYLOR

THOUGH A HOUSEHOLD NAME within Orthodoxy in America and abroad, Father Alexander Schmemann represents more of a cult figure within Protestant evangelicalism as more liturgically and sacramentally minded readers "discover" the richness and robust nature of his works. My own story is hardly different from the countless others I've heard: during a Directed Study on the Eucharist at Fuller Theological Seminary, I read *The Eucharist—Sacrament of the Kingdom* and realized that there was an entire stream of Christian thought of which I had largely been unaware. Father Alexander was not only my gateway into that stream but also continues to serve as my guide and mentor along the journey. Fr. Alexander's legacy has been celebrated most concretely in Orthodox and "higher" liturgical traditions over the last thirty years but little has been done from a truly ecumenical standpoint. Most academic interactions with Schmemann fail to move past the connection he shared with others based on their tradition (e.g., symposiums held by St. Vladimir's and St. Sergius's in Paris) or based on a shared view of the liturgy (see Fagerberg, Kavanagh, Lathrop, etc.). The majority of books engaging Schmemann as a meaningful interlocutor also adhere to this basic principle. The true gift of his legacy, though, is that his teaching and influence, his life and work, and his commitment to the Kingdom of God as understood and revealed through the liturgy crosses all denominational borders and distinctions. Fr. Alexander was thoroughly Orthodox—this was his context, the soil he inhabited, and the air he breathed—but his message was and continues to be meaningful and poignantly relevant for the entire Church catholic.

Fr. Alexander, as he is so lovingly remembered by many Orthodox faithful, was so young when he died (memory eternal) that a *festchriften* was never written in his honor. Similarly, although some of his work has been published posthumously (*The Eucharist, The Liturgy of Death, Journals*, etc.), a comprehensive volume interacting with and celebrating his legacy has not. This book is ultimately an exploration of the far-reaching and long-lasting effects which Schmemann's writing and teaching continue to enjoy some thirty-five years after his death. Written from an ecumenical standpoint by a variety of top scholars from varying liturgical and ecclesiastical traditions, this book represents a unified examination of liturgical theology's most prominent figure.

I began making inquiries with potential contributors and was blessed along the way to hear of Schmemann's vast and lasting influence in the lives and work of these scholars. Some in this volume—like Bruce Morrill and David Fagerberg—have worked extensively with Schmemann, and this volume provided an opportunity for them to return to his life and work anew. Others, such as Don Saliers, were able to provide first person accounts of liturgical theology and studies in the immediate wake of Fr. Alexander, thereby providing a link between his life and his work. The essays contained in this volume represent every corner of the Christian Church and demonstrate the far-reaching effects of Schmemann's thought and teaching.

My simple hope is to help introduce evangelicals and low-liturgical Christians to the riches of liturgical theology and liturgical worship through the lens of Schmemann. One need not join the Orthodox (or Catholic, Anglican, or Lutheran) Church to do so—though you are certainly welcome to do just that! More than anything else, Schmemann provides a way of understanding and living the liturgy that takes Sunday worship from being an experience disconnected from every other part of life.

The goal for this volume is rather simple: to explore Fr. Alexander's work and to continue interacting with him as an ever-important interlocutor, even fifty-five years after the publication of *Introduction of Liturgical Theology*. The volume has been arranged according to four main subcategories: (1) Schmemann in Context, (2) Schmemann and Ecumenism, (3) Schmemann and Liturgical Theology, and (4) Schmemann and Sacraments. In what follows, you will find brief descriptions of each section and chapter. I have resisted the impulse to provide meaningful background information about Fr. Schmemann in this introduction because Mills, Meyendorff, and, to some degree, Schlesinger do this within their own essays.

Schmemann in Context. Two Orthodox scholars have contributed biographical essays to the volume, both of which were first published elsewhere. Fr. William Mills's essay provides the necessary and important historical background to Schmemann's most popular book, *For the Life of the World*. Mills recounts the invitation offered to Schmemann to teach at the 19th Ecumenical Student Conference on Christian World Mission in Athens, Ohio, providing insight into the letters between Schmemann and the conference organizers. Using *FTLOW* as the center-piece, he paints a comprehensive picture, portraying Schmemann's overall concerns and goals and the effect his teaching had on the lives of many gathered (and even more since then). *FTLOW* is frequently touted as Schmemann's most significant book among evangelicals, and this biographical essay will help readers understand the man behind the book even further.

Paul Meyendorff is especially familiar with Fr. Schmemann's work as he was the Alexander Schmemann Professor of Liturgical Theology at St. Vladimir's Orthodox Theological Seminary for twenty-nine years. Additionally, Meyendorff knew Fr. Schmemann, while his own father, Fr. John Meyendorff, was a central figure on staff at St. Vladimir's. Meyendorff has allowed us to reprint the essay he wrote in 2008 commemorating Schmemann's legacy in America. In particular, he outlines the influence Schmemann had in normalizing baptism and Eucharist among the Orthodox in the nascent Orthodox Church in America (OCA).

The final essay in this section was written by Eugene Schlesinger of Santa Clara University on a subject that, prior to his contribution, desperately required attention. Schlesinger explores the connection between Schmemann and *ressourcement*—especially given his connection to the French theologians in the 1940's and 1950's—in order to suggest that (a) a close relationship between liturgical theology and *ressourcement* is both possible and fruitful and (b) that Schmemann's critics need not throw the baby out with the bathwater. That is, Schmemann's historical inaccuracies or deficiencies ought not to negate his work but should be seen through the lens of new data and discoveries after his own research. Schmemann, according to Schlesinger, is still a valuable interlocutor and provides a meaningful link with the modern desire to "return to the Fathers."

Schmemann and Ecumenism. This section captures the ecumenical influence of Schmemann most concretely. While Todd Johnson's essay is formally on liturgical theology, it is the interaction of liturgical theology and free church worship which is foundational to the essay's claims. Three leading scholars—one Reformed, one Free, and one Methodist—combine in this section to point to Schmemann's usefulness amongst Evangelicals (or Kuyperians!) as well as avenues for further conversation and exploration.

As a preeminent Reformed scholar in liturgical theology and the practice of worship, John Witvliet provides an exhilarating look at "Schmemann Amongst the Kuyperians." Drawing on the works of James K.A. Smith,

Nicholas Wolterstorff, Richard Mouw, Matthew Kaemingk, and others, Witvliet highlights areas of congruence between Schmemann and the Reformed tradition, calling his own tradition to a deeper, more robust liturgical theology as well. Over the last decade or more, the trend within the Reformed tradition to delve more fully into the worship and liturgical traditions of the church can be seen explicitly through Smith's *Cultural Liturgies* trilogy, Wolterstorff's most recent books, *The God We Worship* and *Acting Liturgically*, and Witvliet's own corpus. The bedrock of Schmemann's work—and of this essay—is his commitment to vocation and a thick eschatological vision; such a vision is shared, argues Witvliet, by our Reformed brethren.

Todd Johnson's essay highlights the use of liturgical theology within free church worship and argues that a lack of formal liturgy does not render liturgical theology impotent as a lens through which to view the worship of these traditions. Echoing the sentiments of the late, distinguished professor James F. White, Johnson successfully brings the "non-liturgical" churches into fruitful dialogue with liturgical theology. It has long been asked, "What of the millions of Christians who lack a formal liturgy? How should we consider their worship?" and Johnson provides the necessary tools to understand and appreciate their contributions to the liturgical tradition of the one, holy, catholic, and apostolic Church through ritual congruence.

The last essay in this section was written by the esteemed Don Saliers of Emory. Saliers has been interacting with Schmemann throughout his long and illustrious career, most notably in his seminal work, *Worship as Theology*, and in partnership with Bruce Morrill (also of this volume) for the section on Schmemann in Dwight Vogel's (again, also of this volume) *Primary Readings in Liturgical Theology*. Saliers points decidedly to Schmemann's effect on Protestant liturgical theology as being his insistence upon the church's role as "participating in the resurrected life of Christ." For Saliers, joining the paschal mystery in liturgy is one of Schmemann's lasting contributions to liturgical theology and for the entire Church.

Schmemann and Liturgical Theology. It should be no surprise that an entire section—the largest of this volume—is devoted to the subject over which Schmemann is most undoubtedly the father: liturgical theology. Contained within this section are essays by four gifted scholars and the editor of this volume ranging from topics of pastoral liturgical theology to the liturgy of the hours. These essays interact with Schmemann's writings and, through their constructive work, seek to push his research further.

Joyce Zimmerman focuses her attention on the pastoral nature of liturgical theology, insisting that liturgical theology is pastoral at its core and should more appropriately be labeled "pastoral liturgical theology." Liturgy is to be deemed as truly pastoral when it propels the faithful body

TAYLOR—INTRODUCTION   XXV

beyond the words of the text, the gestures of the rite, and the walls of the sanctuary and into the world as co-participants in the life, death, resurrection, and ascension of Jesus. While this is not systematically presented in Schmemann's writings, Zimmerman argues, it is a concept certainly laced throughout, serving as a bedrock for his understanding of liturgical theology. A glimpse into the "pastor's heart" of Schmemann, this essay sets the tone for the whole section.

David Fagerberg has long been one of the most prominent theologians interacting with Schmemann. His dissertation, *What is Liturgical Theology?*, devotes an entire section to "Schmemann as Exemplar" within the field, and in 2008, he was a presenter at SVOTS symposium honoring Fr. Alexander's legacy. In his latest essay, Fagerberg builds off of his work in *Consecrating the World* and beautifully describes what it looks like when liturgy "bursts forth into the world." Fr. Schmemann was fond of criticizing secularism in his writings and here Fagerberg helps us recover an understanding of Christian life with the telos of becoming more "God-like and God-centered." When liturgy bursts forth into the world, breaking free from its textual bonds, there is no longer a division between sacred and profane because all is God's, presenting an opportunity to experience and encounter God's majesty in even the most mundane.

I have contributed an essay to this volume generally, and to this section specifically, on Schmemann's liturgical theology. More concretely, I attempt to demonstrate that it is *The Eucharist—Sacrament of the Kingdom* that should be taken as Schmemann's most important and most significant work. Put another way, *Introduction*, *The Eucharist*, and *FTLOW* should form a trilogy: *Introduction* provides the definition and foundation for liturgical theology and *FTLOW* is the application of liturgical theology to mission and ministry, but *The Eucharist* is the actual doing and working of liturgical theology. Central to this work—and overlooked by the overwhelming majority of scholars engaging with Schmemann—is his use of "the liturgical coefficient." Using the coefficient as an interpretive key, I seek to unpack his liturgical theology through the lens of *The Eucharist* and then unfold the cosmic scope of the Eucharist.

Dwight Vogel's essay follows along the same lines as Zimmerman's, as different notes within the same song. Vogel, too, highlights the participation of the Church in the mystery of Christ through her feasts, and he insists that Schmemann's understanding of *leitourgia* is not the popularized version of "the work of the people" but rather a public work of an individual or group on behalf of the people. This is the meaning of the phrase "for the life of the world." Liturgy is engaged and enacted first and foremost to the glory of God and then on behalf of his creation, for his creation. As such, the liturgy

xxvi   TAYLOR—INTRODUCTION

should then be seen as a guide for holy living rather than an hour or two out of our schedules on a weekly basis; the actions of the rite ought to become the actions of our lives: praise, lament, confession, thanksgiving, proclamation, etc. What we see, hear, taste, touch, and do in the liturgy should be replicated throughout the week.

Notre Dame professor Kimberly Belcher has provided a wonderfully thought-provoking essay on the liturgy of time in relation to liturgical theology. Belcher focuses specifically on the false dichotomy between sacred and profane, movement in and out of holy space/time, and the interplay between Sunday worship and the annual cycle of feasts and seasons. How does our Christian understanding of time interact with life in the present while also remaining encoded with eschatological hope? Belcher provides the answer vis a viz a lovely interaction with Christian and Jewish liturgical texts. Belcher's essay serves as the logical link between liturgical and sacramental theology as it is nigh on impossible to create a separation between liturgical theology and sacramental theology within Schmemann's work; indeed, the division becomes more of a false dichotomy when one sees the trajectory of his overall projects. That said, the final section is devoted to three essays primarily concerned with sacramental theology and the sacraments. Each contributor offers something based on his own research strengths: Morrill on political theology, O'Malley on the rite of marriage, and Guthrie on the sacramental imagination.

Bruce Morrill has been interacting with Fr. Schmemann for over two decades, and as mentioned above, he collaborated with Don Saliers in Dwight Vogel's primer and he also focused heavily on Schmemann in his own text, *Anamnesis as Dangerous Memory*. Here, Morrill revisits Schmemann, arguing that the liturgical is inherently political and that Christian ethics and living are intricately connected with liturgical and sacramental worship. By looking at his *Journals*, Morrill provides insights into the connection between liturgy and life, "faith and politics" in Schmemann's life and thoughts, ultimately arguing that the two cannot be separated.

Timothy O'Malley engages with Schmemann's sacramental understanding of marriage through the lens of Roman Catholic theologian Matthias Scheeben. Schmemann wrote about the Eucharist as being a "sacrament of the Kingdom" and here we find O'Malley using the same reasoning to portray marriage as a similar sacrament. Through this provocative examination of Roman Catholic marriage liturgy, the reader is encouraged to see marriage afresh with the understanding that the consent and blessing of the service are both personal and ecclesial. O'Malley argues that the East and West should not be separated in their sacramental theologies at this point and demonstrates how Schmemann's Orthodox perspective dovetails nicely with the Roman Catholic rite as seen through Scheeben.

Finally, Steve Guthrie enters into meaningful dialogue with Schmemann's work via an exploration of the sacramental imagination. How and where is God present and at work in this world? If God is truly present in all things, it is argued, then he can and should be experienced in both the extraordinary and the mundane. The key to such a sacramental worldview is engaging in worship. Guthrie examines Death within culture and argues that sacramental worship alleviates us of that fear, propelling us out into the world *for the life of the world*. Here, the reader is encouraged to view suffering and death as sacraments because in and through them one encounters the Living God and is transformed. A fitting end to this volume, Guthrie urges Christians to take their worship and living beyond the walls of the sanctuary and out into the world, a world which is teeming with the presence and wonder of God.

A Few Notes On Reading

The essays in this volume can be read individually and collectively. As standalone contributions, each essay brings its own self-contained strengths and academic importance to the intersection of Father Alexander's legacy and ongoing research efforts. Sit with an essay or a sub-section which captivates you and enjoy it for what it is: a sign of gratitude for Schmemann's influence and work. You likely purchased this book because one of the contributors in this volume has written an essay about which you are excited; that is good! Once you have read that essay, however, stay for the rest . . .

There is a cohesiveness to this volume for which I could not have planned or prepared. Each essay has a voice and tone which brings a sense of harmony to the project while allowing for a very diverse range of content and expertise. Borrowing from Schmemann, there is a logic to the *ordo* of the volume, a logic which allows for one essay to strengthen or enlighten another. William Mills's essay on *For the Life of the World* may help elucidate other references to the book within these covers; Dwight Vogel and Joyce Zimmerman both write on matters of liturgical theology which build and enhance one another; David Fagerberg and I have explored the cosmic ramifications or implications of a "liturgy unbound." Reading the volume from start to finish, I hope, will enrich your experience.

These essays have been thoughtfully written for a wide audience. Ecumenically gathered, they are intended as a gift for the whole Church catholic rather than one small ecclesiastical corner. Schmemann's thoughts have begun penetrating non- and low-liturgical traditions as well,[1] making this a book for everyone and not just the liturgically inclined. The essays have been compiled for use in the classroom but also for Mrs. Murphy in the pew. So whether you are an expert in the field, a student in seminary, or a faithful worshipper in the pew, this was written with you in mind.

---

1. The terms non-liturgical and low-liturgical are used here in a descriptive manner and are in no way meant to be pejorative. I believe all worship is liturgical, even when a formal liturgy is absent, but these categories convey something everyone can understand. I am grateful to Dr. Karen B. Westerfield Tucker for helping me articulate this nuance.

PART 1

Schmemann in Context

Alexander Schmemann's
For the Life of the World[1]

A Retrospective[2]

William C. Mills

For the Life of the World will have a broad and continuing significance far beyond the student movements. It represents a major contribution, for nowhere else is this fresh and impelling perspective available to contemporary Western Christianity.[3]

Father Schmemann's book is provocative in many ways. I have been struck by the new perspective it gives on a number of concerns—not the least of which is the life and mission of the Student Christian Movements. He will have nothing to do with the various pietisms and ascetiscims which assume the material world an evil to be renounced, nor will he subscribe to those secularisms which see the Christian mission in terms of catching up with the standards and expectations of general society.[4]

2013 IS A WATERSHED year, for it marks not only the thirtieth anniversary year of the falling asleep of Father Alexander Schmemann but also the fiftieth anniversary of one of the best selling books in Eastern Christendom.

1. Originally published in 2013 and republished here with permission. William C. Mills, "Alexander Schmemann's For the Life of the World: A Retrospective," *Logos: A Journal of Eastern Christian Studies* 54.3/4 (2013) 199–228.

2. I would like to thank Mary Richardson, Joan Duffy, and Kevin Crawford, archivists at the Yale Divinity School Library, for their research assistance.

3. Marketing text on the original book order form for Alexander Schmemann's *For the Life of the World* (1963).

4. Enquist, "We Have Been Given a Gift," 1.

Written as a study guide for the 19th Ecumenical Student Conference on Christian World Mission in Athens, Ohio, *For the Life of the World* has been well received to say the least. It has been translated into over ten languages[5] and is required reading at many seminaries and schools of theology.[6] Even now, fifty years later, this little book, just over one hundred pages, continues to be read, studied, and discussed. This paper will provide the historical, religious, and cultural context of *For the Life of the World* through which to better understand this seminal work.

The Conference

In a two-page typed letter dated February 21, 1963, C. Alton Robertson, Director of the Commission of World Mission of the National Student Christian Federation, officially invited Father Alexander to be the main speaker at the 19th Quadrennial Ecumenical Student Conference in Athens, Ohio. The 19th Quadrennial was a continuation of a series of four-year conferences first sponsored by the Commission on World Mission, formerly known as the Student Volunteer Movement for Foreign Missions.[7] The Commission on World Missions came under a larger umbrella organization called the National Student Christian Federation, with its headquarters in New York City, and was also the representative organization of the United States to the World Student Christian Federation. The National Student Christian Federation was started in 1959 as a larger organizational entity that included many denominational organizations, such as the inter-seminary movement, along with various other student Christian fellowship groups. It served as a wider network of domestic Christian college student and young adult groups across the United States and Canada. When the Commission on World Mission

5. Swedish, Italian, German, Greek, Dutch, Polish, French, Finnish, Japanese, Korean, and Russian. These are the known translations. Other non-authorized or *samizdat* versions of the book may exist but are either unknown or un-catalogued.

6. In a Google search conducted on March 27, 2013, the following seminaries and colleges list *For the Life of the World* as required reading on course syllabi: St. Thomas University, St. Francis University, Seattle University, Furman University, Asbury Seminary, Reformed Theological Seminary, St. Vladimir's Seminary, Holy Cross Greek Orthodox School of Theology, Dallas Baptist Seminary, University of South Carolina, Wycliffe College, Andover Newton Seminary, Southern Methodist Seminary, Sacred Heart Major Seminary, Gordon Cornwell University, and Lipscomb University, among others. These schools represent a wide spectrum—Catholic, Orthodox, Baptist, Episcopal, and Methodist—including both large public institutions as well as small private ones.

7. Richardson, "Guide to the National Christian Federation Archives," 5.

came under the auspices of the National Student Christian Federation, they were the new hosts of the quadrennial conferences.[8]

Robertson's letter emphasizes key themes which were to be highlighted in the conference such as the importance of Word and Sacrament as well as the overarching theme of the conference, "For the Life of the World," focusing on the intersection of the Church and the world, theology and life: "Do not just talk about the Body of Christ as the Body of Christ gathered, but how the Church and the world interact, how they effect each other. Worship and work for the world."[9]

Seven days later, on February 28, 1963, in a brief handwritten note on seminary stationary, Father Alexander accepted Robertson's generous invitation. It is then that he began writing his first and perhaps most important book of his lifetime, which even surprised him years later.[10]

1963 proved to be an important year for Schmemann. In late 1962, after much searching, St. Vladimir's Seminary moved from their original location at 121st and Broadway to 575 Scarsdale Road, a five-acre, tree-lined campus in Crestwood, NY.[11] The seminary was dedicated on Saturday, October 2, 1962, and little over a month later, in late November, Schmemann was made the Dean of the seminary by Metropolitan Leonty (Turkevich), a position that Schmemann would serve until his death in 1983.[12] Then, in March, Paul B. Anderson, a longtime friend of the Orthodox Church, contacted Schmemann, relaying a message from Metropolitan Nikodim (Rotov) of the Russian Orthodox Church.[13] This was the first of many meetings that would eventually lead up to the granting of autocephaly to the Metropolia and the birth of the Orthodox Church in America (OCA). Schmemann contacted Metropolitan Leonty, asking for his advice and Archpastoral blessings, but since his health was failing, he simply told Schmemann, "Receive them with love."[14] And so Schmemann did. This would be the first of many conversations between the Russian Orthodox Church and the Metropolia.

The summer and fall of 1963 were also busy for Schmemann. Not only was he preparing for his upcoming fall classes and lectures at the

---

8. Richardson, "Guide to the National Christian Federation Archives," 6.

9. Typed letter from C. Alton Robertson to Alexander Schmemann.

10. Schmemann, *Journals*, 69.

11. See Meyendorff, *Legacy of Excellence*, esp. 35–40. See also Greeban and Milkovich, "St. Vladimir's Becomes a Permanent Home," 8–11.

12. Schmemann was made dean on November 30, 1962.

13. Paul B. Anderson was a close friend to the Orthodox. For more information about his life and legacy, see his intriguing memoir, Anderson, *No East or West*. See also Miller, *American YMCA*.

14. See Tarasar, *Orthodox America*, 262.

seminary as well as working on the study guide for the conference, but he also attended the Fourth Faith and Order Meeting hosted by the World Council of Churches in Montreal.[15] In mid-October, Schmemann spent two weeks in Rome, serving as an official Observer to the second session of the Vatican Council, where he, together with Greek Orthodox theologian Nicholas Nissiotis, offered comments and suggestions on key working documents of the council.[16] The 19th Quadrennial conference ended a very important year for Schmemann.

One may ask, but why would a largely Protestant Christian organization invite an Eastern Orthodox priest to be the main speaker? Not only that, but *the* first Orthodox speaker. By 1963 Father Alexander had already been teaching at St. Vladimir's Orthodox Theological Seminary for twelve years as an instructor of liturgical theology and church history, served as the dean of students, and worked as a chaplain. During this time, he was also an adjunct instructor of Russian Literature and History at Columbia University, New York University, and at Union Theological Seminary. Father Alexander was also active in talking to youth and young adults on college campuses. Prior to his arrival in the United States, Schmemann was very active in youth work, first in the Russian Student Christian Movement in France as well as one of the three Orthodox members of the Youth Department Committee of the World Council of Churches, which eventually led to the establishment of Syndesmos, the international youth organization.[17] During the summers at his summer home on Lac Labelle, Schmemann often held mini-youth gatherings for the teens and young adults who were staying there, answering questions and talking about the Church and the world.[18] Father Alexander was also familiar with college students on a personal level since his son, Serge, was a student at Harvard University at that time.

In the study guide for the conference, Rev. Philip Zabriskie outlines some key reasons for the focus on a sacramental and liturgical approach to the theme of missions and Church life. He acknowledges that the majority of church bodies in the ecumenical movement in the United States were

15. The Faith and Order meeting was held July 12–26, 1963.

16. See Yves Congar's recently published diaries of the council, Congar, *My Journal of the Council*, 329–31, 382–83.

17. The three Orthodox members of the Youth Committee Department of the World Council of Churches were Alexander Schmemann, Nikos Nissiotis, and George Khodre. Their first organizational meeting was held January 8–13, 1949, in Chateau de Bossey in Switzerland. Syndesmos officially established at a meeting in Paris, April 7–12, 1953. For more information about the early years of Syndesmos, see Possi, *History and Significance of Syndesmos*, 1–2.

18. See Schmemann, *My Journey with Father Alexander*, 93–94.

by and large mainline Protestant Churches, which considered themselves non sacramental, although he does say that this is really not true since, "all churches have some sacramental tradition—either elaborately developed or quite latent—a tradition which includes generally at least significance given to Baptism and the Lord's Supper."[19] He also says that when using the word "sacrament," many people merely think of Church services rather than a sacramental approach or vision of ecclesial life. One major thrust, then, for the 19th Quadrennial conference, was to highlight or hold up a sacramental or liturgical approach to Church life, focusing not so much only on the rites and rituals *per se*, but on the meaning of the rites and rituals, "about the world and God and ourselves."[20] This sacramental vision is further advanced when Zabriskie reminds the students that in the Bible, God acts through objects, through physical actions, and persons, and therefore, the sacramental view should not be that foreign to them if they take time to reflect on it. He says that even the so-called "secular" world has its types of sacraments or liturgical rites, such as shaking hands, kisses, ways of speaking to one another, letters, or touching. Finally, Zabriskie offers three general reasons why the conference highlights the sacramental view: to see what the broad sacramental point of view may say about the world, our freedom in the world, our lives and loves, our hope, and ourselves; to take time and listen to other Christian traditions that have a strong sacramental vision; and to look at our understanding of the word "sacrament."

It is this liturgical understanding of the Church that the conference leaders wanted highlighted during the conference. Zabriskie makes sure to highlight the importance of the missionary perspective too: "It is quite essential that we try, that we seek to understand ourselves, our world, our faith, the Gospel, and that we seek to develop anew a right understanding of the Church's mission. It is essential for the health and integrity of the Church, and, since the Gospel truly testifies to the source of all life, it is essential for the life of the world."[21]

Over the course of four days, from December 27, 1963 to January 2, 1964, thirty two hundred college students, half of whom were international students, gathered together for a week of prayer, dialogue, debate, and discussion at the campus of Ohio University in Athens. Students were divided into 133 Living Unit Groups that served as the heart of the conference. Each Living Unit Group had between twenty and twenty-five students and was interdenominational, intercultural, and international. According

19. *For the Life of the World Student Study Guide*, 9.

20. *For the Life of the World Student Study Guide*, 9.

21. *For the Life of the World Student Study Guide*, 6.

to one participant, the racial and cultural diversity was welcome to some students and surprising to others: "That was the first time I have ever taken communion with anyone of another race, of another nation, or of another denomination."[22] We must keep in mind that the 19th Quadrennial conference took place during the throes of the civil rights movement and race and religion were on the hearts and minds of many people.[23] One participant mentioned in her report that some students were late because their bus from Texas to Ohio was delayed since many restaurants refused to serve the "Negroes" that were on the bus.[24] Furthermore, just two weeks after the 19th Quadrennial, the Rev. Dr. Martin Luther King Jr. delivered a major speech at the National Conference on Religion and Race at the Edgewater Beach Hotel in Chicago.[25]

One of the major aims of the 19th Quadrennial was to show students the true diversity of Christianity in both practice and belief. The conference administration housed the Living Unit Groups in the same dormitories so the students would have plenty of opportunity to mix and mingle during the conference period. Among the students were numbered thirty-one Orthodox Christians and fifteen Roman Catholic. The students ranged in age from eighteen to thirty years old and included a wide range of backgrounds, including nursing, teaching, history, law, missionary work, science, ministry, and forestry. According to a post-conference report from a recently married student couple, "the conference was a microcosm of the world."[26] The conference administration was so overrun with applicants that they reportedly needed to turn away nine hundred students due to lack of dormitory space.[27] Students came from across the United States, including Alaska, some taking buses from as far as California and Texas. Over seventy-eight countries were represented, including Angola, Kenya, England, Germany, Sri Lanka, Syria, Kenya, and Japan. These students also represented the Christian spectrum,

22. Terrill, *ISF Field Trips*, 4.

23. See Feckanin, "Stand Up and Take Note," 15–16. On September 15, 1963, four young girls were killed in a bomb explosion at the 16th Street Baptist Church in Birmingham, Alabama. For more information, see Sitton, "Birmingham Bomb Kills 4 Negro Girls In Church."

24. Terrill, *ISF Field Trips*, 4. The report is a chilling reminder of the racial divide during this time.

25. The conference was held January 14–17, 1963, and included both whites and blacks as well as Christians and Jews. The well known Rabbi and author Abraham Joshua Heschel was the other guest speaker at the conference. King was "Person of the Year" and appeared on the cover of *Time* magazine in January, 1964. For more details about this conference, see Stanford University, "National Conference on Religion and Race."

26. Kallaur and Kallaur, "How it Happened in Athens," 9.

27. See 19th Quadrennial report (1964), 1.

including Methodist, Baptist, Disciples of Christ, Lutheran, Quaker, Roman Catholic, United Church of Christ, Eastern Orthodox, Episcopal, Baptist, as well as non-denominational.[28] This conference was also important for the fact that it was the first time in the seventy-eight year history of the quadrennial conference that Roman Catholics attended—not as "members" but rather as "fraternal brothers and sisters."[29] Representatives from the Peace Corps, the Congress on Racial Equity, and the Student Non-Violent Coordinating Committee were present as well.[30]

While Father Alexander was invited to be the main speaker at the conference, he was not the only one. Since this series of ecumenical student conferences reflected the wide range of Christian traditions there were also a variety of speakers: Milan Opocensky, a senior lecturer in systematic theology at the Comenius Faculty of Protestant Theology, delivered a talk on "The Church in Czechoslovakia Today"; the Rev. Eliezar Mapanao gave a talk on "Bread . . . For the Life of the World"; the Rev. Ruben Alvarez gave a talk on "Injustice and Revolt"; and W. Bonar Sidjabut gave a talk on "Christian Participation in Nation Building."[31] The supplemental talks focused on the social and political implications of Christianity, revealing to many North American students the real trials and tribulations of Christians living in third world countries, many of whom were governed by dictatorships or Marxist governments. As one student, Ross Terrill reported, "Again and again, the insistent challenge of political responsibility hit us full in the face, unexpected yet inescapable, as the impact of the truth often is."[32]

Every morning, after breakfast, Father Philip Zabriskie, an Episcopal priest and longtime member of the student youth movements, lead Bible studies on the infancy narratives in the gospel and their importance for life today.[33] Worship services were lead by the Episcopal Bishop Daniel Corrigan, the Director of the National Council's Home Department. A liturgical highlight of the conference was a large ecumenical Eucharistic service, the first of its kind in the long history of the Quadrennial conferences. The service was lead by Bishop Corrigan and assisted by twenty-four presbyters and twenty-four deacons. They used an edited version of the Eucharist

---

28. See student roster list for the conference.

29. Myers, "National Council of Churches Press Release," 1.

30. Myers, "National Council of Churches Press Release," 6.

31. See 19th Quadrennial Conference promotional flyer for speaker biographies and topics.

32. Terrill, *ISF Field Trips*, 3.

33. See conference schedule.

according to the Apostolic Tradition by Hippolytus.[34] The following is a verbatim reflection on this Eucharistic service by Roger Spinharney from Sheldon Jackson High School:

> At the evening worship of the 30th, we had a service of confession. After which we were instructed to go out and solve any differences we had with any of the people at the conference before taking the greeting of peace. At 10:30 am, on the 31st, 3,000 people gathered in the Alumni Memorial Auditorium for Holy Communion. After the sermon was over with, 24 presbyters from 9 denominations and 24 deacons from 8 denominations went to the stage and were seated with Bishop Corrigan of the Protestant Episcopal Church. Things were started off with the greeting of peace, which was the taking of your neighbors hand and saying, "Peace be with thee" and the other person would respond by saying, "And with thee." Then the person would pass it on to the next person until it had gone through the whole congregation. Then the collection was taken up and then the consecration of the bread and the wine. Then the presbyters and the deacons went out to the congregation to distribute the bread and wine. The communion was held according to the Apostolic Tradition of the early Church, which dates back to 200 AD before the present division of the Church. About the only denomination that did not participate in the communion service were the people of the Orthodox faith. This interdenominational international communion service was the first one in the history of the Church since the Reformation.[35]

Apparently this service was very moving. Some students were worried that gathering three thousand people in one place might make it "circus like" but the opposite was true: "The service, preceded by a half hour of absolute quiet, was deeply moving."[36]

Time during the conference was allotted for denominational worship space as well. The Roman Catholic observers held a series of weekday Masses at nearby St. Paul's Roman Catholic Church, lead by Father Henry Van Kortenaar, a chaplain at the Newman Center at the University of Pittsburgh. One participant remarked, "This will be one of the last Masses you'll hear in

---

34. The text and rubrics for the communion service was prepared by H. Boone Porter of General Theological Seminary in New York. Two hundred chalices were used to distribute communion at this service.

35. Report from Roger Spinharney to Sheldon Jackson High School Sitka, Alaska, dated January 9, 1964.

36. "Holy Spirit at the 19th Quadrennial."

Latin."[37] On a very cold and blustery early morning, the Orthodox students hosted a Divine Liturgy, presided over by Father George Timko[38] and Father Schmemann.[39] The assigned chapel for the Orthodox was too small for the six-hundred students who wanted to witness an Orthodox liturgy, so the conference planners had to find an alternative venue.[40] Father Timko also lead a series of pre and post Divine Liturgy discussions, offering time for questions and answers about the basic structure of the Divine Liturgy and what the Liturgy means for the life of the Orthodox Christian.[41]

The 19th Quadrennial conference was more than merely a religious or spiritual gathering; it really reflected the Church and the world, liturgy, and life together. A guest artist had a large display of her artwork. There was also a Festival of Nations with drummers, ethnic dancing, and the singing of civil rights and folk songs. The Academy-award winning British film *Room at the Top* was shown twice during the week, each time followed by lengthy debate and discussion.[42] Students also solicited funds and raised over $1,500 for Freedom Radio to "educate the Negro" who may be unaware of the larger right for civil rights in the country. Some students signed petitions to Congress and others volunteered to join sit-ins in Washington DC.[43] The spirit of the conference was certainly one of openness, freedom, creativity, and life-giving. As one student reported, "We were experiencing a contemporary stage of the World Council of Churches."[44] Another participant, Leonard Clough, called it an "eschatological experience."[45] Clough went on to say:

> Never have I attended a conference at which so many became
> so deeply involved personally. This was no academic game of
> ping-pong. People wanted to share rather than to debate. Speak-
> ers, both on the platform and in the seminars, led not with their

37. "Holy Spirit at the 19th Quadrennial," 370.

38. Father George Timko was a graduate of St. Vladimir's Seminary and a Navy veteran. He served at an Orthodox mission in Danbury, CT, and eventually moved to Sts. Peter and Paul Orthodox Church in Buffalo, NY. For more information about Father Timko's ministry and life, see Garklavs, "In Memoriam."

39. The Divine Liturgy began at 6:45 am. In their reflections on the conference, Constantine and Arlene noted that it was four degrees below zero.

40. Kallaur and Kallaur, "How it Happened in Athens," 8.

41. Kallaur and Kallaur, "How it Happened in Athens," 9.

42. The movie, based on the novel by John Braine, is a story about the poverty of modern society, including infidelity, lust, and socio-economic struggle.

43. See Spinharney letter.

44. Terrill, *ISF Field Trips*, 2.

45. Clough, "Reflections on the 19th Quadrennial Conference," 2.

chins but with their hearts. There was plenty of disagreement but little point scoring. The Protestant Episcopal Church and the Orthodox Church might claim a majority of the speakers, but there was no ecclesiastical or theological part line.[46]

Ross Terrill also noted the free and open spirit at the conference, highlighting the "signs of the time":

> The conference scene was a highly decentralized one, with scores of creative pockets of activity and encounter all over the place, where no one had planned them but where everyone was free to take part in them. Here, in the conference offices, are 80 vocational resource people, available to talk with those who are wondering what job to seek or what to do next summer. There, in a smoke-filled lounge, is the Peace lobby, members of the NSCF, Peace Concern Committee, the Canadian SCM, Young Friends, the Student Peace, and other groups. . . . Backstage, in the auditorium, in a whirl of costumes and welter of melodies, are students from all corners of the earth, rehearsing songs and dances for the daily presentation of a "Festival of Nations."[47]

It truly must have been quite an experience to gather this amount of students from different cultures, backgrounds, and experiences, gathered together to share their common faith in Christ. The participants were also encouraged and inspired to keep the conference spirit alive, as one participant said:

> We heard so many speeches and participated in discussions on civil rights issues and on problems of the church today that made us want to start becoming involved too, only to return to our University campuses and attempt to find our mission there, amid textbooks and hockey games and dates. I think that I speak for most of us when I say that we have returned home with the realization that we can no longer be content to remain in our Christian ghettos and look out at the rest of the world. We cannot simply dichotomize, calling part of the world "sacred" and another part "secular" and therefore not related to Christian faith and witness. We are called by Christ to be completely involved in his work here, not seeking separation as Christians from the world but rejoicing in our unity with it. We must remember that Christ died, not for the life of the Presbyterians,

46. Clough, "Reflections on the 19th Quadrennial Conference," 2.
47. Clough, "Reflections on the 19th Quadrennial Conference," 1.

or even for the life of the church, but that he died for the life of the world.[48]

A mobile conference bookstore was erected with 7,500 theological and religious books for sale as well as makeshift jewelry and metalwork from the Botolph art center in Boston.[49] They had sculptures, wall hangings, and recordings too. For four days, Ohio University was turned into a makeshift religious commune, where students from across the Christian spectrum worshipped together, discussed, debated, and learned from one another.

The Book

After Father Alexander agreed to speak at the conference, he started on the manuscript. Even though he was the Dean and professor at an Eastern Orthodox seminary, Father Alexander was very comfortable with ecumenical settings and speaking to primarily non-Orthodox audiences. According to pre-publication advertisements for the book, *For the Life of the World* is "to be a book for students which would help us in the Protestant tradition to understand from his perspective the grand source of Christian compassion and joy in the midst of the world's life, the meaning of the Church today."[50] By 1963, Father Alexander was already well known among youth and young adults within the Orthodox and some non-Orthodox circles. In many ways, he had both the charisma and the ability to translate theology into their language. Even the conference chair, Robertson, acknowledged that Schmemann was "very busy and receiving many requests from student groups at this time."[51] Schmemann worked quickly. By April 1, 1963, the conference planners already had the first chapter of *For the Life of the World* in hand for their marketing materials, which were planned for distribution in late summer and fall of that year.[52]

48. Anonymous, undated post-conference report.

49. Spearin, "For the Life of the World," 8.

50. *For the Life of the World* pre-publication book order form (National Christian Student Federation, 1963).

51. Invitation letter from C. Alton Robertson to Alexander Schmemann, dated February 21, 1963.

52. In a letter dated April 1, 1963, from C. Alton Robertson to Rev. B. J. Stiles, Robertson acknowledges that the National Student Christian Movement already had the first chapter of Schmemann's book and was ready to engage in marketing and pre-conference publicity. Stiles was the editor of *Motive Magazine*, a magazine of the Division of Higher Education of the Methodist Church.

As was his custom, Father Alexander worked on the bulk of the chapters while on his summer vacation in Labelle, Quebec.[53] The book was completed on the Feast of the Transfiguration, August 18, 1963[54] and ready for nation-wide sale by September.[55] *For the Life of the World* was first published and sold under the auspices of the National Student Christian Federation and sold $1.45 per copy. After the conference, however, *For the Life of the World* had a life of its own, changing titles and publishers numerous times.[56]

Schmemann did not work completely alone. In the preface to the first edition of *For the Life of the World*, he acknowledges the assistance from Rev. Stephen S. Garmey, an Episcopal priest and one of Father Alexander's former students.[57] Although Schmemann acknowledged Garmey's help, primarily using Garmey's notes, he also admitted that the final version was his alone.[58] The original text of *For the Life of the World* included seven chapters. In 1973, a revised and expanded edition appeared that included two additional chapters as appendices: "Worship in a Secular Age"[59] and "Sacrament and Symbol."

When *For the Life of the World* appeared 1963, it literally had a ready-made audience. Since it was the primary study guide for the duration of the conference, conference participants had either read the entire book or at least part of it. The book also received positive reviews across various

53. Lac Labelle is nestled near Mont Tremblant, northwest of Montreal, where the Schmemanns had a summer cottage.

54. According to the Gregorian Calendar, the Feast of the Transfiguration is cel-ebrated on August 6, but in 1963, the Metropolia was still using the Revised Julian Calendar, and the Feast of the Transfiguration was on August 18.

55. It was first printed in September 1963 and then reprinted again in November 1963.

56. The publication history for this book is long and arduous. First printed by the National Student Christian Federation, it was then published by Herder and Herder Publishers in New York and simultaneously by Montreal Palm Publishers in Canada with a name change to *Sacraments and Orthodoxy* (1965). One year later, it was pub-lished in England by Darton, Longman, and Todd with another title, this time to *The World as Sacrament* (1966). In 1973, St. Vladimir's Seminary Press published an ex-panded edition of the book, including two additional appendices with yet again a new title, *For the Life of the World: Sacraments and Orthodoxy*. Even with the change of publishers and titles, this book has continuously been in print since 1963.

57. Rev. Stephen S. Garmey was the Vicar of Gramercy Park Episcopal Church (1972–2005), a collector of modern Russian art, a musician, an architect, and a sculp-tor. For more information, see Dunlap, "Episcopal Vicar."

58. Acknowledgement page in *For the Life of the World* (1963).

59. Originally delivered at the Eighth General Assembly of Syndesmos on July 20, 1971, at Hellenic College in Brookline, MA, and first appeared in *St. Vladimir's Theo-logical Quarterly* in 1972.

Christian bodies. The Trappist monk and writer Louis (Thomas) Merton wrote an extensive review essay:

> Let the reader be warned. If he is now predisposed to take a comfortable, perhaps excitingly mysterious excursion into the realm of a very "mystical" and highly "spiritual" religion, gold-encrusted cult thick with smoke and incense and populated with a legion of gleaming icons in the sacred gloom, a "liturgy which to be properly performed requires not less than twenty-seven heavy liturgical books," he may find himself disturbed by Fr. Schmemann's presentation. Certainly, *Sacraments and Orthodoxy* will repudiate nothing of the deep theological and contemplative sense of Orthodox faith and worship but the author is intent on dispelling any illusions about the place of "religion" in the world today. In fact, one would not suspect from the title of this book that is one of the strongest and clearest statements of position upon this vexed topic of the Church and the world."[60]

Merton goes on to say that, for Schmemann, there is no real difference when speaking about the Church and the sacraments *per se*; when one speaks about ecclesial life one speaks about the sacramental expression of that life. Therefore, when one speaks about mission, one must also speak about the liturgical impact of that mission: "It is in protesting against false ideas of the Church, her mission, and her relation to the world that Fr. Schmemann makes his most valuable and indispensable contribution to current thought on sacramental theology."[61] Merton had a point that other people have made—namely, that one hallmark of Schmemann's corpus was that he showcased the integral nature of liturgy and life or the Church and the world as he himself states in the preface of the revised edition of the book:

> Our real question is: how can we "hold together"—in faith, in life, in action—these seemingly contradictory affirmations of the Church, how can we overcome the temptation to opt for and to "absolutize" one of them, falling thus into the wrong choices or "heresies" that have so often plagued Christianity in the past? It is my certitude that the answer comes to us not from neat intellectual theories but above all from the living and unbroken experience of the Church which she reveals and communicates to us in her worship, in the *leitourgia*, always making her that which she is: the sacrament of the world, the sacrament of the Kingdom—their gift to us in Christ. And this experience that I

60. Merton, "Orthodoxy and the World," 107.
61. Merton, "Orthodoxy and the World," 107.

tried, not so much to explain or to analyze, but rather simply to confirm in this essay.[62]

Indeed, *For the Life of the World* is not concerned with apologetics, propping up the "Orthodox thinking" about a list of topics which one often finds these days, trying to defend ourselves from the West, from the world, or from anyone who thinks or acts differently than us. What is so refreshing about *For the Life of the World* is its singleness of purpose, revealing the most basic concepts of sacramental vision for life in general, holding up the Eucharist as the source and summit of our faith in Christ. In his pre-conference review of the book, Roy Enquist focuses on what Schmemann has to say to his Western brothers and sisters. He likens it to a real gift that has been given from one brother to another, not forcing himself on the other, but rather as an invitation to come and see:

> Schmemann's book is not so much a thesis to be attacked as a gift from one part of the Body to another. In letting us come with him, behind the iconostasis of reserve which protects Orthodox sacramental devotion, Father Schmemann has, in reality, invited us to share, in some way, in the Sacred Banquet of Life. We have been made guests in an exceedingly venerable part of the house of God. The question is not: Shall we move in and renounce our old home? Nor is it, I trust: Shall we convince our host to remodel and redecorate so his place in God's world will be just like yours or mine? Rather, we have been given a gift. We have been privileged to enter into a world which most of us have never known before—a reflection, incidentally, not on its importance but on our limitations. In being privy to the spirit that animates the life of those who live a sacramental life, we are both privileged and given a new responsibility. Christians, East and West, have not understood each other for over a thousand years. Father Schmemann's book is, among other things, a little sacramental gift that has the power to open up the meaning of the reality of Christ for Eastern Christians in a new and unforgettable way."[63]

As Enquist states, *For the Life of the World* is a gift from one part of the Body of Christ to another, and it has truly been a gift that has kept on giving.

---

62. Schmemann, *For the Life of the World*, 7.
63. Enquist, "We Have Been Given a Gift," 2.

The Lectures

Over the course of the four days, Schmemann delivered four keynote lectures. After lunch, he and Rev. Zabriskie hosted an informal question and answer session together with time for general discussion.[64] Then, at 3 pm, the students convened in the Alumni Memorial Auditorium, where everyone gathered to hear Schmemann speak. The four lectures, largely based on his book, were aimed at the main conference theme of liturgy and life and the Church as mission. A post-conference press release published in the *The Christian Century* reported: "Schmemann made it clear that at this point in the ecumenical movement, apologetics are not needed; what is needed is the confession of the prime role of the Church. For the Christians, there is no alternative to obeying Christ's command, 'Go ye and preach.'"[65] One reason for this particular conference theme on Church and mission was that for years, Christians were going out on mission trips, trying to bring people to Christ, but failed to understand exactly what they were doing; or, as Robertson said:

> Literally hundreds of students have gone out onto these frontiers to invest their lives. But many who have gone out, upon returning to that part of God's people fathered locally in the Church at First Avenue and Main Street, have too often found themselves out of touch, misunderstood, unable to explain adequately what they are doing and why; and, consequently, many have either continued in mission unsustained or have left the Church.[66]

Judging from the various student comments, Schmemann stirred up a lot of emotion in the students and spoke with power.

Schmemann was familiar with the topic of the missionary nature of the Church. Earlier, in 1961, he wrote two essays on missionary activity, one of which appeared as an editorial in the *St. Vladimir's Seminary Quarterly*, simply called "Orthodoxy and Mission,"[67] and one which appeared a little later, in an anthology edited by Gerald H. Anderson, called, "Missionary Imperative in the Orthodox Tradition."[68] This theme of mission, an important one for Schmemann, would later re-appear again in different forms, especially in a keynote speech to young adults in *Concern Magazine*, called,

---

64. See the schedule for the 19th Quadrennial conference.
65. "Holy Spirit at the 19th Quadrennial," 370.
66. Robertson, "*For the Life of the World*—But Why?," 36.
67. Schmemann, "Orthodoxy and Mission."
68. Schmemann, "Missionary Imperative in the Orthodox Tradition."

"The Mission of Orthodox Youth,"[69] which later would be extracted into a popular booklet published by Conciliar Press.[70]

A black and white photo taken at the conference depicts a young Father Alexander[71] in his white collar and suit jacket at the podium against a backdrop of cultural slogans reflecting the signs of the time: WASP, FREE, WAR, IMAGE, THERE. Each of the four lectures, all equal length, focused on the themes of the conference: the missionary perspective, for the life of the word, mission to society, and the Church and the mission.

Schmemann begins his first lecture by reminding the students that he does not plan on giving them "recipe" for missionary work but rather that the overall *raison d' etre* is Church as mission:

> We know that, from the very beginning, to be a Christian meant to be a missionary. The very distinction between these two terms is in itself nonsense. We know it, and this is why we are here. And yet we do not know how to be missionaries. We do not know, not because we have not heard a sufficient amount of lectures and read a sufficient amount of books. This lack of knowledge is deeply rooted in our Christian witness, or rather our weakness as Christians. It is not only on the study of theologies of missions that our missionary activity depends but on something else. And this something else is difficult to present as a recipe. If Christ failed, who are we to succeed? He could not convince the crowds that followed Him and then abandoned Him; He could not convert them. It is difficult to believe that we can, after one, two, three, four conferences finally find adequate methods of mission. I cannot speak here of a theology or a theory of mission that I can offer to you and say, "Go back and apply it now." I have no theory with which you will succeed where your fathers have failed and where generations of missions have failed.[72]

This continued "failure" which Schmemann speaks about was one of the reasons for the theme of this conference to focus on the Church as mission. The conference organizers mentioned that for centuries, Christians have traveled far and wide to establish missions or convert others to the faith, and yet they realized that missionary activity is not just about numbers or people in the pew, it is the reason for our life; Christ came to bring life, not just bigger and better buildings or bell towers.

69. Schmemann, "Mission of Orthodox Youth," 5–9.

70. For a recent analysis of Schmemann's thought on mission and Church life, see Papathansiou, "Church as Mission," 6–41.

71. Schmemann was forty-two years old at the time of the conference.

72. From an unpublished lecture.

In the rest of the first lecture, Schmemann focuses on the fact that in reality, Christianity and the gospel were failures in the eyes of the world; after all, there were very few Christians (as compared with other religious groups) and their leader, Jesus, was crucified. A hero he was not. While Christianity flourished for centuries, it took on forms of the local institutions and failed to be "missionary" in the sense of the gospel but rather just increased its power and authority. While the cross is the vehicle for Jesus' death, it also becomes the source of joy for the Christian, since Jesus defeats darkness, evil, and death itself on the cross: "Does not the Christian message teach us that what we have to do is to hold together in our faith the reality of Christ's failure having its name the cross and also the reality of His victory which has as its name the resurrection? It is not just cross or just resurrection. It seems to me that too often we are tempted by choosing between them."[73] The real missionary activity for the Christian is to embrace the cross of Christ which is both suffering and joy.

After developing the overarching theme of what mission is and what it is not, he emphasizes that Christianity is always *particular* or *personal.* Christ came and healed persons; not society or humanity in general. Schmemann focuses on Boris Pasternak's famous book, *Dr. Zhivago.*[74] The book, Schmemann says, is about one person—Dr. Yuri Zhivago—and Pasternak takes his reader through Yuri Zhivago's life, from the early years, as Yuri watches his mother's funeral, until much later, when Yuri dies. Pasternak does, this Schmemann says, because: "The more you look at one particular man, the more you accept him seriously, the more you *find* him, the more he ceases to be just a case of the general situation. You find that there is no man outside this real, particular man."[75] Schmemann says that this is the miracle of particularity, of real persons with hopes, dreams, fears, sufferings and joys. For the reader, then, Zhivago is not just any doctor but rather a particular doctor with a particular family and particular problems: "The more you look into all these details, the more this other person, Dr. Zhivago, becomes something which you know from inside, a living reality. You realize the depth of the human existence and, in the end, without this being said, you know that we have the story of each man as seen through the story of Jesus Christ."[76] Pasternak does not deal with humanity in general but rather with a human in particular.

73. From an unpublished lecture.

74. Earlier, Schmemann wrote a review of *Dr. Zhivago*. See Schmemann, "Pasternak," 18–25.

75. From an unpublished lecture.

76. From an unpublished lecture.

All of Christian mission, Schmemann continues, rests on the general into the particular: "Not the reduction of the particular to the general, but the constant transformation of the general into the particular, is the beginning, the fundamental beginning of all Christian mission."[77] Basically, Schmemann argues against a merely reductionist approach to missionary activity—one which is as common today as it was fifty years ago. Churches were focusing on numerical growth, more Church buildings, more parishioners in the pews, more seminaries, and more activities and events instead of on just being the Church, being what God meant us to be. Schmemann envisions basic missionary activity as simply seeing the image of God in another person, in honoring people as people and not just some general abstraction:

> He is the one who sits next to me in that long, long ride home in the train and who, at first, is the enemy because he smokes his bad cigar, and then becomes someone whom I have to accept, simply because he is there, and finally, when I make a little effort and ask about his wife and children, he becomes interesting. But still, it is only when finally I make a little effort and ask about his wife and children, [that] he becomes interesting. But still it is only finally, in the morning, when, after that sleepless night, I have to quit him that I have a sense of losing someone. We have met, we have been together. Now this is a victory which cannot be calculated, which cannot be put in any report of any commission or committee. We cannot report this to our churches and organizations and yet, this is the victory that takes place daily. We know, at least with eyes of faith we know, that this is the only foundation on which everything depends.[78]

His words may seem odd given the fact that Christians have worked hard long and hard in the mission field, both domestic and international, for centuries. Yet Schmemann envisions the basis of Christian mission not only as going out and creating more catechumens alone—which is an important element of missionary activity—but rather in the right here and now, through our daily conversations, meetings, encounters with "the other" of which there are so many. If we live our Christian faith at work, at school, at home, whether we are teachers, janitors, nurses, or retirees, we can all be missionaries to those around us.

In his third and fourth lecture, Schmemann turns to the theme of the Church and Society and the Church and Mission. Here, he draws upon

77. From an unpublished lecture.
78. From an unpublished lecture.

themes that are included in *For the Life of the World* (and which also appear in his later writings), the priestly and prophetic nature of our life. He begins by teasing out a theme which he introduces early on in *For the Life of the World*, the priestly character of our life, that we join into Jesus' priestly ministry of offering our prayer and praise to god and fully entering into this priesthood: "Man was to be the priest of a eucharist, offering the world to God, and in this offering, he was to receive the gift of life."[79] In the lecture, he says the same thing in a slightly different way:

> But the priest does not only assume; he also offers to God; he mediates; he knows that the means and the ends of each action is God and His glory. He is offering the sacrifice of praise to God and this is the initial meaning of sacrifice. The sacrifice of praise, the offering to God, is prior to sin and to all the sacrifice of redemption and atonement. If there were no sins, this world would still be a sacrificial world because real love is always sacrificial love, it offers everything it has to the ultimate, to God, to His glory. And God is not only glorified by those achievements that can be evaluated and measured; He is glorified by the very essence of Christian life in the world.[80]

After speaking about the priestly nature of humanity, he then turns to the prophetic. Schmemann says that the prophet was the one who always called people back to God, who reminded people that we are supposed to be in the world but not of the world: "You remember all those Elijah's, Isaiah's, all those men who stood in the midst of the chosen people of God, in cultures and societies, and denounced them. And there are always bearers and messengers of a vision which cannot be simply identified with anything achieved in this world."[81] Yet the prophet is always the one who is disregarded, laughed at, and mocked. The prophets speak the truth and the truth is often difficult—if not sometimes impossible—to accept. The Church does not just have the priestly *or* prophetic functions but both:

> Ultimately, the priestly and the prophetic are not mutually exclusive functions. The real prophet, or the one who opposes, who stands against, can only be a real prophet if he is, first of all, a real priest. He can instill in himself and in other people that hunger for the absolute only if he is, first of all, deeply involved in the priestly function of the Christian mission. The one who jumps into the prophetic without first assuming the priestly

---

79. Schmemann, *For the Life of the World*, 17.
80. From an unpublished lecture.
81. From an unpublished lecture.

will be a false prophet. "Not all who say, 'Lord, Lord,' will enter the kingdom of God," and there is much false prophecy among Christians. In other terms, these two realities are organically connected, and this is what gives the Christian mission to the world and to society its real complexity.[82]

He also brings up a salient point about the prophetic priesthood. The Church has borrowed much of its missionary and growth terminology from contemporary business models, a quantitative approach. Yet implied in this prophetic approach is failure. If one looks at Jeremiah, Hosea, Amos, or Ezekiel, they always stood apart and spoke against Israel for their sin and idolatry, calling Israel back to repentance. The prophets were certainly not part of the inner circle of leaders and rulers; as the author of the Epistle to the Hebrews says: "They were stoned, they were killed with the sword; they went about in skins of sheep and goats, destitute, afflicted, ill-treated of whom the world was not worthy-wondering over deserts and mountains and in dens and caves of the earth" (Heb 11:37–38).

Schmemann also highlights this notion of failure in terms of self-emptying love.[83] He draws upon *The Diary of a Country Priest* by George Bernanos. Overall, the book depicts this priest not as succeeding, but failing:

> In this book, we follow, step by step, the life of a young priest in a small and completely de-Christianzied village in which nothing seems to succeed. He himself is dying of cancer and he fails and he fails and he fails—constantly. But as you read the book, you feel that there is a real progress in grace, and when he finally dies in the room of the prostitute because he went to visit the girl friend of his friend, a defrocked priest—he finally dies in this absurd situation—his last words are: "All is grace" (*tout est grace*). Now every priest—even without going to those extremes, without necessarily dying of cancer in the room of a prostitute— knows that, from time to time—be it on a Sunday morning or sometimes on an evening of a weekday—knows that, in spite of all those failures, everything is grace; and in spite of these visible failures, there is constant growth of grace in this world.[84]

Ultimately, missionary work, according to Schmemann, is nothing other than being faithful to the Church as the Church, as the Body of Christ and the presence of the Kingdom of God in this world, which is revealed to us in the liturgical gathering. It is this—just being what we are supposed

---

82. From an unpublished lecture.

83. From an unpublished lecture.

84. From an unpublished lecture.

to be—that is the true missionary. Yes, there are officially sanctioned missionaries that are sent to establish actual physical new missions, but we are all called to be missionaries since we are all members of one another. Schmemann reminds the participants that no matter what station one finds himself or herself in this world, we are all missionaries, since we are all sent out at the end of the service to "depart" or "go forth" in peace.

The conference certainly ended on a high note. Over the course of four days, students and young adults from around the world prayed together, broke bread, listened to some inspirational lectures, debated, dialogued, and learned from one another. They worshipped and had communion. They were challenged to live out their faith daily—not just on Sunday morning but every day. In many ways, those four days at the 19th Quadrennial conference was a mini World Council of Churches, as students witnessed what it means to be members of one another.

Conclusion

Not all books are the same and surely not all withstand the test of time. Browse any theological library and there are plenty of old, slowly-yellowing, dusty books that have long been forgotten and eventually will not make it to the end of this century. Yet some—like Bonhoeffer's *Cost of Discipleship*, Merton's *Seven Storey Mountain*, or Niehbur's *Christ in Culture*—continue to be read, studied, and re-read, again and again. *For the Life of the World* is one of those books. Yet the question still remains: why? Even Schmemann was surprised at the popularity of this little book. If Schmemann were alive today, he would be shocked that it's still in print. In a very small and unscientific poll, I asked five clergy friends, all unknown to each other, what it was about *For the Life of the World* that they found inspiring. They all answered in nearly the same words: "*For the Life of the World* gave me a vision of what Church is all about." They confessed that even though they learned about the ancient rites and rubrics and the importance of the Typikon, *For the Life of the World* gave them a grand vision of things, a broad view of how liturgy and life, the Church and the world, intersect. They also used the words "organic" and "unified" to describe this vision. Robert F. Taft, the don of liturgical studies of the Byzantine world has called this the "Schmemann phenomenon":

> To what, then, must we attribute this "Schmemann phenom-
> enon": the surprising fascination he and his work still hold
> on the minds and the hearts of those engaged in the liturgical
> enterprise these twenty-five years since his death? I think it is

because, unlike, "all the king's horses and all the king's men," Fr. Alexander was the one who succeeded in putting Humpty-Dumpty together again. He took a decomposed and fragmented vision of liturgy: known by the code name "theology of the liturgy," and transfigured it—the term is not too strong—into a "liturgical theology" expressive of what Christ and his Church is, the "Sacrament of the Kingdom" inchoatively present among us now, in mystery, "For the Life of the World."[85]

I agree. Schmemann's entire *oeuvre*, including *For the Life of the World*, is a simple yet profound vision of our life in Christ. Schmemann was not a liturgical historian and he often was wrong on key liturgical and historical points which have been noted among contemporary liturgical theologians.[86] Yet in all of his sermons, articles, essays, and books, including *For the Life of the World*, we find truth. And as Taft suggests, just because one gets some of the facts wrong does not mean that something is not true; not just truth in general, but the truth of our life in Christ. It is for this reason that *For the Life of the World* has maintained such a long and healthy shelf life, and hopefully will continue to be read, re-read, studied, and discussed well into the future.

---

85. Taft, "Liturgical Enterprise," 174. See also 157–73.

86. Galazda, "Schmemann Between Fagerberg and Reality," 7–32.

Alexander Schmemann's Liturgical Legacy in America[1]

PAUL MEYENDORFF

IT IS AN HONOR for me to be invited to this symposium honoring Fr. Alexander on the twenty-fifth anniversary of his death. As the "Fr. Alexander Schmemann Professor of Liturgical Theology" at St. Vladimir's Seminary, I cannot adequately express the magnitude of the debt and respect owed to him not only by the seminary, which he headed for nearly thirty years, but also by all the Orthodox churches in North America. He left his mark in many areas of church life, he touched countless people through his preaching, his teaching, his numerous lectures at university campuses, and his frequent appearances on radio and television. He was instrumental in the development of the autocephaly of the Orthodox Church in America. More than any other person in his generation, he was the face of Orthodoxy in North America during the last three decades of his life, which was cut short by his untimely sickness and death. My task today, however, is to focus on his liturgical legacy.

Upon arriving in the United States, in 1951, at the invitation of Fr. Georges Florovsky, then the dean of St. Vladimir's Seminary, Fr. Alexander assumed the position of professor of liturgical theology. He quickly became aware of the challenges that lay ahead of him in the New World. Coming out of the rarified academic atmosphere of St. Sergius in Paris, he found quite a different world in the "Russian Orthodox Greek Catholic Church" in America, the so-called "Metropolia." This church, descended directly from the eighteenth-century Russian mission in Alaska, was very different from

---

1. Originally published in SVS Quarterly and republished here with permission.

the émigré Russian community in France in which he grew up. While this church had a smattering of American converts from Western Christianity, most of its members were descendents of Carpatho-Russian, Galician, or Ukrainian origin, primarily immigrants from the Austro-Hungarian Empire in the late-nineteenth and early-twentieth centuries. They had come as economic refugees, settling largely in the coal-mining hills of Pennsylvania and near the steel mills of the industrial Midwest. Many were former "Uniates," who joined the Orthodox Church under the leadership of Fr. Alexis Toth around the turn of the twentieth century. A wave of Russian immigrants arrived subsequently after the Russian Revolution, settling primarily on the West Coast (if they came through China) or on the East Coast (if they came through Western Europe). The High-Russian community, however, was relatively small compared to the earlier immigration, and certainly not as intellectually vibrant as the much larger Parisian one. Many of these Russians ended up in the Russian Orthodox Church Outside Russia (RO-COR, also known at the "Karlovtsy" Synod), and thus remained largely isolated from their fellow Orthodox. Finally, Orthodoxy in America included not only the "Metropolia" but also large numbers of Greeks, Arabs, Serbs, Romanians, Bulgarians, Albanians, independent Ukrainians, and others. Many of these ethnic groups were further split along political lines. And, in an effort to preserve their national and religious identities, the various Orthodox communities became ghettos.

The level of education of both clergy and laity was quite low. In the years following the Russian Revolution, imperial Russian support for the church disappeared. The united Orthodoxy envisioned by Archbishop (and later Patriarch) Tikhon vanished, and the ecclesiastical chaos that followed led to a general fragmentation and decline. It was not until the late 1930s that theological education was restored with the establishment of three seminaries: St. Vladimir's and St. Tikhon's in the "Metropolia,"[2] Holy Cross in the Greek Archdiocese. Of these three, only St. Vladimir's sought to function like the academies in Russia from the very beginning.

The liturgical situation was equally chaotic, not to say decadent. Each of the above groups brought with them their own local traditions, to which they clung as a kind of security blanket in the New World, dominated as it was by foreign, western forms of Christianity. In their ghettoized existence, they each attempted to maintain the inherited language and practices they brought with them. In the case of the "Metropolia," for example, this included the use of Slavonic, a language most found completely incomprehensible.

2. The Metropolia was the direct successor of the Russian Orthodox mission. In 1970, this group was granted autocephaly by the Russian Orthodox Church and became the "Orthodox Church in America."

Since many were former Uniates, their practice was often Latinized. A number of parishes, for example, celebrated daily stipend masses during Great Lent. The musical style varied from the nineteenth-century operatic style of the imperial Russian court to Carpatho-Russian and Galician *prostopenie*. The rich cycle of daily and weekly services was largely reduced to Sunday liturgy alone, often supplemented by a service called the *obednitsa*.[3] As was the case with the other Orthodox in America, communion was normally received only once a year. The typical parish by-law in the Metropolia, for example, prescribed annual confession and communion in order to remain a "member in good standing," i.e., to be entitled to vote at the annual parish meeting. For the few who desired to receive communion more often, confession was required each time. The so-called "priest's prayers" at the liturgy were always recited silently. Sometimes, in order to keep the service moving, they were read in advance or even omitted! Baptisms were performed in private, with only family and friends in attendance, and never in conjunction with the eucharistic liturgy. In seminaries, liturgical instruction was limited to rubrical details, with no thought given to theological or historical factors. Liturgy was simply something one had to do to fulfill the formal requirements of Orthodoxy. No reflection was deemed necessary.

Now, more than half a century later, the picture is vastly different, largely due to the influence of Fr. Alexander. My assignment is to cover his legacy in North America, but much of what I will say will apply, to a greater or lesser extent, to many Orthodox churches across the world, from Finland to Moscow to Beirut.

First, Fr. Alexander established liturgical theology as a legitimate academic and theological discipline. His first book, *Introduction to Liturgical Theology*, remains a classic. It is read not only by students at Orthodox seminaries but also in Roman Catholic and Protestant seminaries and universities. It is, for example, on the required reading list for graduate students in liturgy at the University of Notre Dame, the chief center of liturgical study in America. Schmemann is widely credited with being one of the fathers of the liturgical movement, and I had the privilege of writing a brief article about him in a volume entitled *How Firm a Foundation: Leaders of the Liturgical Movement*.[4]

Fr. Alexander, however, was more than a theoretician. He was first of all a pastor, and for him, scholarship and academic research were but tools needed to accomplish pastoral aims. In fact, he was strongly allergic

3. Essentially a Typika service. Because the structure of the service somewhat resembles the eucharistic liturgy—though without an anaphora or the distribution of communion—it was frequently used as the second, early service on Sunday morning.

4. Meyendorff, "Alexander Schmemann," 300–6.

to academic scholarship for its own sake, as becomes immediately evident when reading his journals. He was interested not in the past, but in the here and now, in the contemporary life of the church. He saw the value of history, of course, but only for the sake of addressing contemporary pastoral issues. And it was precisely in the area of liturgical practice that he left his greatest mark. Allow me to present a few examples.

Baptism

The Orthodox "tradition" (with a small "t") that he inherited considered baptism as an essentially private rite. Baptisms were typically performed in private homes rather than in church, with only family and friends in attendance. I myself was baptized in this way in our small apartment on rue Lauriston in Paris. Baptism was understood to be somehow essential for one's membership in the church, but in America, it was primarily a party to celebrate a new birth. The focus was on the cute baby, the beautiful baptismal robe, and then the food and drink that followed.

Fr. Alexander set about to change this in the first book he wrote in America, *Of Water and the Spirit*. Here, he argued forcefully that baptism is primarily an ecclesial event, marking the incorporation of a new member into the church, the Body of Christ. As such, it should be conducted not in a private home but in church. And because it is by nature a corporate, ecclesial event, it should, where possible, be celebrated in conjunction with the eucharistic liturgy—precisely because he understood the celebration of the eucharistic liturgy by the local parish community to be the full manifestation, the realization, of the Church into which the candidate, whether child or adult, is being incorporated. Ideally, therefore, the entire parish community should be present to welcome and to celebrate with its newest member.

As strongly and forcefully as he would argue this point, however, he was never dogmatic. He would condemn such liturgical abuses with his inimitable gusto in the classroom one day, then happily perform the baptism of an infant relative at a home—giving no indication that he considered the practice to be abusive—the next. As a pastor, he was well aware that he had to begin in the same place as his flock, and it was in private conversation, as well as in his seminary classes, that he could vent his frustrations and forcibly express his own vision.

Needless to say, not all were (or, even today, are) prepared to hear or accept this vision. Certainly, in America at least, baptisms are now typically celebrated in church. All too often, however, they are still performed in private, for family and friends, apart from the Sunday liturgy. But many priests, particularly those who studied with Fr. Alexander, never lost sight of his vision, and many parishes, particularly in the Orthodox Church in America, now celebrate baptisms as part of the regular Sunday liturgy; and Holy Saturday, which has the original paschal, baptismal vigil, is often the occasion for the reception of adult converts. However, there are others, including bishops, who continue to condemn such practices as innovations, and who resist any changes whatsoever.

The Eucharist

Perhaps the most significant impact of Fr. Alexander was on eucharistic practice. Having been formed in the rich theological atmosphere of St. Sergius, and having been influenced by Frs. Nicholas Afanasiev and Cyprian Kern, he understood the eucharist to be the center of church life, the fullest manifestation of the Church in a particular time and place. Upon coming to America, he consistently and energetically sought to implement this vision in parish life, and this is where he left his greatest mark.

The challenges were great. Eucharistic reception was infrequent, typically as an obligation just once a year. The liturgy was usually conducted in Church Slavonic, a language that was totally incomprehensible to the average parishioner. The "priest's prayers" were read silently. Preaching was virtually non-existent. More generally, the Church was experienced by most as an ethnic club, whose chief purpose was to help foster one's cultural identity as a Russian, Carpatho-Russian, Ukrainian, Serb, Greek, etc. And the liturgy itself was a tool to accomplish this—thus becoming a manifestation of this fallen world rather than a foretaste of the Kingdom to come.

Because the challenges were so great, Schmemann had to attack the problems on many fronts. He did so, first of all, by his personal example. For him, there was no greater joy than to stand at the eucharistic altar, and this joy was there for all to see. He had the deep intuition that what would draw people to Christ was not rules, laws, obligations, or threats but a positive, joyful experience and vision of the Kingdom, which is already granted to us here in this world—if we are ready and willing to accept it. It was this joy that he sought so hard to transmit in both the written and spoken word for all of his life.

Everything that he did was guided by this fundamental vision. He struggled to make the liturgy available in a language accessible to the people, hence his involvement in the development of English texts of the liturgy. He actively promoted the recitation of the "priest's prayers" aloud, particularly the anaphora, pointing out that these prayer in fact belong to all the faithful, the priestly assembly. He encouraged more frequent and regular reception of the eucharist, which raised additional questions about the connection between the sacraments of confession and communion. It is hard to overstate how revolutionary such an approach appeared to be back in the 1950s and 1960s!

Fr. Schmemann's legacy is most pronounced precisely in the dramatic change in eucharistic practice. In 1992, as chairman of the OCA's liturgical commission, I conducted a survey of OCA clergy. The results were startling: 80 percent read all or part of the eucharistic anaphora aloud; 95 percent encouraged frequent communion; and 39 percent celebrated baptisms in conjunction with the eucharistic liturgy (although 69 percent would do so if the local bishop allowed it and provided guidelines!).[5] Though I have no statistics for other Orthodox jurisdictions, I have personally witnessed large numbers of regular Sunday communicants in nearly all of the parishes I have visited over the years—Greek, Antiochian, Romanian, Russian . . . and, increasingly, even Serbian!

Confession and Preparation for Communion

In the Slavic liturgical tradition in which Schmemann was raised, the sacrament of confession was required each time before receiving communion. When communion was received only once a year, this posed little difficulty; but with a more frequent reception of communion, this posed a tremendous challenge. The clergy would be overwhelmed by the huge number of penitents, the faithful would resent much more frequent confession, and confession itself would become merely a routine formality, stripped of much of its content. Adding to the confusion was the lack of a clear consensus among all Orthodox about the very meaning and necessity of confession. Orthodox practice varies widely. For the Slavic churches, confession is generally a formal requirement; the faithful are expected to confess once a year to maintain their "good standing" in the church. Among those who follow Greek practice, confession never became a legal requirement, and the vast majority of the faithful have never experienced the sacrament of confession. This is particularly the case for Greek Orthodox living in the West, as they do not have ready access to monastic spiritual elders, to whom the faithful would typically go for confession, and they would almost never consider going to their parish priest.

The pastoral challenge was great, indeed. In order to encourage more frequent communion, Fr. Alexander had to sever the one-to-one connection

5. See Meyendorff, "Liturgical Path of Orthodoxy," 43–64.

between confession and communion. Even more importantly, he needed to restore a deeper understanding of confession. In most parishes of the Slavic tradition, the once-a-year requirement for confession meant that on Holy Thursday (the traditional day for one's annual communion), the faithful would typically line up for confession. I personally witnessed one occasion when the Holy Thursday liturgy began over two hours late because of the rush of last-minute penitents. Administered in such a way, each annual confession could last only one or two minutes and consisted of a few quickly uttered prayers, several routine questions by the priest, and the prayer of absolution. This was a process that edified no one.

In some Orthodox traditions, preparation for communion requires not only confession but also up to a week of fasting and abstention from marital relations. This not only makes frequent communion virtually impossible but also leads to the temptation to think that, by performing such feats of asceticism, one is made worthy of the reception of communion. This potential danger led Fr. Alexander to compose one of his most strident articles, "Holy Things for the Holy: Some Remarks on Receiving Holy Communion."[6]

In order to address these problems and to encourage more frequent communion, in 1972, Fr. Alexander prepared a report on the subject to the Holy Synod of the Orthodox Church in America.[7] He concludes by making a number of recommendations, all of which were adopted by the bishops. In particular, he proposed the introduction of "general confession" as a supplement to the customary individual confession. This proposal, which severed the one-to-one link between confession and communion, made much greater eucharistic participation by the faithful possible. In addition, because general confession included an "enumeration by the priest of all acts, thoughts, and desires with which we offend the holiness of God, the sanctity of our neighbor, and the sanctity of our own soul,"[8] it provided an opportunity to teach the faithful about the nature of sin as something more than simply the violation of some commandment or rule. I vividly remember his classes in pastoral theology in which he described how parishioners would approach their yearly confession and have no sins whatsoever to confess—after which they would stand there, waiting to receive absolution from the priest, so that they could fulfill their annual obligation and remain "members in good standing" (i.e., be eligible to vote in the annual parish

---

6. Published as an appendix to the revised second edition of Schmemann, *Great Lent*, 107–33.

7. Schmemann, *Confession and Communion*.

8. Schmemann, *Confession and Communion*, 16.

meeting). The introduction of general confession was thus an important step for those Orthodox coming out of the Slavic traditions, but it certainly did not solve everything. For Fr. Alexander was keenly aware of the problematic history of penance and confession in the Orthodox Church. He was well aware that modern society had largely lost its understanding of sin, and that contemporary Orthodoxy did not have a clear understanding of the nature and purpose of the sacrament of confession. How often in his *Journals* he complains about people's misconceptions about confession, about their treating him as a kind of guru who could resolve all their personal problems! This was an area, however, in which he did not find the time for further work or reflection.

Challenges

Needless to say, not all Orthodox in America were comfortable with what Fr. Alexander said or did, even within the Metropolia, known since 1970 as the Orthodox Church in America. There was certainly resistance to the use of English, to the recitation of the "secret" prayers aloud, to baptismal liturgies, to presanctified liturgies in the evening, to more frequent communion, etc. The opposition generally came from those who simply wished to preserve the customs with which they grew up and which they identified with traditional Orthodoxy—making no distinction between tradition with a capital "T" and local traditions with a lower case "t"—and it came from all levels of church life, from bishops to lay people. Little did they understand that what Fr. Alexander was proposing was a return to an authentic Orthodox tradition that restored baptism and the eucharist to their central place in church life, integrating liturgy and theology, liturgy and life.

To his great credit, Schmemann knew that things could not be changed overnight, that patience was needed because the faithful needed preparation and time to digest these changes. I remember vividly how, in class, he would angrily condemn the then-common practice of celebrating one memorial service after another after the liturgy on Sunday. Don't people know that the deceased are already commemorated during the eucharistic liturgy, that our participation in communion is the best way to express our unity with and our love for them? But the next Sunday, he would, without a single complaint, happily preside over a panikhida.[9] He was ever the teacher and pastor. While guided by his strong and clear vision of what should be,

---

9. The Russian term for the memorial service for the dead, essentially an abbreviated funeral service.

he was always gentle and patient in implementing it—an example that was not, unfortunately, followed by all those who followed him.

In the years since his passing away, the debate which he started has not ebbed. There are still those who continue to resist what they call his "innovations." I recall an article that appeared in a diocesan journal not long ago which condemned the reading of prayers aloud and defended the silent recitation of the anaphora—on the basis that Hannah's prayer (1 Sam 1:13) was uttered in silence![10] As I have already indicated, however, it would not be an exaggeration to say that much of what Fr. Alexander taught has entered the mainstream within the Orthodox Church in America. In recent decades, more frequent participation in communion has become normative in a number of other jurisdictions as well—even in some parishes of the Serbian dioceses in America (through former students at St. Vladimir's Seminary). In other respects, however, liturgical practice in these jurisdictions has been less affected by his work.

Sacramental Vision

Perhaps Fr. Alexander's greatest contribution, however, is not so much in these very practical aspects of liturgical life but rather in the development of an overarching vision about the very essence of Christian life as it is expressed in the Church's liturgy. He clearly saw the challenges that secularism posed for the church. In his writings and, in particular, his talks, he constantly argued for a sacramental view of life, in which one's ecclesial and secular life remained one, integrated whole. He strenuously argued against a disincarnate and dualistic spirituality as well as against those who sought to reduce the Church merely to this world and its problems. No work of his expresses this vision more clearly than *For the Life of the World*,[11] originally a series of lectures given to a non-Orthodox Christian audience and generally regarded as his best and most influential book. Allow me to cite from his introduction:

> How can we "hold together"—in faith, in life, in action—these seemingly contradictory affirmations of the Church, how we can overcome the temptation to opt for and "absolutize" one of them, falling thus into the wrong choices or "heresies" that have so often plagued Christianity in the past?

10. Heckman, "On the Silent Prayers of the Liturgy," 24–25, 36.

11. Schmemann, *For the Life of the World*, second edition (1973). The first edition appeared in 1963.

> It is my certitude that the answer comes to us not from neat in-
> tellectual theories, but, above all, from that living and unbroken
> experience of the Church which she reveals and communicates
> to us in her worship, in the *leitourgia* always making her that
> which she is: the sacrament of the world, the sacrament of the
> Kingdom—their gift to us *in Christ*.[12]

This was the fundamental vision that guided all of Fr. Alexander's work. His
goal was never to alter the liturgy in any way or to return to some Golden
Age but rather to make the liturgy transparent—thus, capable of revealing
the Church as the manifestation of the Kingdom and us as its citizens. It was
this more than anything else which enabled him to experience the liturgy as
pure joy—a joy that he radiated to those who benefitted from his presence
and which continues to shine in the written words he has left behind, as well
as in the countless persons whom he continues to touch.

12. Schmemann, *For the Life of the World*, 8.

The Quest for Liturgical Meaning

Schmemann, Ressourcement, and Scholasticism

Eugene R. Schlesinger

"Every revolution carries within it the seeds of its own destruction"
—Princess Irulun, *Dune*.[1]

"We shall not cease from exploration
And the end of all our exploring
Will be to arrive where we started
And know the place for the first time."
—T. S. Eliot, "Little Gidding."[2]

Introduction

The early twentieth-century was a time of great ferment for both the Catholic and Orthodox theological communities living in France.[3] The latter was diasporic, and the former, if not at the margins of ecclesial

---

1. *Frank Herbert's Dune.*

2. Eliot, *Four Quartets*, 59.

3. For more on Russian emigration after the Bolshevik Revolution and the charac-ter of the diasporic community, see Meyendorff, "Postscript," 145–48; Taft, "Liturgical Enterprise," 161–62; and Denysenko, *Liturgical Reform after Vatican II*, 35–48, 94–99. On the French *ressourcement* movement, see, for example, Mettepenningen, *Nouvelle Théologie*, 172–84, and Gabriel Flynn, "Introduction," 1–19. Also note the treatment of their mutual relationship in Louth, "French *Ressourcement* Theology and Orthodoxy," 495–507.

existence, was soon to be viewed with serious suspicion.[4] Nevertheless, this was a period of immense creativity and lasting influence as both communities turned to Scripture, the church fathers, and liturgy as sources for theology, breathing new life into a discipline which had come to be dominated by the manual tradition.[5] This *ressourcement* was seen as a breath of fresh air in the musty environs of an ossified scholasticism,[6] recovering the vitality of the first Christian millennium.

Alexander Schmemann, educated at *L'Institute de Théologie Orthodoxe Saint-Serge*, drew and benefited from this unique period of creativity and cross-pollination.[7] As is well-known, his works frequently cite such *ressourcement* figures as Daniélou, Congar, and Bouyer.[8] More significant than his engagement with *ressourcement* types, though, is his methodological appropriation of their priorities in his works on liturgical theology, which hinge upon a quest for the liturgy's immanent meaning and its relevance as not just a source for but also the context of theological reflection.[9] Schmemann has helped to remind us that the Christian faith is properly located within the life of the church and that theology's validity as an academic discipline depends upon that life. This is a welcome reminder, and it has gained significant traction in what has been dubbed the Schmemann-Kavanagh-Fagerberg-Lathrop school of liturgical theology.[10]

4. For example, see Garrigou-Lagrange, "La nouvelle théologie où va-telle?," 126–45. See also Pope Pius XII's encyclical, *"Humani generis,"* which many believed contained condemnations of Henri de Lubac's, *Surnaturel : études historiques*, but which de Lubac always insisted could not have been directed towards him (de Lubac, *At the Service of the Church*, 71). Nevertheless, a pall of suspicion remained over the *nouvelle théologie* enterprise until fairly well into the Second Vatican Council. See de Lubac's account of this in *At the Service of the Church*, 67–68, and *Vatican Council Notebooks* (particularly his account of the ante-preparatory and preparatory phases of the Council).

5. A classic programmatic statement of this sensibility remains. Daniélou, "Les orientations présentes de la pensée religieuse," 5–21.

6. As we shall see, I believe that a renewed evaluation of scholasticism is in order. Nevertheless, such was the perception.

7. See Louth, *"Ressourcement* and Orthodoxy"; Taft, "Liturgical Enterprise," 163–64; Fisch, "Schmemann's Theological Contribution to the Liturgical Renewal of the Churches," 4–6; and Denysenko, *Liturgical Reform*, 9, 35–40.

8. See, for example, the introductions to Schmemann, *Introduction to Liturgical Theology*, and Schmemann, *Of Water and the Spirit*, as well as his comments about the "liturgical 'resourcement' of theology" in Schmemann, *Liturgy and Tradition*, 11–12.

9. Schmemann, *Liturgical Theology*, 11; Schmemann, *Eucharist*, 10, 13, 27–29; Schmemann, *Liturgy and Tradition*, 18, 49–68.

10. This trajectory is found in the works of Schmemann himself and carried forward in such works as Kavanagh, *On Liturgical Theology*; Fagerberg, *Theologia Prima*; and Lathrop, *Holy Things*. The terminology of a Schmemann-Kavanagh-Fagerberg-Lathrop

Nevertheless, as research into the liturgy—and, especially, its origins—has advanced, significant challenges to the Schmemann-Kavanagh-Fagerberg-Lathrop trajectory have arisen.[11] In what follows, rather than lodging a defense of Schmemann, I shall engage with his thought and his priorities in light of these criticisms. More specifically, I want to re-contextualize these critiques as themselves continuous with Schmemann's priorities and methodology. Far from being destructive to his vision, they present an opportunity for refinement. Finally, I shall suggest that a renewed appreciation for scholastic theology could present a viable way forward in light of these developments.

Schmemann and Method: History and Text

Throughout his career, Schmemann sought to recover the authentic theological meaning of the liturgy, and, in this endeavor, he seems to have faced two primary intellectual *bêtes noires*: a theological method that abstracted the liturgy from theology entirely and baroque allegorical interpretations of various liturgical acts.[12] The former severed the vital motive force from the theological enterprise while the latter distorted the liturgy's meaning by reducing it to something akin to a medieval passion play—each moment corresponding to some event in the life of Christ. In place of these two erroneous positions, Schmemann's consistent conviction was that liturgy, the church, and the theological enterprise were all inextricably linked, and that the retrieval of their intrinsic connection was needed for the church to continue to thrive.[13]

---

school appears in Aune, "Liturgy and Theology 1," 46–68, and Aune, "Liturgy and Theology 2," 141–69.

11. See, for example, Bradshaw, "Difficulties in Doing Liturgical Theology," 181–94; Johnson, "Can We Avoid Relativism in Worship?," 135–55; Aune, "Liturgy and Theology 1"; Aune, "Liturgy and Theology 2"; and Aune, "Current State of Liturgical Theology," 209–29.

12. On abstraction from the liturgy see, for example, Schmemann, *Liturgical Theology*, 9–11; *Of Water and the Spirit*, 7–12, 76–77; *Eucharist*, 13–14, 161; *Church, World, Mission*, 21–22; and *Liturgy and Tradition*, 11–18, 61–65. On the avoidance of allegorical interpretations of the liturgy, see Schmemann, *Liturgical Theology*, 14; *Of Water and the Spirit*, 12, 110–11; *Eucharist*, 14, 30–31; and *Liturgy and Tradition*, 102–3, 115–29. See also Taft's suggestion that Schmemann actually had a great affinity with the allegorical mystagogical tradition but just never quite realized it (Taft, "Liturgical Enterprise," 173–74).

13. See the previous note, along with Fagerberg, "Cost of Understanding Schmemann in the West," 179–207, and Taft, "Liturgical Enterprise," 166, 175. In this regard, Schmemann was highly influenced by the emergent eucharistic ecclesiologies of Nicholai Afanasiev, Aleksei Khomiakov, and Cyprian Kern. See further Denysenko, *Liturgical*

To achieve this retrieval, Schmemann deployed two techniques. One was to attend carefully to the liturgical texts themselves in order to draw out their immanent intelligibility from them rather than impose foreign constructions upon them.[14] The other was a turn to history, recognizing that the liturgy has developed and complexified over the centuries, seeking a more basic meaning beneath those accretions.[15] Indeed, citing Filaret, the Archbishop of Chernigov, Schmemann goes so far as to say: "A theory of worship in the Church which does not rest on historical data is in itself false, and is also harmful in its consequences."[16]

By attending to a sort of liturgical archaeology, Schmemann sought to retrieve lost meanings of the liturgy, such as the paschal character of baptism,[17] the ecclesiological character of the Eucharist,[18] or the intersection of eschatology and time in the Typikon.[19] This turn to history led Schmemann to seek a more formal *ordo* which lay behind the various material permutations of liturgical development.[20] For Schmemann, though, the basic meaning of the liturgy is about the eschatological disclosure of the church as the body of Christ and the church's entry into the Kingdom of God.[21] This is the vision that animates Schmemann's project: the re-integration of the church, liturgy, and eschatology in a coherent synthesis based upon the church's liturgical tradition.[22]

Reform, 87–94, and Plekon, "Church, the Eucharist and the Kingdom," 119–43.

14. Schmemann, *Liturgical Theology*, 14, 28–39; *Of Water and the Spirit*; *Eucharist*, esp. the programmatic statement on 13–14; *Liturgy and Tradition*, 61–65, 69–88, 115–29. Attentive readers will recognize "immanent intelligibility" as a signal of where this essay is heading vis-à-vis scholasticism.

15. For example, Schmemann, *Liturgical Theology*, 16–18, 28–71, and Schmemann, *Of Water and the Spirit*, 15–16, 37–38, 109–15.

16. Schmemann, *Liturgical Theology*, 17.

17. Schmemann, *Of Water and the Spirit*, 37–38.

18. Schmemann, *Eucharist*, 11–26; *For the Life of the World*, 26–28.

19. Schmemann, *Liturgical Theology*, 40–71.

20. Schmemann, *Liturgical Theology*, 17–18.

21. Schmemann, *Of Water and the Spirit*, 109–29; *Eucharist*, 27–63; *For the Life of the World*, 26–46; *Church, World, Mission*, 10–11, 149–55, 210–15; *Liturgy and Tradition*, 115–29. See further Plekon, "Church, Eucharist, Kingdom"; Fagerberg, "Cost of Understanding Schmemann in the West," 195–203; Denysenko, *Liturgical Reform*, 99–113.

22. Schmemann contends that the separation of liturgy from theology is one of the greatest ills plaguing the church and academy (Schmemann, *Liturgical Theology*, 9–15).

Schmemann's Project and the Problem of History

Schmemann's historical reconstruction of the liturgy and its meaning was based upon the prevailing scholarly opinions of his time.[23] However, in the intervening years, historical scholarship on the liturgy has advanced considerably, often leaving these older understandings behind as inadequate to the data.[24] For example, in Schmemann's articulation of the underlying *ordo* of the liturgy, he is clearly indebted to Gregory Dix's influential theory of the "shape" of the liturgy, which reconstructed a formal liturgical structure undergirding the various material differences and developments the liturgy took.[25] A Dixian theory of liturgical development sees a fairly straightforward progression from Jewish liturgical forms, whether the Seder or the synagogue, to more fully developed Christian liturgies, a perspective which Schmemann also evinces.[26] Yet so linear a progression is no longer tenable in light of what we now understand to be an almost staggering diversity of liturgical practice in early Christianity.[27] Moreover, the influence of Graeco-Roman forms upon Christian liturgy is also becoming clearer, complexifying the question of the influence of Jewish forms upon Christian practices.[28]

Another example is Schmemann's appeal to the *Apostolic Traditions* and his attribution of the document to Hippolytus of Rome.[29] Though formerly the *Apostolic Traditions* was judged to be a witness to third-century liturgical practice in Rome, a judgment which significantly informed twentieth-century liturgical reforms (of which the Catholic Church's *Rite of Christian Initiation*

23. See, for example, his judicious sifting of evidence and opinions regarding the emergence of the "liturgy of time" in Schmemann, *Liturgical Theology*, 40–43.

24. These issues are explicitly documented in articles such as Bradshaw, "Difficulties in Doing Liturgical Theology"; Johnson, "Can We Avoid Relativism in Worship?"; Aune, "Liturgy and Theology 1"; Aune, "Liturgy and Theology 2"; and Aune, "Current State of Liturgical Theology."

25. For example, Dix, *Shape of the Liturgy*. See Schmemann's direct appeals to Dix in *Liturgical Theology*, 17–18, and *Eucharist*, 13.

26. Dix, *Shape of the Liturgy*, 48–82; Schmemann, *Liturgical Theology*, 40–71; *Liturgy and Tradition*, 15–17.

27. For but a few examples, see Bradshaw, *Search for the Origins of Christian Worship*; Klinghardt, *Gemeinschaftsmahl und Mahlgemeinschaft*; McGowan, *Ascetic Eucharists*; *Ancient Christian Worship*; "Rethinking Eucharistic Origins," 173–91; "'FIRST REGARDING THE CUP,'" 551–55; "Naming the Feast," 314–18; and Chilton, *Feast of Meanings*.

28. Klinghardt, *Gemeinschaftsmahl und Mahlgemeinschaft*; Klinghardt, "'Nehmt und eßt, das ist mein Leib!,'" 37–69; McGowan, *Ancient Christian Worship*, 24–55; as well as the essays in Klinghardt and Taussig, *Mahl und religiöse Identität im frühen Christentum*.

29. Schmemann, *Eucharist*, 112.

of Adults is perhaps the foremost instance),[30] this claim's historical basis is now not only dubitable but has simply been disproven. The *Apostolic Traditions* is almost certainly a composite document drawn from geographically diverse communities, leading Paul Bradshaw to conclude that it is "most improbable that it represents the actual practice of any single community," much less third-century Rome.[31] While the theology of *Apostolic Traditions* may be quite defensible, and perhaps even *should* inform contemporary liturgies, this influence can no longer be understood as a historical re-pristination. At the very least, it cannot provide a historical basis for claims such as Schmemann's. This does not invalidate Schmemann's proposals, but it does require a rethinking of their relationship to history.

All of this leads Bradshaw to conclude that all too often liturgical theology tends to "rest upon bad history or no history at all."[32] As a result, it has been too free with its definite article in describing "the liturgy," as if there were a uniform tradition rather than polyphony, and has tended to ignore the bi-directionality of traffic between liturgy's "*theologia prima*" and doctrinal theology's "*theologia secunda*."[33] This latter insight is crucial, for it forces a recontextualization of the principle of a *lex orandi*, which informs the *lex credendi*.

This recontextualization works on a couple of levels. First, Bradshaw notes that even Prosper of Aquitaine's famous appeal to the *lex orandi* was actually meant to bolster a theological case in which he had first appealed to papal decree. The liturgy provided support, but the pope's authority was the actual basis of Prosper's argument.[34] Indeed, in most appeals to the *lex orandi* one already has doctrinal norms in mind for which one looks for support in liturgical texts, and unexamined principles of selectivity tend to drive determinations of what is "essential" to the liturgy (and hence carries

---

30. Catholic Church, *Rite of Christian Initiation of Adults*. See also Peter McGrail's excellent treatment of the context for the emergence of these revised rites and the problematic status of the history it purported to reconstruct (*Rite of Christian Initiation*). Johnson's discussion of the history of Christian initiation and the twentieth-century revisions is quite nuanced, detailed, and sympathetic (*Rites of Christian Initiation*).

31. Bradshaw, *Origins of Christian Worship*, 80–83.

32. Bradshaw, "Difficulties in Doing Liturgical Theology," 193–94.

33. The terminology of primary and secondary theology is Aidan Kavanagh's, but in developing this differentiation, he is developing convictions basic to Schmemann. See Kavanagh, *On Liturgical Theology*.

34. Bradshaw, "Difficulties in Doing Liturgical Theology," 186–87. See also Aune's discussion of the problems attending appeal to the "*lex orandi*" ("Liturgy and Theology 1," 65–68).

authoritative weight) and what is not (and hence should not be brought to bear on doctrinal norms).[35] Second, as Bradshaw explains:

> Attractive though such a distinction between primary and secondary theology sounds, its vision of the former is a highly romantic one. It is doubtful whether many worshippers have ever engaged in an act of *pure* primary theology. When Christians gather on a Sunday morning to worship God, they do not come with their minds a *tabula rasa*. On the contrary, they come together with their religious attitudes and expectations already formed by secondary theology as a result of the catechesis that their particular ecclesiastical tradition has given to them over the years; and they usually participate in a liturgical rite that itself has been shaped and honed by secondary theological reflection in order to give expression to particular doctrinal convictions.[36]

All of this leads Michael Aune to conclude that liturgical theology's future lies in a different direction than the one charted by the "Schmemann-Kavanagh-Fagerberg-Lathrop line."[37] The agenda proposed by Aune is twofold: "'Liturgical theology' needs to be both more *historical* and more *theological* in its content and character."[38]

That liturgical theology must be more attentive to the fruits of historical research is undeniable, but this contention itself must be historically contextualized because it is not at all a novel idea. To be sure, we can no longer appeal to "Hippolytus" for evidence of ancient Roman practices of initiation or anaphora. We must recognize that no straight line can be drawn from the synagogue to the church's liturgy. Moreover, the diversity of early Christian worship is so strong that the search for an immutable *ordo* or "shape of the liturgy" is complexified to say the least.[39]

But we must also resist the tendency to measure the scholarship of past generations by the canon of our own achievements, as though our intellectual forebears were simply methodologically sloppy or inattentive to

---

35. Bradshaw, "Difficulties in Doing Liturgical Theology," 187–88.

36. Bradshaw, "Difficulties in Doing Liturgical Theology," 191.

37. Aune, "Liturgy and Theology 1," 48.

38. Aune, "Liturgy and Theology 1," 47–48.

39. Note Johnson's defense of a more simple ordo in Lathrop's scholarship ("Can We Avoid Relativism in Worship?," 150–51), as well as Bradshaw's judgment that Lathrop's "categorization may be a little too neat and tidy, a little over-systematized to fit the full facts of history, yet it offers a promising avenue for future exploration" ("Difficulties in Doing Liturgical Theology," 186).

evidence.[40] In the case of Schmemann, it is clear enough that he recognized the diversity of early Christian worship, writing:

> We know of course that worship has passed through a long and complicated development, and that the contemporary uniformity of liturgical norms in Orthodoxy is a comparatively late phenomenon. The Church has never believed that complete uniformity in ceremonies and prayers is an obligatory condition of her unity, nor has she ever finally identified her *lex orandi* with any particular "historical" type of worship.[41]

Later in the same work, Schmemann notes that the *Typikons* which govern worship are amalgams of historical and local developments.[42] So while current research is showing us that the diversity of early Christian liturgy is more profound than Schmemann would have imagined, it is not as if he ignored the reality of diversity.

Indeed, in many ways, the recognition of historical problems with the "Schmemann, et al." line of liturgical scholarship are themselves the fruit of that line of inquiry. Schmemann returned attention to the liturgy and its history, and that attention has uncovered new evidence of which Schmemann was not aware. Nevertheless, by pioneering this inquiry, Schmemann laid the ground work for these subsequent developments. The proper way to honor his legacy is to follow the research where it goes, for had it been available in his day, he would have drawn upon it himself.

Moreover, while some of Schmemann's ideas about the origins of certain liturgical practices are no longer tenable, we must also recognize that,

40. Indeed, Aune's historical perspective is somewhat marred by his appeal to LaCugna, *God for Us*, for his characterization of pre-Nicene theology (Aune, "Liturgy and Theology 2," 146–47, 155). Recent patristics scholarship has exposed the inadequacies of LaCugna's work, premised as it is upon the century-old and now quite debunked typology of Theodore de Régnon. See, for example, Ayres, *Nicaea and Its Legacy*; Barnes, "De Régnon Reconsidered," 51–79; and Barnes, "Augustine in Contemporary Trinitarian Theology," 237–50. I raise this somewhat ironic point not because I believe it invalidates Aune's basic agenda but simply to illustrate that scholarship is always moving forward, making attentiveness to the fruits of historical research a moving target.

41. Schmemann, *Liturgical Theology*, 16. See Fagerberg's judgment that those who would see Schmemann's appeal to the *lex orandi* as somehow appealing to "an ancient and universal practice" is a grave misunderstanding ("Cost of Understanding Schmemann in the West," 190–92). Hence, that "ancient liturgical practice was not as uniform as we thought" is not destructive to Schmemann's fundamental conviction. Instead, the *lex orandi* is less a theory about the liturgy qua liturgy; rather, it is a conviction about the church's faith, which is expressed in (not necessarily derived from) the church's liturgies. It is only by considering the question outside of the overall and integral perspective of the church's life that such a misunderstanding is able to arise.

42. Schmemann, *Liturgical Theology*, 28–39.

by and large, his attention was on later developments anyway, particularly the "Byzantine synthesis."[43] By the time of this synthesis, a good deal more uniformity was obtained, and Schmemann's proposals about the theology operative in those rites ought to be evaluated on their own merits rather than scuttled on the shoals of the diversity that characterized an era earlier than where he lodges his main contentions. For that matter, it would be a mistake to assume that liturgical theology is governed by a principle of "primitivism," as though straightforward repristination of a bygone golden age were all that is in view.

So much for history. Aune contends that the future of liturgical theology will also need to be more theological. Once more, this is absolutely correct, but it needs to be contextualized. Aune's contention is that the theology to which the study of the liturgy must be attentive is one of divine self-communication.[44] He believes that the priority of divine initiative has been occluded in liturgical theology, which has tended to focus upon ecclesiology instead of God's self-communication.[45] And yet, this is not so much a matter of liturgical theology being less than explicitly theological as it is a matter of Aune thinking that a different theological supposition is in order. Schmemann's formula intertwining church, Eucharist, and eschatology is quite theological; it is just not the same as what Aune sees operative in the liturgy.

That said, though, Aune is quite right (and here he follows Bradshaw and Johnson) to insist that liturgical theologians recognize that there are indeed extra-liturgical suppositions at play and informing their formulations of the theology operative in the liturgy. One's engagement with the liturgy is always already informed by such matters as kerygma and catechesis. Indeed, Schmemann himself tends to import theological assumptions into his reading of the liturgy, such as when he develops an account of humanity as priest, prophet, and king with reference to the sacrament of chrismation. Importantly, Schmemann argues that the royal, priestly, and prophetic offices are anthropological principles, intrinsic to humanity's nature as created. The sacraments of initiation give a share in Christ's threefold office, yes, but this is because—even more fundamentally—the threefold office is the primordial calling of humanity.[46] As Nicholas Denysenko notes, Schmemann imports a particular definition of what a Christian is, rooted in a theological anthropology, onto the rites, but "does not establish how the initiatory rites communi-

---

43. See, Schmemann, *Liturgical Theology*, 116–67.
44. Aune, "Liturgy and Theology 1," 151–58.
45. Aune, "Liturgy and Theology 1," 156.
46. Schmemann, *Of Water and the Spirit*, 71–108.

cate the imparting of these gifts."[47] Similarly, Denysenko notes "Schmemann's reference to the 'Fathers' as a collective entity," however, "Schmemann does not identify which particular 'fathers' conceived of the Eucharist as 'sacrament of sacraments.'"[48] So again, Schmemann has a *theolegoumenon* in mind and attributes it to his sources (the liturgy in one case, the "fathers" in another), but in both instances, he is importing this *theolegoumenon* rather than drawing it exclusively from said sources.

From my perspective, *that* Schmemann imports extra-liturgical theological categories into his explanation of the liturgy is not a problem. If we take seriously the fact that—at least in its theologically normative pattern—sacramental initiation is preceded by catechesis, or at least by kerygma, it is unavoidable that previously imparted theological formulations inform one's engagement with the liturgy.[49] What this recognition does, though, is open space for a more explicit interaction between theological categories native to the liturgy and extra-liturgical categories. In other words, this is already happening; by recognizing it, we have the opportunity to do it in a more coherent and methodological manner.

Scholasticism and the Quest for Meaning

In this connection, I believe that a re-engagement with scholastic theology presents an important aid to advancing Schmemann's theological agenda. To be sure, in many ways, the *ressourcement* movement was positioned as a reaction against scholasticism, but it is important to recognize that, at least among the Catholic *nouveaux théologiens*, it was never a repudiation of scholasticism as such. Indeed, many of the movement's controversies evolved around the question of how best to interpret that scholastic *par excellence*, Thomas Aquinas.[50] The *ressourcement* did not seek to repudiate Thomas but

---

47. Denysenko, *Liturgical Reform*, 46–47.

48. Denysenko, *Liturgical Reform*, 102, citing Schmemann, *Of Water and the Spirit*, 106.

49. Note that the theologically normative rite is the one by which adult converts are brought into the church (i.e., the *RCIA*). The application of the sacraments of initiation to infants is a theologically warranted extension of this normative pattern. Schmemann is aware of this principle (*Of Water and the Spirit*, 15–20). Even apart from the ancient catechumenate and its modern restoration, the New Testament records baptism occurring in response to the gospel's proclamation.

50. See de Lubac, *Surnaturel*, esp. 421–71, and Garrigou-Lagrange, "La nouvelle théologie." See also the discussion in Mulcahy, *Aquinas's Notion of Pure Nature and the Christian Integralism of Henri de Lubac*, and Hütter, "*Desiderium Naturale Visionis Dei,*" 81–183.

rather to retrieve an authentic teaching obscured by the subsequent manual tradition. Whether or not the *nouveaux théologiens* were correct in their assessment of Aquinas (or, for that matter, of early modern theology) is beside the point.[51] What matters is that there need be no antipathy between *ressourcement* and scholasticism.

That said, Schmemann's criticisms of and disdain for "school theology" is well-documented and consistent. His most basic complaint about scholastic theology was its separation from and tendency to overlook the church's liturgical experience.[52] On this score, he is almost certainly correct: the church's life must be taken seriously as the source and context of theological inquiry. Nevertheless, it should be born in mind that, at least in scholasticism's medieval form, the scholastics were men of deep devotion and piety, who engaged in more than writing disputations. The same Thomas Aquinas who produced the *Summas* was also a priest who celebrated the Mass, wrote liturgical poetry, and produced biblical commentaries. Whatever the state of the theology manuals against which Schmemann reacted, the example of Aquinas demonstrates that there is nothing about scholastic method that *requires* this separation of liturgy and theology.

Schmemann's other criticisms included the tendency of scholastic theology to focus reductively upon questions of validity rather than exploring the fullness of liturgical and sacramental acts.[53] For instance, rather than exploring the rich and polyvalent symbolism of water and the notion of an entrance into the fullness of life that is the Kingdom of God, the minimum requirements of proper matter and form became the focus in the theology of baptism.[54] Such minimalism also led to losing sight of the eschatological and ecclesial meaning of the Eucharist.[55] Once more, the concern is a valid one (no pun intended), but does not necessarily undermine the scholastic enterprise. After all, questions of validity do not stem from a downgrading of the sacraments' importance but rather quite the opposite. Yes, there is

51. On this front, due to the nature of the French Jesuit scholasticate at his time, the somewhat idiosyncratic theological formation de Lubac received is relevant. See Kerr, *Twentieth-Century Catholic Theologians*, 67–70. Dominicans (such as Yves Congar and Marie-Dominique Chenu), however, were in a different situation vis-à-vis early modern scholasticism.

52. Schmemann, *Liturgical Theology*, 9–10, 14–15; *Liturgy and Tradition*, 13–14, 55–56, 61–62; *Eucharist*, 12–14, 161; *Of Water and the Spirit*, 12, 76–77; *For the Life of the World*, 135–36.

53. Schmemann, *Eucharist*, 116; *Of Water and the Spirit*, 38–40; *For the Life of the World*, 67–68.

54. See Schmemann, *Of Water and the Spirit*, 37–70, 109–30.

55. See, for example, Schmemann, *Eucharist*, and *Liturgy and Tradition*, 69–88. See also his exposition of the eucharistic liturgy in *For the Life of the World*, 23–46.

a fullness of life bestowed through baptism. This then raises the question: has this person been baptized? Have *I* been baptized? Assuming that some rite was performed, this becomes a question of validity. If the minimalism of validity is used to undercut liturgical and theological fullness, it is a misuse of that question, but it does not invalidate (pun intended, this time) the question altogether.

A final, related criticism of scholasticism is its tendency to "dismember" the coherent whole that is a liturgical act in order to inquire as to its discrete elements. An instance of this is a focusing in upon real presence, sacrifice, and communion in a consideration of the Eucharist rather than attending to its entire *Gestalt*, in which case, key dimensions of the sacrament (such as its ecclesial nature and eschatological orientation) are overlooked.[56] Nevertheless, there is nothing wrong with treating separate questions separately. Indeed, this is sometimes the only way to advance in understanding.[57] The problem is not with differentiating questions but rather with excluding relevant questions from one's inquiry or with losing sight of the coherence of the constituent elements of a thing.[58]

In this way, we have come to the crux of the matter: the contribution of scholasticism to theology. It is one thing to suggest that (negatively) the liabilities Schmemann sees with scholastic thought are not intrinsic to it and another thing to suggest that (positively) scholasticism could contribute to his enterprise. As I noted above, Schmemann's vision of liturgical theology is, above all, the pursuit of the theological meaning of the church's liturgy.[59] The interrogation of meaning and the pursuit of understanding is precisely the provenance of scholastic theology, making it a potentially fruitful interlocutor for liturgical theology.

Above all, scholastic theology is concerned with the intelligibility of doctrine and the divine mysteries. This may be seen in the first ten articles of the *Summa theologiæ*'s *Prima pars*, which inquire as to whether or not sacred doctrine is a science (i.e., whether it is concerned with real knowledge).[60] It also informs the perspective of Vatican I's Constitution on the Catholic Faith, *Dei filius*, which commends that reason, aided by faith, pursue "some understanding, and that most profitable, of the mysteries,

---

56. See Schmemann, *Eucharist*, 116, 207, 214.

57. This principle is exemplified in Lonergan, *Insight*.

58. See Lonergan, *Insight*, 270–95, with its account of the intelligibility of "things," as distinct from the "bodies" which might compose them.

59. "The elucidation of the meaning of worship" (Schmemann, *Liturgical Theology*, 14). See also Schmemann, *Of Water and the Spirit*, 15–16, 76–77, 152, and *Eucharist*, 27–30.

60. Aquinas, *Summa Theologiæ*, 1.1.1–10.

whether by analogy from what it knows naturally, or from the connexion of the mysteries with one another and the final end of humanity."[61] When Schmemann pursued the meaning of the liturgy, he was, without realizing it, pursuing the same end as scholastic theology.

This principle is also discernible in the question of eucharistic presence. Regarding the presence of Christ's body and blood in the sacrament, Schmemann both affirms the reality and castigates the Western scholastic notion of transubstantiation as a way of talking about it. So, for instance, he finds the scholastic talk of substance, accidents, and the change of the former to be worthless for the faith experience of the church, preferring instead the simple liturgical confession that "this is truly Thine own most pure Body . . . this is truly Thine own precious Blood."[62] This confession, he believes, is sufficient such that "any attempt to *explain* the conversion, to locate it in formulas and causes, is not only unnecessary, but harmful."[63] Yet this characterization, especially when coupled with an approving quotation of Khomiakiv's statement that transubstantiation winds up reducing the sacrament "into a certain 'anatomical miracle'" having to do with "the tasting of 'sacred matter,'"[64] demonstrates that whatever Schmemann is displeased with, it is not the doctrine of transubstantiation.

At issue are the propriety of two distinct matters: doctrinal development and speculative elaboration.[65] To begin with, in the Catholic Church's official teaching, transubstantiation is simply a word, not an explanation. Its first appearance in the magisterium—at the Fourth Lateran Council—is quite minimal: "His body and blood are truly contained in the sacrament of the altar under the forms of bread and wine, the bread and wine having been changed in substance [*transubstantiatis*], by God's power, into his body and blood."[66] Similarly, in the later affirmations of the Council of Trent, the church "openly and without qualification professes that, after the consecration of the bread and wine, our lord Jesus Christ, true God and true man, is truly, really, and substantially contained in the propitious sacrament of the holy eucharist under the appearance of those things which are perceptible to the senses,"[67] with the further statement:

---

61. Tanner, *Decrees of the Ecumenical Councils*, 2:808.

62. Schmemann, *Eucharist*, 162.

63. Schmemann, *Eucharist*, 222–23.

64. Khomakiov quoted in Schmemann, *Eucharist*, 235.

65. What I have in mind here is roughly equivalent to the functional specializations of "doctrines" and "systematics" in Lonergan, *Method in Theology*, 295–353.

66. Tanner, *Decrees of the Ecumenical Councils*, 1:230.

67. Tanner, *Decrees of the Ecumenical Councils*, 2:693.

> By the consecration of the bread and wine, there take place
> the change of the whole substance [*conversionem fieri totius
> substantiae*] of the bread into the substance of the body of
> Christ our Lord, and of the whole substance of the wine into
> the substance of his blood. And the holy catholic church has
> suitably and properly [*convenienter et proprie*] called this change
> transubstantiation.[68]

In none of these statements is "transubstantiation" used as an explanation. Instead, it is used to affirm the reality that the eucharistic elements
truly are Christ's body and blood. Essentially, they are meant to uphold
the reality confessed in Schmemann's preferred formula (see above). They
state nothing further, nor do they demand assent to any further propositions. As Schmemann recognizes, the language of transubstantiation arose
in response to the Berengarian controversy, which raised the question of
whether Christ is in the sacrament "mystically" or "really."[69] The doctrinal
force of transubstantiation is simply to avoid the Berengarian rejection of
the reality of Christ's body and blood in the sacrament while also avoid-
ing any crude literalisms (such as those found in the oath imposed upon
Berengar at Rome in 1059, which affirmed the tearing of Christ's flesh with
the teeth of the faithful) in that avoidance.[70]

Seen in this light, the term "transubstantiation" is nothing more than a
doctrinal affirmation, which developed within a particular set of historical
circumstances in response to a particular problem. The fact of the matter
is, once the challenges that provoke further refinements of language (or
speculative elaborations) have arisen, there is no putting the genie back into
the bottle. Once Berengar raises the question of whether Christ's body is in
the sacrament mystically or really, the challenge can no longer be met by
re-stating the liturgical confession, "this is truly Thine own most pure Body
. . . this is truly Thine own precious Blood," for it is precisely the meaning
of these words that is under question. Nor can we simply say that this is
a bad question: it has been asked and it demands an answer. In the West,
transubstantiation was that answer, and it is simply a way of unambiguously
affirming the meaning of that more primitive confession.

The Catholic Church's official doctrine answers the question thus
without requiring any particular speculative commitments of those who

---

68. Tanner, *Decrees of the Ecumenical Councils*, 2:695. Later in the canons, on the
Eucharist, the fathers use the language, "a change which the catholic church most aptly
[*aptissime*] calls transubstantiation" (*Decrees of the Ecumenical Councils*, 2:697).

69. Schmemann, *Eucharist*, 223; Kilmartin, *Eucharist in the West*, 97–102; and de
Lubac, *Corpus Mysticum*, 144–46, 152, 226–30.

70. See Kilmartin, *Eucharist in the West*, 99–100, for the oath.

would believe the Church's teaching, though the more complex elaboration provided by figures such as Thomas Aquinas gives further insight into the intelligibility of this simple doctrine. For contrary to popular opinion, transubstantiation has nothing whatsoever to do with anatomical changes or a physical conversion of elements (to use the terminology Schmemann drew from Khomiavov above). This is demonstrated by considering Thomas Aquinas's teaching on the real presence, which affirms that the whole Christ is entirely present under each of the sacramental species in their entirety,[71] that this presence is not local,[72] and that what happens to the host or chalice (e.g., motion, fraction) does not happen to Christ himself.[73] Put into a more contemporary scientific idiom, Christ's presence in the sacrament has nothing to do with atoms, molecules, or chemical composition.[74]

Hence, we must differentiate between the notion of transubstantiation as such, which is affirmed in doctrinal formularies, but without any speculative elaboration, and theological inquiry into the doctrine, which appeals to a speculative apparatus in order to promote understanding of the doctrine. The former is essentially the same as the liturgical confession Schmemann upholds: in response to a new challenge, new ways of speaking are developed. The notion of transubstantiation adds no new meaning to the primitive ways of speaking, but rather closes off false understandings that were left open due to the ambiguities of language. The latter is not formally defined, nor are the faithful required to hold to it. It does, however, avoid some of the very reductive crudities which Schmemann criticizes. The existence of those crudities—and of Schmemann's apparent misunderstanding of what transubstantiation means—demonstrates the ongoing importance of speculative positions designed to demonstrate the intelligibility of doctrinal norms.

In all of the foregoing, my intent is not to suggest that Orthodox theologians ought to adopt Western scholastic positions on the real presence. Instead, it is to show that (1) scholasticism is not so inimical to the enterprise of liturgical theology as Schmemann seems to have thought it was, and (2) that the intent of scholastic theology is the same as that of liturgical theology: to give an account of meaning and intelligibility. As I said above, Schmemann's pursuit of the theological meaning of the liturgy was, essentially, a scholastic enterprise. Indeed, his tendency to collocate

71. Aquinas, *Summa Theologiæ*, 3.76.2–3

72. Aquinas, *Summa Theologiæ*, 3.76.5

73. Aquinas, *Summa Theologiæ*, 3.76.3, 6.

74. For an excellent contemporary restatement of the Thomistic doctrine in the terms set out by Lonergan's epistemology and metaphysics, see Mudd, *Eucharist as Meaning*.

the church, the Eucharist, and eschatology is an example of pursuing an understanding based upon the *nexus mysteriorum*, which the First Vatican Council advocated in *Dei filius*.

At the same time, this is not a call for a return to scholasticism *tout simple*. Rather, what I propose is a sort of *ressourcement* scholasticism (or perhaps a scholastic *ressourcement*). What I mean by this is straightforward enough. Schmemann's turn to the liturgy as a locus and context for theological intelligibility is, I think, a permanent achievement. There should be no turning back the clock on it for the theological enterprise: no return to a cleavage between theological reflection and the church's life of worship. Moreover, Schmemann is right to point us to the need to pursue the fullness of meaning latent in our liturgies. While I have defended the propriety of inquiring as to the minimum requirements of validity for the sacraments, we must avoid any myopia in this question which would lose sight of the maximal import of the sacraments. Maximal meaning—rather than minimal validity—ought to be regarded as normative, and it is there that theological reflection should be lodged. Moreover, though it is simply a matter of good methodology to consider separate questions separately, the pursuit of theological understanding should keep in mind the whole, the interconnection of these separate elements, the *nexus mysteriorum*.

At the same time, liturgical theologians should not be afraid of engaging in the speculative enterprise of faith seeking understanding, for though the liturgy is slow to change, the world is not. New challenges and questions arise, and in meeting these exigencies, speculative theology serves an important role.[75] Indeed, by seeking the theological meaning of the liturgy, they are already engaged in theological speculation.

Conclusion

The liturgical *ressourcement* of Alexander Schmemann remains a milestone of recent theological endeavor. But like all theological endeavors, it was historically contingent, limited by the understandings available to Schmemann in his historical-cultural-intellectual environment. Its ongoing validity depends upon what subsequent scholars (within their own historically limited horizons) do with it.

---

75. Schmemann was quite attuned to the currents of contemporary civilization and frequently spoke to them. It is often at these junctures, however, that his unacknowledged speculative flourishes would come out, such as the theological anthropology that Denysenko notes he appeals to in explaining the rite of chrismation. See Schmemann, *Of Water and the Spirit*, 81–108, and Denysenko, *Liturgical Reform*, 45–47.

By turning our attention to the liturgy and its history, Schmemann has sown the seeds for calling into question some of his particular formulations, as research into the liturgy's origins has shown that the ritual practices of early Christianity were far more diverse than Schmemann ever anticipated, making appeal to "the" liturgy as a theological source somewhat problematic. Moreover, this discovery of liturgical polyphony has also demonstrated that straightforward appeal to the liturgy for theological content is also a fraught enterprise: it is nearly impossible to build a systematic theology upon the liturgy alone, for the liturgy is varied, speaks with multiple voices, and is subject to multiple meanings.[76] Moreover, any engagement with the liturgy is always already conditioned by "secondary" theological reflection.

This recognition presents us with the opportunity to consider once more the role of speculative theology in the enterprise of liturgical theology. The *ressourcement* has retrieved great riches of biblical, patristic, and liturgical wisdom while, for its part, scholastic theology presents a specialized discipline for interrogating theological meaning. In the modern twentieth century, they parted ways (for a variety of reasons), but in the post-modern, twenty-first century, they must work in tandem. Each without the other is incomplete. But the two of them together present the best hope for achieving their one common goal: to set forth the authentic meaning of the new life given by God, through Christ, and realized in the church by the power of the Holy Spirit.

76. Bradshaw, "Difficulties in Doing Liturgical Theology," 188, 190–94.

PART 2

Ecumenical Essays

Schmemann among the Kuyperians

Christian Worldview, Sacramental Worship, and Discerning Cultural Engagement in Ecumenical Conversation

John D. Witvliet

Resonances Across Christian Traditions

For the past thirty years, since I was an undergraduate at Calvin College in Grand Rapids, Michigan, I have been reading Schmemann among the Kuyperians.

For many readers of this volume, I need to explain this reference. Abraham Kuyper (1837–1920) was a prolific Dutch Reformed pastor, theologian, journalist, and politician who, in a single lifetime, pastored two congregations, founded a university, served as Prime Minister of the Netherlands, wrote several volumes of theology and devotional literature, and helped to found a Reformed denomination—all as an expression of his distaste for modernism and his embrace of a world-engaging vision of Christian discipleship.[1]

Kuyper's vision for a Christian way of life, most famously articulated in his 1898 Stone Lectures at Princeton Theological Seminary, was influential in shaping the mission and ethos of Calvin College and Calvin Theological Seminary where I studied and where I now teach.[2] This vision promotes an all-encompassing Christian spirituality which aspires to engage every sphere of life, not just church life, in Jesus' name. In Kuyper's words, "no single piece of our mental world is to be hermetically sealed

---

1. See Bratt, *Abraham Kuyper*, and Wood, *Going Dutch in the Modern Age*.
2. Kuyper's Stone Lectures are still in print. See Kuyper, *Lectures on Calvinism*.

off from the rest, and there is not a square inch in the whole domain of our human existence over which Christ, who is Sovereign over *all*, does not cry: 'Mine!'"[3] If Jesus is Lord of all creation, if God created everything good, then each dimension of creation and culture offers potential for Christian redemptive engagement. This means that vital Christian discipleship is not equated with church ministry but rather can be expressed in any field of study and in every aspect of life—fertile theological soil for Christian liberal arts education. There are still Calvin College students that keep a tally of how often this Kuyper quotation is heard on campus during their Calvin years.

This Kuyperian tradition is merely one strand of the much broader Reformed and Presbyterian tradition. The world's 200 million plus Reformed and Presbyterian Christians are a loosely connected tapestry with strands that are identified with any number of quite different theologians (e.g., Calvin and Knox, Owens and Edwards, Warfield and Nevin, Kuyper and Barth), confessions (e.g., Westminster and Belgic, Barmen and Belhar), movements (e.g., ranging from conservative neo-confessionalism to appropriations of more progressive liberation theologies), and international associations (e.g., World Communion of Reformed Churches and the International Conference of Reformed Churches) across many cultural contexts and denominations in over 200 countries.

Think of these Kuyperian Reformed voices as roughly analogous to an order within the Catholic Church (though with less institutional definition). Just as the Benedictines and Jesuits have particular charisms and institutions, so too Kuyperian Reformed Christians have been animated by the charism of Kuyper's all-encompassing vision of the world as created good by God, distorted by sin, and redeemed by Jesus Christ—a charism which inspired and has been sustained by a variety of institutions, including journals (e.g., *Reformed Journal*, *Perspectives*, and *Comment*), non-profit organizations (e.g., the Center for Public Justice), key publishers (including those that ensure Grand Rapids is a prominent location in theological bibliographies), and colleges and seminaries (e.g., Calvin College, Dordt College, the Institute of Christian Studies, International Association for the Promotion of Christian Higher Education).

The influence of this "Neo-Calvinist" vision (which, confusingly, is distinct in tone and emphasis from a more recent group of "New Calvinists"[4]) is not restricted to Dutch Reformed theologians and their

3. Kuyper, "Sphere Sovereignty," 461.

4. Smith, *Letters to a Young Calvinist*, is an interesting place to see the difference, with Smith writing letters from a Neo-Calvinist (Kuyperian) perspective to an audience of New Calvinists.

heirs. Through the writings of Richard Mouw, Corneluis Plantinga Jr., Nicholas Wolterstorff, Albert Wolters, Michael Goheen, Calvin Seerveld, George Marsden, Mary Stewart Van Leeuwen, John Bolt, Charles Colson, Vincent Bacote, Steve Garber, Andy Crouch, and many others, Kuyperian discussions of "Christian worldview" and "Christian cultural engagement" have been quite common in a variety of mostly Protestant settings, including several dozen Christian colleges which are rebounding from a heritage of pietistic disengagement from the culture. The vigorous range of recent Protestant initiatives aimed at stimulating a workplace spirituality (the "faith and work" movement) are frequently informed, at least indirectly, by this vision. Over time, especially in the United States, this strand has become less linked with Dutch ethnicity, a process likely to continue with the recent publication of many more English language translations of both Kuyper and his associate Herman Bavinck.

In what may come as a surprise to many readers of this volume, several writers influenced by this Kuyperian strand of Reformed Christianity have taken a shine to Alexander Schmemann. Schmemann's *For the Life of the World* appears on various online "top books of all time" lists and in the footnotes of college-level textbooks on Christian worldview.[5] Most obviously, the influence is seen in a video curriculum on a Christian worldview with the very same title—*For the Life of the World*—as Schmemann's famous book. This is not accidental. The DVD explores "how God's purposes are woven into every area of our lives: family, work, art, charity, education, government, and all creation,"[6] a direct echo of Schmemann's call to perceive the world anew in light of a radically transfigured vision of the kingdom of God. In his review of the curriculum in *Christianity Today*, Andy Crouch notes how it weaves together "insights from Dutch theologians Abraham Kuyper and Herman Bavinck" alongside "Schmemann's breathtaking sacramental view of ordinary life."[7] This is precisely the juxtaposition I find so fascinating and instructive.

To be sure, when I travel to the North American Academy of Liturgy, there I encounter the Alexander Schmemann of *Introduction to Liturgical Theology* and *Liturgy and Tradition*, the Schmemann feted by David Fagerberg, Robert Taft, Gordon Lathrop, and Bryan Spinks as the key catalyst for the emergence and growth of the discipline of liturgical theology. But when

---

5. See, for example, Naugle, *Introduction to Christian Worldview*, 162–63; Naugle, *Worldview*, 46–54; Bartholomew, *Contours of the Kuyperian Tradition*, n57; Bartholomew, *Where Mortals Dwell*, n33; and Goheen and Bartholomew, *Living at the Crossroads*, 19.

6. *For the Life of the World* (2015).

7. Crouch, "Abraham Kuyper Goes Pop," 72.

I travel back home to Calvin College, there I encounter a variety of voices who quote select pages from Schmemann's *For the Life of the World* but have likely never engaged *Introduction to Liturgical Theology* and may have only a passing acquaintance with the Orthodox liturgical tradition which grounds Schmemann's life and body of work. It is this experience of convergence and divergence that offers promise for greater ecumenical understanding and growth for my own tradition, and perhaps also for readers of Schmemann in other traditions.

Why exactly is Schmemann received so well among these Kuyperians? Let me count the ways.

First, like Kuyper, Schmemann frequently uses the metaphor of vision to describe an all-encompassing construal of the world. When Schmemann argues that "there is no point converting people to Christ if they do not convert *their vision of the world and of life*,"[8] it sounds so much like the "world and life view" talk of Kuyper and his heirs that it is hard to fathom that there isn't a hidden Q source feeding both streams of writing.[9] When Schmemann calls his Orthodox readers to embrace the ways that the Christian faith "posits a vision of man, world, nature, matter, entirely different from the one which in fact shapes not only their lives but their mental and psychological makeup,"[10] and argues that "the eternal task of the faith and of the Church is . . . to enable us to see once again what we have forgotten how to see, to feel what we no longer feel; to experience what we are no longer capable of experiencing,"[11] a Kuyperian heart is strangely warmed. Neither Schmemann nor Kuyper were satisfied with the "idea" of Christianity or with Christianity's "ideas." They both testify to the radical and pervasive vision of God, truth, beauty, and the cosmos offered to us in Christ—the "apprehension of the world as God's world."[12] In this vision, there is no divide between sacred and secular. All of reality is charged with the glory of God, yet without any hint of pantheism. For both, those who are grasped by Kuyper's or Schmemann's writing, I notice how, in the words of David Naugle, evocations of a Christian worldview have a "mysterious way of opening up the parameters of the Bible so that

8. Schmemann, *Journals*, 16. See also "East and West May Yet Meet," 128.

9. For explorations of use of the term worldview/Weltanschauung in Orthodox thought, see Counelis, "Relevance and the Orthodox Christian Theological Enterprise," 35–46, and Chryssavgis, "World as Sacrament," 1–24.

10. Schmemann, "East and West May Yet Meet," 136. For a broader history of the concept, see Naugle, *Worldview*.

11. Schmemann, *Celebration of Faith*, 2:161.

12. Schmemann, *Journals*, 20.

believers might be delivered from a fishbowl-sized Christianity into an oceanic perspective on the faith."[13]

Second, Schmemann and—at least parts of—the Kuyperian tradition share a vivid, Trinitarian *sursum corda* ("lift up your hearts") rhetoric about our encounter with the living God in light of Christ's ascension. For Schmemann, the liturgy of the Eucharist is a "journey of the Church into the dimension of the Kingdom, . . . the presence of Christ," a liturgy bequeathed to us by early Christians who realized that "they must ascend to heaven where Christ has ascended," and that this "ascension was the condition of their mission in the world."[14] For Kuyper, the Reformation intended to "lift up [believers'] eyes again, on high, to the real sanctuary, where Christ, our only priest, ministers at the only real altar," and to insist that the church would "again become the outer court from which believers could look up and onward to the real sanctuary of the living God in heaven," in which, in spite of the "curtain stretched before the eye," what remains possible for us on earth is "a mystical communion with that real Church [in heaven], by means of the Spirit," confident that "Christ, in human form, in our flesh, has entered into the invisible, behind the curtain; and that, with Him, around Him, and in Him, our Head, is the real Church, the real and essential sanctuary of our salvation."[15] A dissertation could explore all the ways these views diverge, but it is important to note that they both, echoing key themes in their own historic traditions, cultivated a Trinitarian vision which comes into vivid focus through the ascension.[16]

Further, both Schmemann and the Kuyperian tradition approach this vertical language with appropriate suspicion of Platonic dualism. Among Orthodox voices, Schmemann would be among the most ambivalent about monastic withdrawal from cultural engagement and the most critical of the Platonic "mysteriological" piety of parts of the Orthodox tradition (especially associated with Maximus the Confessor, Germanus of Constantinople, and Nicolas Cabasilas).[17] When Schmemann laments "the

13. Naugle, *Worldview*, 342.

14. Schmemann, *For the Life the World*, 28; *Eucharist*, 177; and several dozen other similar passages.

15. Kuyper, *Lectures on Calvinism*, 60–61.

16. The ascension is a key theme in Reformed theology, though its prominence in liturgical theology, spirituality, and practice has varied widely over 400 years. Arguably more than some of his heirs, Kuyper—along with Herman Bavinck—was intent upon a seamless and vivid integration of this vision across his devotional, theological and liturgical writings.

17. See Schmemann, *Liturgy and Tradition*, 123–24; *Journals*, 220–21; Louth, *Modern Orthodox Thinkers*, 207–9; and Larin, "Fr. Alexander Schmemann and Monasticism," 301–18.

transposition of the experience of the Church from an eschatological to a mysteriological key," where "Plato turns out to be stronger than the Bible," asserting that "people do not understand that eschatology is interest in the world, whereas mysteriology is indifference to the world,"[18] Kuyperians feel right at home. When looking for a natural bridge between Orthodoxy and Reformed Christianity, the Schmemann-Kuyper bridge is far less wide than the massive gap between the sensibilities of most Reformed theologians and this mysteriological tradition.[19]

Third, Schmemann returns frequently to a three-fold creation-fall-redemption meta-narrative description of the history of the cosmos. Schmemann writes:

> First, God has created the world. . . . To claim that we are God's creation is to affirm that God's voice is constantly speaking within us and saying to us, "And God saw everything that he had made, and behold it was very good." . . . Then there is a second element, inseparable from the first: this world is fallen—fallen its entirety; it has become the Kingdom of the prince of this world. . . . All is created good; all is fallen; and finally . . . all is redeemed. It is redeemed through the incarnation, the cross, the resurrection and ascension of Christ, and through the gift of the Spirit of Pentecost. Such is the intuition that we receive from God with gratitude and joy: our vision of the world as created, fallen, redeemed. Here is our theological agenda, our key to all the problems which today trouble the world.[20]

If given this quotation without attribution, I suspect that the vast majority of Calvin College graduates, even those with advanced degrees in theology, would probably guess that this was written by Al Wolters, Richard Mouw, Michael Goheen, or Craig Bartholomew. But there it is in Schmemann, repeatedly. The force of this construal, by affirming the essential goodness of creation, is to ensure a soteriology that is wide, deep, and all-encompassing, inspiring Christian engagement not only in private devotional practice but in every area of culture and creation care. Reformed voices hear Schmemann

18. Schmemann, *Journals*, 314.

19. Louth, *Modern Orthodox Thinkers*, 208–9. It would be a fascinating project to compare various Reformed-Orthodox "bridges." This Kuyper-Schmemann bridge is built around the vision of a Christian worldview and world engagement. Another quite different, but nevertheless complementary bridge was featured in many Reformed-Orthodox official ecumenical dialogues, focusing primarily on Trinitarian theology. See Torrance, *Theological Dialogue Between Orthodox and Reformed Churches*.

20. Schmemann, *Liturgy and Tradition*, 98–99. See also Schmemann, "Between Utopia and Escape."

testifying "Christ came not to replace natural matter with some supernatural matters, but to restore it and to fulfill it as the means of communion with God," and echo back with Bavinck's own, frequent "grace restores nature" refrain: "Grace is opposed not to nature, only to sin. . . . Grace restores nature and takes it to its highest pinnacle."[21] Both Schmemann and the Kuyperians aim their critique at other, more pietistic impulses within Protestantism that pull back from world engagement.

Fourth, Schmemann develops his vision by polishing his rhetoric about creation and humanity, celebrating the world as a sacrament of God, and human beings as *"homo adorans"*—priests of a new creation.[22] This resonates strongly with Reformed confessional claims that "the universe is before our eyes like a beautiful book in which all creatures, great and small, are as letters to make us ponder the invisible things of God,"[23] and that "because by faith I am a member of Christ and so I share in his anointing," an anointing to serve, Christ-like, in the offices of prophet, priest, and king.[24] It also resonates with an Augustinian impulse that sees the heart as the orienting aspect of humanity, showing how our identity is grounded in desire—in what we love and aspire to embrace. In fact, in his recent survey of Kuyperian themes, Craig Bartholomew writes, "Like Kuyper, Schmemann calls us to think of humans as priests who bless God in thanksgiving and worship."[25]

Fifth, Kuyperians cherish Schmemann's call for a pervasive, 24-7 spirituality, a domestic and workplace spirituality with a profound sense of connection between faith and daily life.[26] This is where Schmemann's *For the Life of the World* meets Plantinga's *Engaging God's World*.[27] Schmemann's own testimony—that he "was profoundly conscious of being in God's presence at another, more humble kind of altar: the sacred desk of his little office at home"—sounds very Kuyperian.[28] When Kuyperians discover those tender passages where Schmemann voices gratitude for such quotidian joys as "snow sparsely illumined by street lights, windows with cozy light behind them, little Alexandra, like a little ball rolling on that snow," and testifies that "all of these are gifts from God!—All from God; all about Him," we feel like

21. Schmemann, *Of Water and Spirit*, 49, and Bavinck, *Reformed Dogmatics*, 3:577. See Jan Veenhof, *Nature and Grace in Herman Bavinck*.

22. Schmemann, *For the Life of the World*, 15.

23. *Belgic Confession*, s.v. "Article 1."

24. *Heidelberg Catechism*.

25. Bartholomew, *Contours of the Kuyperian Tradition*, 117.

26. Plekon, "Liturgy of Life."

27. Plantinga, *Engaging God's World*.

28. Lazor, "Father Alexander Schmemann."

we have entered a redeemed Narnia, deeply resonant with the devotional dimensions of Kuyper's *Be Near Unto God*.[29] Both write with an existential urgency and an awareness of how a profound Trinitarian theological vision impacts ordinary human experience.[30] In particular, this vision grounds resistance to hyper-spiritual escapism, and makes us more, not less engaged in the things of this world, delighting the graces that abound around us in acts of justice, beauty, creativity, and genuine human community and resisting every form of injustice and violence. Indeed, once you love the Kingdom of God, "you cannot avoid loving all creation."[31]

Importantly, this very same 24-7 vision would lead many Kuyperians to be sympathetic with Bruce Morrill's critique of Schmemann's reluctance to speak with specificity about the church's engagement with injustice and poverty and his neglect of the dynamic interactions between vibrant liturgical participation, aching solidarity with the world's pain, and specific interventions designed to bring healing, hope, and sustenance. In Morrill's view, Schmemann is far more eloquent about the church's "ascent" in liturgy than its "descent" to Christ-like service.[32] While there is a significant variance among Kuyperians in terms political and economic philosophy, there has long been strong conviction that sacrificial service and redemptive responses to the pain, poverty, and violence in the world should be among the highest priorities for Christian communities.

Overall, these five interlocking themes reveal a profound resonance between Schmemann and the Kuyperians. I have found no evidence that Schmemann was aware of the existence of Kuyper and his heirs, and I have often wondered how Schmemann would have interpreted these similarities and the extent to which it would have mitigated his sense that Western attempts at overcoming the sacred-secular divide were completely unsuccessful. What would he have made of Protestant voices who were addressing so

29. Schmemann, *Journals*, 147, and Kuyper, *Be Near Unto God*.

30. Peter Galadza frames *For the Life of the World* as an "existentialist Orthodox sacramental theology," because of the way it foregrounds themes of fear, hunger, joy, death ("Twentieth Century and Contemporary Orthodox Sacramental Theology," 441).

31. Schmemann, *Journals*, 174.

32. Morrill, *Anamnesis as Dangerous Memory*, 73–138, and "Review of Schmemann's *Journals*," 187–89. In Schmemann, the accent is on ascension: "The Church must go into the world in all its reality. But to save the world from social injustices, the need first of all is not so much to go down to its miseries, as to have a few witnesses in this world to the possible ascension" (*Liturgy and Tradition*, 135). It is striking to ponder the history of the 1963 conference that gave rise to *For the Life of the World*, where that message was set inside an event framed primarily as a stirring call to the church to engage the needs of the world.

many of his same concerns with such similar language? And how might we account for their similarities?

The most obvious reason for the similarities is that both writers stand within traditions deeply influenced by biblical and patristic sources. Both were formed intellectually in communities that were simultaneously a part of and yet resistant to the pervasive effects of modernity and post-Enlightenment rationalism. Beyond this one very specific reason that their resonances could be so easily recognized is that Schmemann's most vigorous account of his world-engaging worldview was delivered to a largely Protestant audience, and, even while delivering a stunning apologia for Orthodox liturgy, he spoke in terms that his audience could readily understand.

More specifically, he wrote *For the Life of the World* for the 3200 students (roughly half from outside the United States) that gathered in Athens, Ohio during Christmas break of 1963 for the ecumenically-oriented Protestant student conference on Christian World Mission.[33] The title for the conference and book was assigned by the organizers, who invited Schmemann to "not just talk about the Body of Christ as the Body of Christ gathered but how the Church and the world interact, how they affect each other. Worship and work for the world."[34] Conference organizers were intent upon simultaneously promoting a liturgical, sacramental vision for churches and a deep engagement of the church with the ills of society. Media coverage of the event emphasized the latter point, missing the juxtaposition of sacramentality and missiology that the conference (and Schmemann) achieved. The *New York Times* story title read: "Students Hear Churches Chided on Inactivity in Changing World," quoting Schmemann's conviction that "Christ came to save the whole man and not part of him."[35] One reviewer who did grasp the potency of the approach was Thomas Merton, who explained: "It is in protesting against false ideas of the Church, her mission, and her relation to the world that Fr. Schmemann makes his most valuable and indispensable contribution to current thought about sacramental theology."[36] To bring this into a Reformed seminary curriculum, Schmemann's book was written to address a question at the heart of missiology, and his answer arose from the

---

33. For a perspective on these gatherings, see Evans, *Journeys that Opened Up the World*, 29, 107, 192. Much of the rhetoric around the 1963 conference for which Schmemann wrote *For the Life of the World* is aimed at a resistance to Puritan separation from the world.

34. Letter to Schmemann from C. Alton Robertson, February 21, 1963, quoted in Mills, "Alexander Schmemann's For the Life of the World," 202.

35 Handler, "Students Heart Churches Chided on Inactivity in Changing World."

36. Merton, "Orthodoxy and the World," 107.

heart of sacramental theology and liturgy without squelching his enthusiasm for the missiological force of the conversation.

Tensive Poise in an Eschatological Mode

As an heir to this Kuyperian tradition, I am profoundly grateful for these resonances and the specific ways that Schmemann can help us hear our most familiar language in fresh ways, approaching some stubborn internal debates anew. In the history of Dutch Calvinism (and its diaspora all over the world), there has often been strong—though sometimes hidden—clashes between those who cherish "common grace" and those who cherish "the antithesis": the "positive Calvinists" and the "Antithetical Calvinists," those who love accenting how we are "in the world" and those who love accenting how we are "not of the world."[37] While Kuyper and Bavinck held these twin themes together, their heirs have often been better at either one but not both, treating being "in the world" and "not of the world" as two sides of a teeter-totter. Especially in periods of more intense insularity or cultural fragility, we spend our institutional energy bouncing up and down—from one journal's editorial page to another, from one generation to another, from one congregation to another—on this teeter-totter.

Schmemann shows the value of ensuring that both motifs are amply narrated in his many passages which point simultaneously to the problems of godless secularism and pietistic sentimentalism, often with a profound sense of urgency:

> Christianity is by definition ambiguous: on the one hand . . . "for God so loved the world" . . . on the other, "Don't love the world, not what is in the world." . . . If "God so loved the world" is unrelated to "do not love the world," it becomes a dark negative maximalism and a true heresy. But the Church is unable any longer to discern that heresy since the key to that discernment (and I will repeat it to my dying hour) is in the eschatological essence of Christianity. It means, precisely, to discern, here and now, in our midst—the coming Kingdom in the joy of Christ who ascended into heaven. Hence the two dead-ends of contemporary Christianity: Love of "this world" (i.e., without "don't love the world") and hatred of this world (i.e., without "and God so loved the world"). Two dead-ends, two apostasies, two heresies).[38]

---

37. Bratt, *Dutch Calvinism in Modern America*.

38. Schmemann, *Journals*, 334.

On the one hand, Schmemann argues for a radical rejection of this-worldly theology, liturgy, and spirituality, where the world sets the agenda for theology and liturgy, as a surrender to secularism and the powers of the age. On the other, he argues for a radical rejection of the spirituality of escape, individualistic spiritualism, and a self-righteous denial of the world.

This tensive interweaving of loving and resisting the world not only animates a great deal of his corpus but also describes a lot of his own life. It is the unifying theme of his journals, which are worth citing at some length.

> Conservativism is sad and heavy; revolution is scary and frightening. . . . It is quite frightening when Christianity itself turns into heavy law or becomes revolutionary. The whole meaning of Christianity is to soar upwards, out of this rhythm, this course, these dynamics of the world. Christianity makes it possible to live by the truth of revolution inside the law and by the truth of the law inside revolution. Christianity is the *"coincidentia appositorum,"* the synthesis of law and religion, their fulfillment in each other. . . . Christianity is freedom from conservatism and from revolution. Hence a "rightest" Christian is as frightening as a "leftist" one, and I know why I sway to the left when dealing with the rightists and to the right when I am with leftists.[39]

> The Right is incompatible with today's Gospel [lection]: . . . "sick and in prison and you did not visit Me." . . . The Left is incompatible with the prayer of thanks: "Great are You, O Lord."[40]

> The idea of the Church . . . lies in taking us away from activity ("let us put aside all earthly cares"), in making us commune with a new life, eternity, the Kingdom. And the idea of the church, the principle of its life also demands that we would bring into the world this experience of a new life so that we would purify this world, illumine it with the non-worldliness of the experience of the Church. Quite often the opposite happens: we bring activism into the Church, the fuss of this world, and submit the Church, poison its life with this incessant fuss. What happens is not that life becomes Church, but the Church becomes worldly.[41]

In contrast to so many of us who work only one side of this rhetoric, Schmemann offers a more balanced model, affirming our desire to engage culture, but also warning us against being entirely swallowed up by it.[42] The rhetori-

39. December 8, 1975 (Schmemann, *Journals*, 99).

40. March 5, 1978 (Schmemann, *Journals*, 191).

41. February 18, 1982 (Schmemann, *Journals*, 313).

42. This posture is a single sentence summary of the work of James K. A. Smith's

cal pattern nurtures the practice of discernment, which always involves the judicious expression of both "yes" and "no."

Yet this rhetorical symmetry is not merely an end in itself, as if we should be content to floor the gas and brake pedals of our ecclesial and theological engines simultaneously. The goal is not mutual contradiction. Rather, both emphases serve a larger eschatological goal. Both the "against the world" and "for the world" motifs find their resolution, fulfillment, and redemptive force in the same Jesus Christ and in the fullness of God's kingdom being revealed to us. To press the point further, what we Kuyperians need to realize is that both concerns serve a missiological aim that is aimed squarely at the ultimate eschatological reality of an entirely redeemed cosmos in Christ.[43] We hold on to each motif not as an end in itself, not as the source of our ultimate identity, but rather as a tool to help us faithfully point to the future kingdom into which we are being invited.

The Liturgical Gap

So far I have mentioned almost nothing of liturgy, and the insights I have named from Schmemann are insights that are typically addressed in a Reformed context by systematic, not liturgical theologians. The reason is quite simple, I think. Many Kuyperians who read Schmemann give very little evidence of having participated in Orthodox liturgies or of having been immersed in the largest part of Schmemann's corpus, which explores so many aspects of Orthodox liturgy.[44] Kuyperians have tended to read Schmemann selectively, appreciating his cosmological and eschatological vision while neglecting the Eucharistic, liturgical basis for it.

The problem is not that Kuyper himself was uninterested in ecclesiology and liturgy. To the contrary, he wrote his dissertation on a Reformation church order and wrote extensively about liturgy and ecclesiology.[45] Nor is the problem necessarily with the Reformed tradition as a whole, which features robust confessional claims about the ascension and the sacraments and at least several key historical models for pairing rich, sacramental worship with redemptive cultural engagement and social witness.

---

influential trilogy, discussed below.

43. For more on this, see Papathansiou, "Church as Mission," 6–41. For Protestant echoes of this missiological vision, see Senn, *Witness of the Worshipping Community*.

44. Notable exceptions include Payton, *Light from the Christian East*, and Letham, *Through Western Eyes*.

45. Wood, *Going Dutch in the Modern Age*.

Rather, the problem, in my view, is with later Kuyperians who took one of Kuyper's own key ideas, "sphere sovereignty" (a vision of differentiated responsibility in which no one sector or dimension of life—whether the state, the church, or the family—is sovereign over another) and applied it in such a way that it sometimes functioned to not only differentiate but also practically obscure close ties between the church, liturgical participation, and other areas of cultural engagement. For the sake of resisting an ecclesial totalitarianism, the tradition unwittingly came close to severing the connection between liturgical imagination and Christian political, social, and cultural engagement. Thus, later Kuyperian reception of Schmemann is similar to the later Kuyperian reception of Kuyper himself, showing far more interest in their cosmological vision, and their invitation to cultural engagement than to the liturgical, ecclesial, and even devotional life that grounds, inspires, and informs this engagement.[46]

Yet, as readers and contributors of this volume would surely argue, neglecting Schmemann's distinctive liturgical vision is like reading Augustine without pondering his vision of the Trinity or engaging Luther without engaging his theology of the cross. It misses the central, animating source of his vision. Indeed, as Schmemann clarifies in the opening paragraphs of *For the Life of the World*: "It is my certitude that the answer comes to us not from neat intellectual theories but above all from that living an unbroken experience of the Church which she reveals and communicates to us in her worship, in the *leitourgia* always making her what she is."[47] Liturgical worship is, for Schmemann, the source that "capacitates" the robust worldview that the Kuyperians affirm.[48]

Here we confront the vexing problem of genuine ecumenical encounter. For all the learning and sharing that does happen throughout the body of Christ, we can all too easily miss the depth of our differences and thus fail to truly listen and receive. Schmemann himself encountered this challenge in his participation in the Hartford Statement discussions of the mid-1970s, which led him to nearly decline the invitation to contribute to the volume of essays that emerged out of that project.[49] Schmemann said of the encounter:

---

46. I have explored this concern in Witvliet, "Institutional Church and the Mission of Calvin College," 18–21; in a series preface to Abraham Kuyper, Witvliet, *Our Worship*; and in a brief introduction to Abraham Kuyper, Witvliet, "Worship of the Reformed Church and the Creation of Its Service Book," 59–61.

47. Schmemann, *For the Life of the World*, 8.

48. A turn of phrase adapted from Denysenko, *Liturgical Reform After Vatican II*, 102.

49. Schmemann, "East and West May Yet Meet," 126.

> It was the experience, familiar to me since my first contacts with the ecumenical movement, of the Orthodox transplanted as it were into a spiritual and mental world radically different from his own; forced to use a theological language which, although he understands it, is not his language; and who, therefore, while agreeing on one level, experiences and realizes on another level the frustrating discrepancy between that formal agreement and the totality of the Orthodox vision.[50]

So, too, when Kuyperians engage Schmemann, there is an agreement on one level but also a profound (frustrating) discrepancy that must be named. There is, obviously, a profound gap between Reformed Protestant and Orthodox liturgies, a gap large enough that should cause those of us who readily quote Schmemann to pause and wonder whether we have truly grasped the depth of his subversive vision. Perhaps we should all be required to witness a few annual cycles of Orthodox liturgical celebrations before quoting Schmemann much more, or at least to temper our assumptions of profound congruence without naming this gap more explicitly.

Closing the Gap: A Reformed Vision for Reconnecting Liturgical Worship and Worldview

I am tempted to conclude this essay with a litany of Kuyperian Reformed engagements with Schmemannesque cosmological and eschatological concepts that miss the liturgical and ecclesial themes that are so central to his work, and to point out how this tendency reflects broader Reformed weaknesses in those areas. I will save that extended lament for another occasion. What I want to do here, instead, is to celebrate that there is also a minority report to notice: the vein of work by Nicholas Wolterstorff, Leonard Vander Zee, Hans Boersma, James K. A. Smith, Matthew Kaemingk, and others to strengthen the tenuous connection in Kuyperian Reformed discourse between liturgical participation, Christian worldview, and redemptive cultural engagement.[51]

When I hear David Fagerberg explaining that, for Schmemann, theology, liturgy, and piety are inseparable—like "three atoms that make up a molecule"—and then asking those us in the West "if once upon a time the East was westernized for having let liturgy, theology, and piety drift apart, cannot

---

50. Neuhaus, *Against the World For the World*, 128.

51. There are also many other veins of Reformed renewal, in very different parts of the Reformed tradition. Michael Horton, including Ward, *Reformed Sacramentality*, Michael Horton, Ronald Byars, For more on this, see Witvliet, "YALE."

the reverse happen and the West be easternized by bringing liturgy, theology and piety back together?"[52] I am immediately grateful for this minority report within the Kuyperian Reformed tradition, and I live and labor in the hope that it will be fruitfully received and practiced in the years to come.

Nicholas Wolterstorff has led the way over the past forty years. In 1981, his Kuyper lectures at the Free University of Amsterdam featured a prophetic announcement, "Justice and Worship: The Tragedy of Liturgy in Protestantism," which conveyed "the possibility that a rhythmic alternation of work and worship, labor and liturgy is one of the significant distinguishing features of the Christian's way of being in the world"[53]—a thesis developed in conversation with Schmemann himself. In Wolterstorff's words: "What is especially appealing in Schmemann's thought is his intense aversion to dividing up reality into the 'spiritual' versus the 'material,' the 'sacred' versus the 'profane,' the 'supernatural' vs. the 'natural.'" Citing the famous Schmemann passages about humanity as the priest of creation, Wolterstorff concludes that Schmemann's vision is one that links worship and work, liturgy and life as two inter-related aspects of humanity's gratitude to God.[54] Since then, Wolterstorff's vision for liturgy has unfolded in a rich series of essays and books, including his distinctly Reformed contribution to the very subdiscipline of liturgical theology which Schmemann inspired, *The God We Worship: An Exploration of Liturgical Theology.*[55]

The sacramental dimensions of a reconstituted Reformed liturgy, worldview, and cultural engagement synthesis are explored further by Leonard Vander Zee in *Christ, Baptism, and the Lord's Supper.* Vander Zee explicitly links the processional quality of Schmemann's vision of liturgical participation with the robust ascension themes in John Calvin and James Torrance, affirming the sacramentality of the cosmos, and the dramatic ways that sacramental celebrations are occasions which convey "all the benefits of Christ's finished work at a depth of human need that the Word alone cannot touch."[56] Quotations from Schmemann anchor the culminating chapter of Vander Zee's manifesto for the recovery of robust Eucharistic practice.[57]

Hans Boersma's *Heavenly Participation* affirms the value of Christian cultural engagement but also argues that contemporary Protestants have

52. Fagerberg, "Cost of Understanding Schmemann in the West," 183, 206.

53. Wolterstorff, *Until Justice and Peace Embrace*, 147.

54. Wolterstorff, *Until Justice and Peace Embrace*, 149, 151.

55. Wolterstorff, *God We Worship*, and Wolterstorff, *Hearing the Call*.

56. Other Reformed voices, outside the Kuyperian strand, have developed similar themes. For one recent example, see Ward, *Reformed Sacramentality.*

57. Zee, *Christ, Baptism, and the Lord's Supper*, 202, 212, 219, 224, 239. See also Billings, *Remembrance, Communion, and Hope.*

failed to realize how this engagement is ultimately sustained by "setting our minds on things above." Like Schmemann, he directly confronts any simplistic natural/supernatural binary and argues for a sacramental vision of the world grounded in vibrant Trinitarian theology, prayer, and liturgical practice. Responding to a functional bifurcation of heaven and earth in so much of Protestant faith and piety, Boersma argues that "for a sacramental ontology, heaven and earth are not like two essentially unconnected stories in which the bottom half at best vaguely resembles the top half " and that "with a sacramental ontology, one can be grateful for created reality precisely because, as a sacrament, it really makes present the heavenly reality of God himself."[58]

Schmemann's vision has been central to the explicit project of reconnecting worship and worldview, liturgy and life in James K. A. Smith's influential trilogy *Desiring the Kingdom*, *Imagining the Kingdom*, and *Awaiting the King*, and the more popular treatise, *You Are What You Love*.[59] Like Schmemann, Smith affirms a vision of human beings as "homo adorans," worshiping beings whose capacity for love orients all of life. Like Schmemann, Smith offers his readers a tour of the liturgy, explaining its formative force in Christian life and witness. And his *You Are What You Love* culminates with a luminous quotation from *For the Life of the World*, adding his amen to Schmemann's poetic acclamation that "to bless the Kingdom [liturgically] is . . . to declare it to be the goal, the end of all our desires and interests, of our whole life, the supreme and ultimate value of all that exists," in which the church "expresses the agreement of the Church to follow Christ in his ascension to the Father," a posture we receive as "Christ's gift to the church."[60]

Most recently, Matthew Kaemingk develops a poignant vision for the interplay of liturgy and life, sacramental participation and Christian political engagement in his *Christian Hospitality and Muslim Immigration in an Age of Fear*—perhaps the clearest sign that some of the unintended weaknesses of Kuyper's sphere sovereignty theme are being overcome.[61] While this volume primarily focuses on principled pluralism and Christian engagement in public life, Kaemingk demonstrates how it is very possible overcome Kuyperianism's temporary allergy against engaging liturgy, developing a robust chapter on the how Christian public wor-

58. Boersma, *Heavenly Participation*, 186–87.

59. Smith, *Desiring the Kingdom*; Smith, *Imagining the Kingdom*; Smith, *Awaiting the King*; and Smith, *You Are What You Love*.

60. Smith, *You Are What You Love*, 189–90, quoting Schmemann, *For the Life of the World*, 29.

61. Kaemingk, *Christian Hospitality and Muslim Immigration in an Age of Fear*.

ship forms believers for participation in pluralistic public life. Drawing on themes in Wolterstorff, Mouw, Smith, and myself, Kaemingk shows how liturgical participation engages our deepest desires, our longing for God, and, through the mystery of divine action, trains us in the dispositions and practices needed for faithful participation in public life. Liturgy trains us—it transfigures us—to confront and engage death, to learn humility, to lament, and to express hope. In contrast to those whose political engagement is motivated from within, in "raising Christ's cup, [Christians] drink from a spring that does not come from within but from without."[62] Along the way, he notes the strong indebtedness this cluster of writers has to the life and thought of Schmemann.[63] Here is a Reformed public theologian who sees how a robust Schmemannesque liturgical vision contributes quite specifically to Christian efforts to resist fearful nationalism and tribalism—much as it also potentially could to efforts that resist poverty, violence, and racism, promoting vital spirituality in the workplace.[64]

None of these Reformed voices simply adopt Schmemann uncritically. One notable difference is their tendency to describe liturgical worship and sacramental participation as *one* indispensable place of formation and joyful communion with the triune God rather than as *the* primary or only place of such access. Schmemann uses the definite article, the Kuyperians use an indefinite one.[65] For Schmemann, liturgical participation is the singular source which capacitates the luminous Christian worldview. For the Reformed, it is rather the *interaction* of private and liturgical prayer, personal and communal Bible reading, personal and communal social witness and service that mutually reinforce this vision. (In fact, Schmemann's own writings participate in this interaction, helping us see things about our liturgy we may have missed, or that we would be motivated to reform in some way.)

For his part, Schmemann would likely have been amused or puzzled by the Reformed liturgy that sustained Kuyper and his heirs. He may well have argued that the Reformed don't see the liturgy as a singular source of

---

62. Kaemingk, *Christian Hospitality*, 236.

63. Kaemingk, *Christian Hospitality*, 206n17.

64. See Willson, "Heart of Worship," as well as his additional forthcoming contributions on this theme.

65. See an interesting parallel here with Bruce Morrill's critique that Schmemann sees signs of the kingdom "only in the liturgy" whereas, in Morrill's view, liturgical participation forms participants to perceive signs other signs of the kingdom, too, including kenotic deeds of service (*Anamnesis as Dangerous Memory*, 134). Or see Don E. Saliers, who argues that it is "the worship of God in cultic enactment and service of God in life that constitutes the 'primary theology'" on which liturgical theology is based (*Worship As Theology*, 16).

this vision because of the kind of liturgies we have.[66] While many of us are grateful for how much more our liturgical life draws on patristic practices, instincts, and sensibilities than in some earlier Reformed generations, even our more recent efforts at liturgical reform would have seemed quite inadequate to him. Given his occasional, stern rebuke of "thematic" Protestant services focusing on societal concerns, he would have been mortified that a DVD-curriculum named after his book might lead pastors to preach and organize worship services based on the themes of the curriculum!

The massive challenge for Kuyperian Reformed Christians, as Schmemann surely would have helped us see, is that even the best efforts to reconnect worship and worldview, liturgy and life fall flat if a community's liturgical practices are but a tepid, flattened out vestige of the church's great liturgical heritage—a Spirit-graced Trinitarian, Eucharistic procession into "heaven on earth."

Indeed, we Reformed Christians need to face the massive challenges we have in our liturgical life. In contrast to Orthodoxy, we do not have a stable or common liturgy. We live, move, and have our being in the wild, woolly world of liturgical deregulation, where congregations frequently exercise their enormous freedom to change or adapt liturgical patterns, quite often by watering down or displacing the central practices of Word and Sacrament, and the vision of the Lord's Supper as nothing less than a participation in the body and blood of our ascended Lord through the Spirit. We may well produce luminous, robust, comprehensive Trinitarian liturgical books (e.g., *Book of Common Worship*, *Worship Sourcebook*), rich and vital veins of congregational song and liturgical art, but they are too often used by 23 percent of congregations 23 percent of the time. The effect is similar to engaging in physical exercises on, say, six days scattered throughout the year—it's enough to remind us we have some underused muscles but not enough to form or shape them in any meaningful way. Further, when worship practices are stable and robustly Trinitarian, it is often because of the agency of a local pastor or a musician who insists on such practices during their tenure, only to have a decade or two of robust practice quickly set aside by successive leaders.

Underneath all of this is a still deeper concern. Many congregations are not all that eager to participate in worship by "setting their minds on things above" (Col 3:1). Many have never really been invited to engage with a luminous Trinitarian vision of the kingdom and liturgical participation. Many seem to lack the internal theological enyzmes to be able to digest it, and thus many are are perplexed rather than awakened by Robert

---

66. See Spinks, "From Liturgical Theology to Liturgical Theologies," 231–49.

Taft's Schmemannesque vision that, even in an humble village, we might worship in an "atmosphere of profuse symbolism, through which the supernatural splendor of the inaccessible divine majesty and holiness is approached," where we would "witness the exaltation and sanctification of creation, the majestic appearance of God who enters [us], sanctifies [us], divinizes [us] through the transfiguring life of his heavenly grace," allowing us to live "habitually within a liturgical ambiance that encompasses one in body and soul, transfigured through faith into a concrete vision of spiritual beauty and joy."[67]

All of this makes us susceptible to the culminating concern Schmemann voiced in *For the Life of the World*—that churches would respond to secularism by merely attempting to offer "help" rather than immersing believers in the life-changing vision of the kingdom of God. Let us frankly acknowledge that the worship life of many Protestant congregations reinforces rather than resists the self-centeredness and nationalistic tribalism of our consumerist age.

Those of us called to serve as liturgical theologians in a consumerist, voluntarist, deregulated context are thus confronted by the question: "What is our vocation when we glimpse the compelling sacramental vision for the life of the world disclosed in the church's classic Trinitarian liturgies but find ourselves in a place where the liturgical practices that capacitate that worldview are so uneven?"

Some Reformed Christians have responded to this question by joining the small but steady stream of Protestant pilgrims making their way into the Orthodox (or Catholic or Anglican) communion, not infrequently because they have read Schmemann. These are people I deeply admire, who have been grasped by the sheer gospel beauty of this vision, and who testify to their sense of call to this profound pilgrimage.

One such pilgrim is New Testament theologian Edith Humphrey, who was received into the Orthodox Church while teaching at a Presbyterian Seminary. Her *Grand Entrance: Worship on Earth as in Heaven* offers one recent, theologically-rich, testimonial vision for such a conversion, echoing Schmemann's own ascension motif, conveying the beauty and force of reverential entrance into the presence of the triune God through liturgical participation. She argues that Protestant worship, in spite of some notable

---

67. Taft, "Mrs. Murphy Goes to Moscow," 386–407. Interestingly, within parts of the Reformed-Presbyterian tapestry, these appear not only in the liturgical movements represented by, say, the *Book of Common Worship*, but also in certain parts of the tradition worldwide, influenced by the charismatic and Pentecostal movements. Often, though, that "heaven on earth" spirituality is not primarily mediated through the Word and Table but through music.

Trinitarian accounts of ascension by Calvin and others, features nearly intrinsic obstacles to a genuinely heavenly vision of worship, including its therapeutic orientation, its undue focus on community, its concern for novelty, and its focus on self-fulfillment rather than divine encounter.[68]

Another such pilgrim is philosopher Terence Cuneo, whose *Ritualized Faith: Essays on the Philosophy of Liturgy* weaves together analytical insights about the nature of liturgical participation with poignant autobiographical reflections about his own journey to Orthodoxy. He describes the tepid ways that Protestants often shape funerals and mark the occasion of Easter, then notes his astonishment at Orthodox Pascha: "While standing during the Paschal liturgy, I sensed, for the first time ever, a fit between the actions being performed in an Easter service and the significance of that which was being celebrated."[69] These conversion narratives are prophetic invitations to all Protestants, to ponder deeply the gaps in our life and witness and our own call to respond.[70]

Others of us live out our baptismal vocation differently, embracing a sense of call to serve within our baptismal tradition, resolving to maintain robustly Catholic and Orthodox reading habits as a matter of theological principle, and doing our best to commend liturgical celebrations that invite the gift of Trinitarian participation—even in the rocky soil of American voluntarism and seemingly unrestrained liturgical deregulation. Pray for us!

We embrace this vocation for any number of reasons, including our gratitude for the strengths of Christian formation and witness that are present even in our liturgically uneven tradition, and especially the way our tradition as a whole—in its liturgy, catechesis, devotional practices, social witness, and cultural engagement—capacitates a worldview and way of life so recognizably similar to many of the most compelling features of Schmemann's vision. We also recognize that even in traditions with more consistently robust Trinitarian, sacramental worship, there are vexing temptations and complications with rubricism, escapism, fundamentalisms on the left

68. Humphrey, *Grand Entrance*, esp. 159–79.

69. Cuneo, *Ritualized Faith*, 210. Much of Cuneo's work is developed in conversation with Wolterstorff and also features twenty or so references to Schmemann along the way. It would be fascinating to compile a trail of such personal testimonies about Orthodox Paschal vigils—Cuneo's, alongside John A. Jillions (Jillions, "Connecting Liturgy and Spirituality," 91–108), Schmemann's own testimonials about liturgical participation in his journal, and Sergei Bulgakov's testimonial, published in a volume Schmemann edited as a young theologian (Bulgakov, "Meditations on the Joy of the Resurrection," 299–304).

70. These pilgrimages echo the narratives of Gillquist, *Becoming Orthodox*; Gillquist, *Coming Home*; and Green, *Facing East*.

and right, as well simple indifference—complications of which Schmemann is a compelling witness.

There are signs of hope and opportunity that sustain us in this calling: congregations who deeply embrace both a profound sacramental and missional calling, pastoral leaders and theologians eager to deeply integrate Trinitarian liturgy, theology, spirituality, and pastoral ministry, and global voices which prophetically challenge the narcissism, consumerism, nationalism, and tribalism that shapes too many North American Christian sensibilities. And we are further sustained and inspired by constructive conversations outside our tradition, including the very kinds of engagements included in the volume you are holding.

Along the way, we make mistakes. Pressed by the demands of this challenging existence, at times we slip and treat Orthodoxy, as Schmemann himself once wryly noted, as a little "mystical vitamin" we take when feeling ill,[71] treating Orthodoxy as a "marginal supplier of valuable but unessential 'mystical' and 'liturgical' contributions."[72] At times, we theologize about liturgy and try to explain it rather than to follow Schmemann's lead in "taking a stab at the meaning epiphanized in the liturgy"—the first order prediscursive theology, which precedes analytical second-order theology.[73] And yes, in spite of his protests, we do "plan thematic services," engaging in a level of liturgical creativity which seems offensive to those steeped in a posture of receiving the liturgical inheritance of the church rather than improvising new liturgical responses to current challenges and events.

For those called to this tensive vocation, let me close by suggesting that Schmemann offers us yet one more resource. That is, he offers us even more than an influential theological method, more than a cluster of memorable theological motifs, and more than his compelling Eucharistic vision. For he also offers us the witness of his often conflicted life. For every luminous experience of a vision of the kingdom of God, he also experienced profound anger, frustration, and disappointment at the failure of so many—including those in his own community and tradition—to embrace this vision. He was forever lamenting "fuss."

Those of us who are Protestant liturgical theologians, are, in a strange but striking way, called to a similar path. Just as he lived as a cultural exile in the West as a theologian of the East, with a poignant sense of "inner

71. Schmemann, "East and West May Yet Meet," 131.

72. Schmemann, "East and West May Yet Meet," 134

73. Paraphrased from Robert Taft's affirmation of David Fagerberg (Taft, "Liturgical Enterprise," 80–81).

distance,"[74] so, too, many of us negotiate an "inner distance" with the voluntarism, consumerism, and sentimentality of our context. For Schmemann, this inner distance gave rise to his crescendo of critique about secularism of the West as well his equally intense crescendo of critique about his own communion and especially the "Super-Orthodox." And it wasn't just his vision that created this restlessness but also the dynamic tension of his overlapping roles, as he served simultaneously as both a prophetic theological educator as well as a pastoral leader and administrator.[75]

But this does not mean that he was defined by despair or cynicism, an ever-present temptation for any idealistic theologian. Ultimately, a profound eschatological vision elicits not only disappointment but also brighter joy, a sense of deep hope, and pastoral poise. And Schmemann surely leaves us with many clues about how his profound experience of Paschal joy also elicited in him the kind of pastoral poise needed for sustaining his pastoral, prophetic ministry. His life shows us how, in God's providence, experiences of disequilibrium and restlessness can be redemptive—how the restlessness of an Orthodox seminary dean could end up being so inspiring and sanctifying decades later for a group of restless Protestants, quirky Kuyperians among them.

In the middle of a secularizing culture and an ossifying church, the Spirit graced Fr. Schmemann with a stunning vision of the Eucharistic kingdom of God and the capacity to convey the vision with bouyancy and prophetic urgency. Regardless of our Christian vocation among God's people, may God's Holy Spirit grant those same gifts to many today, even as we are being pulled, inexorably, into the radiant light, beauty, and goodness of the kingdom of God.

74. Schmemann, "East and West May Yet Meet," 128.

75. See Galadza, "Schmemann Between Fagerberg and Reality," 19. This insight warrants more attention. It is easier to be a prophetic critic of liturgical practice if you are not in charge of it! See also several references to Schmemann's writing style in Morrill, *Anamnesis*, 73.

Liturgical Theology as Ritual Congruence

Todd E. Johnson

It is most appropriate to engage the topic of liturgical theology in a *festschrift* in honor of Alexander Schmemann. His *Introduction to Liturgical Theology*,[1] written in Russian in 1961, on the eve of the Second Vatican Council, and released in English in 1966, almost exactly three years after the promulgation of *Sacrosanctum concilium*, became the touchstone for the North American conversation about the nature and method of liturgical theology, in particular the debate between Geoffrey Wainwright and Aidan Kavanagh.[2] At the core of this early discussion on the theological nature of the liturgy was the central place of the dictum *lex orandi/lex credendi*; inviting the question of the relationship between the Church's prayer and the Church's belief. If one were to consider the scant treatment this received in the massive work of Italian scholar Cyprian Vagagini, *Il senso teologico della liturgia: saggio di liturgia teologica generale* (1957),[3] one can see Schmemann's singular influence in this direction. It is Schmemann who provided the categories for liturgical theology in the English-speaking world for decades to come.

---

1. Schmemann, *On Liturgical Theology*.

2. See Irwin, *Liturgical Theology*, 40–48.

3. Lex orandi/lex credendi is treated in a very short section, well into Vagaggini's tome, in the section, "Lex Orandi Lex Credendi: Reciprocal Influences between Faith and Liturgy" (Vagaggini, *Liturgical Dimension of the Liturgy*, 529–41). Schmemann is not mentioned in this volume (fourth edition, 1976).

Schmemann's work arises out of the work of the Liturgical Movement and the renewed interest in historical documents, their meaning, and their application to the contemporary church. In the past, "liturgics" was considered either the academic study of historical liturgical documents or the pastoral/practical (what Schmemann calls "the study of rubrics") dimension, often the following of a church's canons,[4] the Liturgical Movement changed this, with Schmemann declaring:

> [The Liturgical Movement's] substance lies in the genuine discovery of worship as the life of the Church, the public act which eternally actualizes the nature of the Church as the Body of Christ. . . . It is a return from the pietistic and individualistic understanding of worship to worship once more conceived as the eternal self-revelation of the Church.[5]

Schmemann's concerns were neither primarily historical nor rubrical, they were ecclesial. He was concerned that a lack of understanding of the liturgy's meaning and purpose created a deficient—if not anemic—church.

Schmemann continues by suggesting that the analogical mystagogy which has served the church in the past is no longer sufficient, as those explanations result in an often "elementary and in many ways superficial and arbitrary symbolism."[6] Instead, liturgical theology is to be the "elucidation of [the liturgy's] theological meaning." In Schmemann's paradigm, liturgical theology is tasked with giving a theological foundation for the meaning of "worship and the whole liturgical tradition of the Church."[7] Schmemann offers this conclusion:

> If liturgical theology stems from an understanding of worship as the public act of the Church, then its final goal is to clarify and explain the connection between this act and the Church, i.e., to explain how the Church expresses and fulfills herself in this act.[8]

In Schmemann's paradigm, the object of theological reflection is not a particular liturgy but rather a liturgical action done within the context of "the" liturgical tradition.[9]

4. Schmemann, *On Liturgical Theology*, 9.

5. Schmemann, *On Liturgical Theology*, 13–14.

6. Schmemann, *On Liturgical Theology*, 16.

7. Schmemann, *On Liturgical Theology*, 17.

8. Schmemann, *On Liturgical Theology*, 17.

9. Most liturgical historians in the twenty-first century would not maintain that one could identify a singular or "UR" liturgy that could be called "the" liturgy, or even

As Kevin Irwin points out, Schmemann, like many of his contemporaries, privileges the liturgical tradition of the first few Christian centuries as being exemplary for all Christian practice.[10] Yet Schmemann does not expect liturgical uniformity, diachronically or synchronically, as diversity naturally occurs over time and geography—even within the Orthodox Churches, which are often seen as more uniform. Instead, Schmemann focuses upon the *ordo* of the Church. By this, he does not mean primarily the *ordo* of a particular liturgical rite but instead the rhythm or cycle of rites that comprise the *ordo salutis* for the life of the church: Initiation (baptism and chrismation), Eucharist, "the Liturgy of Time" (the daily, weekly, and yearly rhythms of prayer),[11] and the "Liturgy for the Sanctification of Life" (the consecration of space and time, along with people, through the on-going prayer of the church).[12]

Liturgical Theology and "Non-Liturgical" Churches

As I said, it is not surprising that liturgical theology would be addressed repeatedly throughout this volume. It might be more surprising, however, to address the relationship of liturgical theology to "Free Church worship"; those worship patterns that neither reflect the historic *ordo* valued by Schmemann nor even a valuing of historical worship traditions. Does that mean that such worship is either devoid of theological content or intent? Is it exempt from the desire to fortify and enrich the Church through a more robust understanding of the meaning of its ritual gatherings? I would argue not.

Therefore, the question at hand is one of method. The emerging discipline of liturgical theology has always privileged those traditions that have more traditional liturgical forms in no small part because liturgical theology has been done in the main by and for those in traditions with historically traditional liturgies. The result is that liturgical theology, as defined by its early proponents, seems to be almost irrelevant to those traditions we identify as

---

a singular—let alone apostolic—liturgical tradtion. Most would maintain a diversity in liturgical practice throughout the history of the church, even if not especially in the first two centuries. See Bradshaw, *Search for the Origins of Christian Worship*. To Schmemann's credit, he does not expect uniformity, except in a general *ordo* of practice.

10. Irwin, *Liturgical Theology*, 44.

11. That being the offices of daily prayer, weekly Eucharist on the Lord's Day, and the feasts and fasts of the liturgical calendar.

12. Schmemann, *On Liturgical Theology*, 26. This last theme of cosmic sanctification echoes the theology of Maximus the Confessor in his *Mystagogia* in which the liturgy of the Eucharist affects the redemption of the cosmos. This was expounded in Schmemann's most popular book, *For the Life of the World*.

"Free Church worship" traditions,[13] those with fluid rather than fixed liturgies, and those who would be more likely to pair Word and Music as the two poles of their worship, "Word and Turntable"[14] rather than Word and Table. These traditions locate their liturgical roots historically in the revivals of Europe and North America. They would theologically privilege the primacy of the sermon over other ritual acts of worship and tend to evaluate their rituals in terms of their kerygmatic effectiveness and their evangelical appeal. These are traditions whose pervasive pragmatic *modus operandi* has been defined as *lex agendi/lex orandi*.[15] The application of liturgical theology has either been apologetic from the inside, arguing for a more apostolic practice and interpretation by those of the Free Church tradition,[16] or critical from the outside.[17] In either case, there is a challenge to the definition of "worship" and whether or not Free Church worship is actually worship.

Exploring Free Church Worship

Almost three decades ago, when assuming my first call to parish ministry, I was asked by a member of my new congregation if I played golf. Informing him I did not, he quickly provided me with a set of golf clubs and some wisdom: "Learn to play golf and you will spend a lot more time with people in this church." After my first few attempts at golfing with church members, I realized that unless I *really* learned to play golf, I would be on the course with people from the church but spend very little time with them,

---

13. For the sake of consistency, "Free Church worship" will refer to the liturgical tradition arising out of evangelical and free churches, but it could be found in any number of churches—even churches with liturgical texts and traditions. Whereas, "free church" refers to churches of the free church tradition, which is an ecclesial (and not liturgical) distinction, both terms are distinct from the Evangelical Free Church, which is the name of a specific denomination, as well as the International Federation of Free Evangelical Churches, which is in an ecumenical and international body that gathers churches from the free church (ecclesial) traditions in Europe and the Americas.

14. Dr. David Lemley is to be credited for this phrase.

15. Ruth, "Lex Agendi, Lex Orandi," 386–405.

16. Of those from the inside who have applied liturgical theology to Free Church worship, the first is Robert Webber. His work has been consistent in trying to hold in tension the benefits of the evangelical fervor of Free Church worship together with the classic four-fold *ordo* of worship. Compare Webber, *Worship Old and New*, and Webber, *Ancient-Future Worship*. An even stronger critique of Free Church Worship comes from Pentecostal theologian, Simon Chan, who argues, following Schmemann and using liturgical theology, that deficient liturgy (read: non-traditional worship) leads to a deficient church. See Chan, *Liturgical Theology*.

17. For example, see Senn, "Worship Alive," 194–224.

and our conversations would be reduced to "I think you are over there, and I am over there—way over there!" So I proceeded to take golf lessons. My instructor was a wise and rigid man, schooling me in the technique and philosophy of the game. He informed me that there are people who every day play a game a lot like golf, but it's not golf. For example, he said there are people who tee the ball up, hit it somewhere (but not where they wanted to hit it), grab a second ball, say the magic word "Mulligan," and drive another ball as if they never hit the first one. This, he said, was a game a lot like golf, but it's not golf.

I think of those lessons today because of the intense debates surrounding corporate worship. Many of the conversations about worship sound very much like, "I am here and you are *way* over there," or, "You are playing a game a lot like worship, but it's not worship." Particularly in the past two decades, with the proliferation of so many "new" forms of worship, the question of what is truly worship and what is "a lot like worship" is hotly contested in liturgical circles.[18] The issue of normativity and innovation in worship is compounded in the so-called "non-liturgical" or Free Church traditions. In most traditions, if one seeks liturgical normativity, one simply turns to the appropriate denominational documents, worship manuals, or hymnals. But by definition, Free Church worship is not bound by such texts, if they have them at all. In exploring this ritual territory, I realized that texts and traditions have little authoritative traction in the free churches, so if liturgical scholarship was to be of any assistance to them, it would be a theological—and not a historical—resource that would be the most relevant.

This raises the question: What sort of vision of a Free Church theology of worship—or Free Church liturgical theology[19]—would work best to both assess the theological intent and content of Free Church rites as well as to place Free Church rites in discussion with the broader conversation of liturgical theology? Those who have been most aggressive in bringing Free Church worship into the larger liturgical conversation have often been the most aggressive in pushing for liturgical conformity with the classic liturgical tradition, especially the four-fold *ordo*, acceptance of the rhythms of the church year, a more sacramental approach to liturgy and life, and so on.[20] What they have done less well is ask what contribution the Free Church

18. For example, see Lathrop, "New Pentecost or Joseph's Britches?," 521–38, and Ross, "Joseph's Britches Revisited," 528–50.

19. There is no small variety of approaches to this discipline known as liturgical theology. For two attempts at taxonomy of liturgical theology, see Vogel, *Primary Sources of Liturgical Theology*, and, Irwin, *Liturgical Theology*, 44–81.

20. See Webber and Bloesch, *Orthodox Evangelicals*.

tradition of worship offers to our ecumenical understanding of worship, and specifically the field of liturgical theology.

From the other end, there has been a critique of the historical assumptions used by liturgical theologians to define the *ordo* of the liturgy. Although initially begun by liturgical historians in general terms,[21] the question of the *ordo* was applied more directly to liturgical theology as a method of re-envisioning the task and method of liturgical theology by Michael Aune in a comprehensive two-part essay.[22] Aune is explicit in identifying his agenda: "My thesis is this: 'liturgical theology' needs to be both more *historical* and more *theological* in its content and character, thus requiring a rethinking of how we regard the liturgy-theology relationship."[23] Later, when Aune enfleshes what he considers to be better historical and theological work, he identifies those elements which present a "clearer understanding in depth of why and what we do in worship." These building blocks—or *Bausteine*—of worship were the Sanctus, the epiclesis, the reception of communion, and the Lord's Prayer.[24] Although Aune's work may be helpful in moving the conversation from an idealized *ordo* or liturgical paradigm which one can reference in doing liturgical theology for liturgical traditions, these *Bausteine* have little to do with Free Church worship, serving more as a critique than a theological engagement with it.

Liturgical Theology and Free Church Worship

How would one go about applying liturgical theology (as intended by Schmemann) to revitalize the Church, to Free Church worship without dismissing patterns of Free Church worship? First, most liturgical theology starts with a question of the *ordo* or prescribed structure or order of worship for its basic meaning, and Free Church worship—though it may have routinized patterns of worship—would not have what Schmemann understood as *ordo*.[25] Second, there is an inherent vagary in the term "worship" as it is understood in the Free Church traditions. Because the womb of North American Free Church worship was not the church but the evangelistic

---

21. In particular, Bradshaw, "Difficulties in Doing Liturgical Theology," 181–94, and Johnson, "Liturgy and Theology," 203–27.

22. See Aune, "Liturgy and Theology 1," 46–68, and Aune, "Liturgy and Theology 2," 141–69.

23. Aune, "Liturgy and Theology 1," 47–48.

24. Aune, "Liturgy and Theology 2," 143.

25. Ellis, *Gathering*, 25–36. Interestingly enough, Ellis argues for a Word-Table *ordo*, even though the Word is frequent and the Table infrequent.

meeting, its intention was evangelism, not worship *per se*.[26] Likewise, as free church Protestants began to incorporate these frontier patterns of ritual into their church life, they created a variety of "services" of which one was explicitly the Sunday morning worship service, that together with the Sunday evening prayer service, the Wednesday evening Bible study, the hymn sing, the testimony service, and the evangelistic service created a fully orbed pattern of ritual life. All of these services had elements native to worship—scriptures read and proclaimed, prayers spoken and sung, and times of fellowship, including repentance and forgiveness. Yet only one was considered to be *the* worship service. Furthermore, as the church has lost its central place in many family calendars, these extra services have all but disappeared, given a lack of attendance, and these multiple ritual emphases collapsed into the Sunday morning "service," now left to be a multi-purpose (rather than single-purpose) ritual, leaving "worship" to be defined operationally, not theologically.

This leads to a third and related issue: that most scholars of liturgy who examine Free Church worship are not from, or even sympathetic to, Free Church worship. Therefore, their analysis both imports their values upon it, defining Free Church rituals from the outside, and ignores any clues of what these rituals mean to the people on the inside.[27] As James White pointed out, Protestant worship in general must be studied anthropologically, not textually. The true text of Protestant worship is the event. There is no guarantee that any Protestant tradition's liturgical texts will be used—or used in the prescribed fashion—privileging participant observation over textual analysis as a methodology.[28] White further stated that to ignore the Free Church traditions is not only to ignore or dismiss more than half of the Christian population in North America but also to do so at the peril of academic integrity and the disregard for the movement of God's Spirit in the world.[29]

At this point, I feel obliged to offer a historical proposal of whether "Free Church worship" and "liturgical worship" might be of the same genus but of different species. Upon examining the origins and trajectory of Free Church worship, it might be safest to say that Free Church worship and liturgical worship are both part of the genus of corporate Christian ritual, but Free Church worship is characterized more (but not exclusively) by intentional focus on communicating about God from person to person,

26. For the history of evangelical worship patterns in the United States, see Schmidt, *Holy Fairs*, and White, *Protestant Worship*, 171–91.

27. Ross, "Joseph's Britches Revisited," esp. 543.

28. White, *Protestant Worship*, 13–24.

29. White, "How Do We Know It Is Us?," 55–65.

while liturgical worship is characterized more (but not exclusively) by intentional focus on interacting with God. Both traditions see "worship" as building up the body of Christ, with Free Church worship emphasizing quantitative growth and liturgical worship accenting qualitative growth, but neither exclusively so.

This latter tendency runs deep in the Free Church tradition. One finds an interesting test case by examining the ritual pattern of George Whitefield's preaching service used in his open-air preaching. Whitefield would begin by intoning a Psalm, but it appears this was done more to draw a crowd than to begin in prayer. Whitefield would then read a passage from the Bible and proceed to preach. His sermons would often conclude with an invitation and a prayer.[30] Whitefield's preaching ritual appears to be a different animal than even Zwingli's Prone liturgy, and certainly from the Prayer Book pattern of the Church of England used in Whitefield's church. It appears that this truncated form of the liturgy of the Word was more influential on early Methodist itinerants, Asbury and Coke, than was Wesleyan liturgical practice and theology.

At first blush, it seems that it is Whitefield who, though primarily thought of as a preacher, may have been one of the most influential liturgical reformers by virtue of the imitation of his preaching pattern in North America and its gradual growth and development, including music, prayers, and other, more traditional liturgical elements. Is it possible that Free Church worship is the evolutionary development (or mutation, take your pick) of a new species of Christian ritual? This would imply that using the theological criteria utilized to evaluate liturgical worship would distort the nature and intent of Free Church worship.

A contemporary example of this sort of reconsideration of the nature of free church rituals would be the almost uniform ritual patterns in mega-churches. A survey of the ritual patterns of some of the most 'notable' churches in North America revealed an almost universal order among these communities.[31] They begin with a block of music between twenty and thirty-five minutes long. Often there will be informal welcome, testimony, collection of tithes and offerings, or prayer interspersed in this time offered by members of the worship band or praise team. This portion ends making a sometimes-abrupt shift to the sermon, which lasts between twenty-five and forty-five minutes. There is an informal sending forth, with the rare occasion of a closing song or songs.

30. Stout, *Divine Dramatist*, 66–86.

31. Eldridge, "Mega-Church and Its Micro-Liturgy."

This pattern of ritual is not new to the evangelical tradition. For the better part of the last century, Sunday School programs began with all ages gathered together to sing, have a brief time of prayer, oftentimes take an offering, and then be dismissed to individual classes for catechesis. Music was used to prepare a receptive hearing, tilling the soil of the soul, preparing for the seeds of the Gospel to be sown in the Sunday School lessons to follow.[32] It appears that the template for what is called worship in today's most popular churches is drawn from rituals of Christian education, whose purpose is to evangelize and catechize much more than worship per se. Certainly, these rituals were in no way connected to the traditional four-fold pattern of Word and Table worship. Is it really fair to the churches using these ritual patterns, then, to hold them accountable for the expectations of efficacious worship from another pattern? This digression is offered as a caveat, simply to suggest that what is being proposed as liturgical theology is stretching the term "liturgical" to its broadest possible meaning.

Building Blocks of Free Church Worship?

Given this broad historical survey, are there biblical *Bausteine* that might be proposed for consideration for Free Church worship? Would not churches practicing these contemporary forms of worship privilege the authority of the Scriptures, in particular the New Testament, over any liturgical tradition? I would suggest such building blocks may be found in Paul's First Epistle to the Corinthians. Especially as Paul does not use the term "worship" in 1 Corinthians but instead the term "gathering," which would certainly apply to the Free Church rituals described above.

1 Corinthians is the record of Paul's attempt to redirect a church he feels is drifting off course. At the outset, Paul identifies the reason for his correspondence as the fissures growing in the foundation of the community leading to factions (1 Cor 1:10). These divisions are evident in the various people given allegiance by the community (1 Cor 1:12–13), the segregation of the 'haves' from the 'have nots' at their communal meals (1 Cor 11:21–22), and the valuing of the various gifts that people bring to the community, arguing that no gift is unnecessary or unimportant (1 Cor 12:22–25).

It appears that there were two particular gifts in the Corinthian church that were problematic enough to warrant extended attention: prophecy and speaking in tongues (1 Cor 14:6–25). As Paul describes these two, tongues is a form of ecstatic speech which appears to lack meaning outside of the

32. For more examples of these ritual models, see Johnson, "Video: Monstrance for a New Millennium," 17–19.

individual speaking in tongues and does not "build up the body"—either qualitatively (edifying the believers) or quantitatively (attracting unbelievers)—as it does not appear to be distinct from ecstatic speech in other religions (1 Cor 14:8). On the other hand, speaking a word of prophecy is a clear articulation of God's truth, correcting the faithful and convicting the unbeliever. This, Paul proposed, could build up the body both spiritually and numerically. Prophecy is distinct from tongues with the notable exception of when tongues are interpreted which, according to Paul, is the gift that those who speak in tongues should pray for (1 Cor 14:13).

It is in this context that Paul offers his advice for the gatherings of the Corinthian church. In doing so, Paul continues the two central themes of this epistle: unity within diversity and the building up the body of Christ. Paul begins with what appears to be an obvious assumption: each person is expected to bring something to contribute to the community's gathering (1 Cor 14:26). Each contribution (whether a hymn, a teaching, a prophetic word, a word in tongues) is to be offered for the building up of the body as well as to the glory of God (1 Cor 10:31). This implies that worship leadership is primarily the coordination and orchestration of the gifts and offerings of the people, although there is no explicit mention of liturgical leadership in these gatherings. Paul assumes that worship is not only corporate but that it is essentially so. If one should come and not contribute his or her gift—or not even attend at all—the building up of the community will be deficient.

Next, Paul underscores the interdependent nature of the gifts that people offer, resulting in the whole of the service of worship. There is such a level of interdependence that if some gifts are absent, others may not use their gifts. In particular, Paul instructs that if someone speaks in a tongue, they should only contribute it to the gathering if there is someone there to interpret the tongue, for everything is done for the glory of God and the building up of the community. If there is no one to interpret, those with a tongue to speak should speak it to God in silence, for an un-interpreted utterance will not build up the body (1 Cor 14:28).

Paul understands these services to be empowered by the Spirit but also that they have limited spontaneity. Twice, Paul states that worship should reflect the nature of God, being orderly, as God is a God of peace and decency (1 Cor 14:33, 40). To this end, Paul prescribes a sequence with which the contributions of this gathering should take place—tongues, interpretations, prophecy, revelations—all offered for the building up of the community to the glory of God, decently and in order.

A summary of Paul's instructions might be distilled to a few salient points that help us identify the defining qualities of Christian worship. That is, Christian worship is an interdependent offering of gifts by all members of the community, done in an orderly fashion, for the building up of the body to the glory of God. I would not advocate that we follow these instructions slavishly or literally. I would have problems applying this teaching to communities that currently have neither tongues nor prophecies. I would further have difficulty applying Paul's principal of "decently and in order" literally to women who are expected by Paul to be silent in these gatherings (1 Cor 14:34). I do believe, though, that the principles above—that Christian worship is a corporate, interdependent, ordered gathering gifted by the Spirit—can help us in our worship planning, leading, and participation today. These *Bausteine* are qualities, however, not liturgical elements as Aune proposed. This actually makes them more appropriate to Free Church worship while still remaining applicable to liturgical worship.

Paul: Liturgical Consultant for Contemporary Churches

This loosely defined *ordo* of qualities is not a description of Free Church worship. Instead, these qualities could identify (with biblical authority) the building blocks of Free Church worship for the health of the Church, following Schmemann's agenda. I would suggest this interpretation: when people plan worship they should do so with the question, "What sequence of actions do I want to lead the people through for the worship of God and the building up of the community?" These are not such actions as *sing* or *clap*, *stand* or *kneel*, but instead *praise, confess, adore, proclaim, give thanks*, etc. Each of these actions should be in a logical sequence. This requires carefully considering what one wants each congregant to do at every point of the service to worship God. This would suggest asking how what the congregants are doing now logically follows what they just did and logically leads to what they do next, from the beginning to the end of the service. It also holds each choice up to the criteria of how it builds up the body and glorifies God. It is not enough to be a vehicle for self-expression, evangelism, or edification.

Those leading worship services would need to ask how they can resource their people so that they are able to do those actions of worship successfully, that God might be glorified and the community strengthened. And those who go to worship should go with the expectation that they will be the primary actors in the worship service. They are going to contribute their gifts to the worship of God by the entire community; without their contribution, their community's offering will be less than it otherwise could be. The leaders of worship, then, are not worshipping for people, but are empowering them to worship God.

This approach to understanding worship through the eyes of Paul's writing to the church at Corinth does not imply a style or format. Those from traditions with more fixed liturgies would be able to identify the actions being offered to the congregation for their execution and the intent behind them, and would allow them to chose variable elements that make sense for that day, given the season of the Church Year, the Scriptures being read, and the events in the life of the church. Those from Free Church traditions could still begin with a song set but would require the song set to be seen primarily as congregational song, and each song would be chosen in sequence for its theological content and the act of worship it suggests. For example, one could open with a song calling God's people to worship, followed by an invocation of God's presence in that time and space, leading to a celebration of God's presence in their midst, and so on—with this entire sequence accomplished through congregational song.

Developing a Liturgical Theology for Free Church Worship

The above description is more a theology of worship, a prescriptive theological definition of how to worship, even for Free Church worship. But what about a liturgical theology from Free Church worship? Liturgical theologians have, more often than not, traced the origins of liturgical theology back to Prosper of Aquitaine's appeal to the intercessions of the Good Friday liturgy as a defense against a creeping Pelagianism. In his identification of the intercession's appeal for God's grace—rather than an appeal to the righteousness of the believers—Prosper famously writes, *"legem credendi lex statuat supplicandi"* (the law of supplication determines the rule of faith).[33] This has been infamously reduced to the adage "lex orandi/lex credendi" (the law of prayer determines the law of faith). Most liturgical theologians have followed Schmemann's lead of a normative apostolic *ordo* that forms those who pray it into a normative apostolic faith.

There are also those, on the other hand, who suggest that a more proper interpretation is that the norm of faith determines the norm of prayer—that faith arises from theology—contrary to what Schmemann and his followers believe, that theology arises secondarily from liturgy. It was the genius of the late Jesuit theologian Edward Kilmartin who identified the reciprocal

33. The actual meaning of this phrase in its original, longer form may not actually refer as directly to the liturgy, but to the convergence of Scriptures, tradition and the liturgy. For a detailed exegesis of Prosper's phrase, see De Clerk, "'Lex orandi, lex credendi,'" 178–200. Further, with the recent work of Joseph Novak, we now have a fuller understanding of *lex supplicandi* than simply a liturgical *ordo*. See Novak, "Revaluing Prosper of Aquitaine in Contemporary Liturgical Theology," 211–33.

relationship between faith and prayer, where both are constantly changing, influenced by each other as well as outside influences. Kilmartin summarized this relationship writing: "The slogan 'law of prayer/law of belief' leaves in suspense which magnitude might be the subject, and which the predicate in particular instances. Consequently, it seems legitimate to state the axiom in this way: *the law of prayer is the law of belief, and vice versa*."[34] Although most people have been in agreement with Kilmartin that this is a dynamic, reciprocal relationship, few have sought to apply this relationship pastorally to the needs of churches whose worship and theology is in a state of flux. The needs of Free Church worship provide an opportunity to do just that. I would suggest three links implied by this reciprocal relationship that will identify the trajectory a Free Church liturgical theology should develop.

The first link is the link of congruence between belief and prayer, or perhaps better said, belief and rite. The term congruence does not imply a primacy of one over the other but instead implies the need for constant pastoral monitoring and careful theological reflection. The principle of congruence asks the questions: Are you saying and doing what you believe? Are you believing what you say and do? What do you intend to accomplish with this ritual, theologically and pastorally? Evidence of incongruence should lead to pastoral correction from within—not theological correction from without.

Let me explain by way of illustration. I was once in attendance at a large evangelical church on "Baby Dedication Sunday." The Pastor of Family Ministry was presiding over this part of the service and invited over a dozen couples to come forward to the front of this church with their infant children. The families stood in a semicircle facing the minister. He explained how this rite had no spiritual blessing or benefit to the children in any way but instead was an opportunity for the parents to dedicate themselves to the raising of these children. The pastor never held nor touched the children at any time, lest they be seen as receiving some sort of blessing. He reiterated that this rite has nothing to do with salvation. The pastor then began to pray, "Bless, O Lord, these children, that they might come to know Jesus Christ as their savior." This pastor has made two incongruous statements, one "liturgical" and one "theological." Which one is correct? The task of liturgical theology in this proposed approach is not to privilege one over the other but to bring the two into compatibility. The fact is, one is formed by both catechesis and ritual, and you are mal-forming people to the extent that there are contradictions and inconsistencies between them. The task of liturgical

---

34. Kilmartin, *Christian Liturgy*, 97. It should be noted that such reciprocity was found in Vagaggini's work and never denied by Schmemann.

theology in Free Church worship would be to help ministers choose those signs, words, and gestures that best express their belief within their community as well as evaluate those that are already in use.

The second link is between the story of God and the story of people. Christian worship, like Jewish worship before it, has always had both a narrative quality and a narrative logic to it.[35] The God we worship is the God of Abraham, Isaac, and Jacob; Eve, Miriam, and Mary. Chronology is not incidental. God is a God who has acted in history, and worship of God begins with telling the story of God's work in the world. It is into this larger, cosmic story of God's creating, redeeming, sustaining, and finally consuming, that the stories of every tribe and nation, woman and man are told.[36]

The implication of the narrative quality of Christian worship has three direct consequences on Free Church worship. First, worship ought to have a logical beginning, middle, and end. It ought to have a narrative flow that has a gospel purpose to it. Once, while offering a consultation to a church having issues with worship style, I suggested that they take the previous week's bulletin and cross out the musical selections and the sermon. I then asked what was left. What should remain is a prayer with a logical beginning, middle, and end. The question of musical or homiletic style is secondary to the question of whether the insertion of those elements helps or hinders the narrative flow of the people's prayer that day. Surveys of contemporary worship patterns has revealed that many "traditional contemporary" churches (i.e., Calvary Chapel, Vineyard, etc.) have what might be called modular liturgies, plugging elements into the ritual in a regular sequence but without any narrative logic. Emerging churches tend to move beyond this and offer a sort of collage, with elements at times occurring simultaneously.[37] This will address the question of gatherings that are orderly, reflecting God's nature, following Paul's criteria.[38]

Second, this link suggests that the reading of the Scriptures is a non-negotiable element of Free Church worship, as one cannot tell God's story without God's story. As a tradition that prides itself on biblical faith, it is regularly critiqued for the absence of biblical reading in worship. It is obvious

35. For example, Paul Bradshaw's assessment of the narrative quality of Jewish prayers, see Bradshaw, *Two Ways of Praying*, 45–56.

36. This is certainly a position held by Robert Webber in his later works. For him, "Worship does God's story." See Webber, *Ancient-Future Worship*, 29.

37. See Cherry, *Worship Architect*.

38. This is not to say that there is no logical arrangement of elements in contemporary worship patterns. Often, the paradigms that guide this worship arise out of interpretations of the architecture and liturgies associated with the temple in Jerusalem. See Lim and Ruth, *Lovin' on Jesus*.

that free churches consider themselves to be grounded in the Bible. Yet, in many churches, from Whitefield on, the reading of Scripture has been secondary to the proclamation of Scriptures. This tendency has evolved to the point where it is not uncommon to have no explicit reading of the Bible in Free Church worship.

Third, this link invites us to consider our stories within the context of God's story. Baptist scholar Martin Stringer suggests that when we hear God's story in worship, it speaks to our story, creating a third, entirely new story of our life in Christ.[39] It is important to note with Stringer that we do not invite Christ into our lives. Instead, we are invited to place our lives into a life greater than our own, that of the life of Christ and his work of redemption. Frequently, however, a congregation's ritual life orbits primarily around the personal story of the individual and is often less connected with principles of the Reign of God and more with success in terms of personal growth and self-fulfillment.

This second link leads to our third and final link of liturgical theology in the Free Church worship tradition, which is reflection of the life of Christ in the life of his disciples. In Romans 12:1 (one of the two most quoted proof texts for defining worship), after Paul has laid out the mysterious plan of God's salvation in chapter 11, he invites a response which is one of sacrifice, surrendering yourself to something greater—not thinking of yourself more highly than you ought, offering your gift for the greater good—and all in praise of God. It is this spiritual theme of sacrifice that led the early Christians to choose the term "liturgy" to describe what they did when they worshipped. A liturgy was not just the work or service of the people but work on behalf of the people; a public service and a response to serve and care for the other.[40] As we remember the earlier practices of collections of offerings in the early centuries of the Church, some of the gifts (bread and wine) would be used for the celebration of the Lord's Supper, some would be set aside to feed the clergy as their pay for the week, the rest would be given to the poor. When the bread and wine would be processed forward to be consecrated, it symbolized all the people's offerings. When the gifts were consecrated, a blessing was invoked on the gifts *and* the people. This was the people's liturgy: worshipping God, supporting the church, and serving the world. All of this begins with the posture of sacrifice. This theme of sacrifice is marked on us at the beginning of our walk as a disciple for, as Paul writes in Romans, we have been buried with Christ in baptism (Rom 6:3–4) to

39. Ross, "Joseph's Britches Revisited," 542. See also Ruth, "Rose By Any Other Name," 33–51, esp. 46–51.

40. For a discussion on the interpretation of this term, see Aune, "Liturgy and Theology 1," 61–65.

enter new life in Christ. Although many free church rites lead into baptism, they are less likely to offer an opportunity to affirm one's baptismal pledge as a life of sacrifice to God.

Traditionally, this was the purpose of the Table, but it need not necessarily be so. For example, when I was a seminary student, I would do pulpit supply in a small Southern Baptist church. Each week, people were invited to bring their offerings forward as a reminder of the time they first came forward to confess their faith and receive baptism, affirming once again their commitment to follow Christ as Lord. It is less a matter of "how" than a matter of "that" an opportunity for God's people to affirm their ongoing commitment to be part of God's ongoing story in the world is afforded. As Luther pointed out in his day, a theology of glory, *theologica doxa*, worship for our sake, is not Christian worship. Only a *theologica cruxis*, a theology of the cross, a sacrifice of self, will lead to Christian worship.[41] But of course, we are now being prescriptive, imposing an interpretation on a tradition, bordering on a theology of worship again.

Summary: A Liturgical Theology of Congruence

This study has led me to offer two general comments by way of conclusion. First is one of nomenclature and the second is one of methodology. In terms of nomenclature, I believe it is appropriate to once again open up the question of defining worship. James White suggested that authentic Christian worship was defined by three factors: gathering in Christ's name, an expectation of encountering the divine, and an embrace of a variety of forms and styles.[42] My concern is that heading in this direction moves the term "worship" closer to the term "spirituality," which becomes so broad in meaning that it means very little. Within the academy, I would prefer to maintain a narrower definition of worship, using the term "service" as a more accurate description of the Lord's Day ritual in the free church tradition. What a congregation chooses to do on the Lord's Day may very well fit traditional understandings of worship, but it may just as well be a ritual of education, edification, evangelism, or spiritual experience. Regardless, they would all have in common that the ritual executed on the Lord's Day was that community's service to God and service to the community in God's name. This would require liturgical theologians to ask the question of the community's intention before entering into evaluation or critique of such a ritual. None of the range of rituals described would necessarily be excluded by Paul's

---

41. See Kolb, "Luther on the Theology of the Cross," 443–66.

42. White, "How do We Know it is Us?," 64–65.

qualifications that everything be done for the qualitative and quantitative growth of the gathered community.

Second, in terms of method, I would like to suggest that liturgical theology ought to be a method of assessing congruence in two directions. The first is internal congruence. Is there a compatibility of all the ritual elements in the service with the intention of the service? In particular, this raises the question of the congruence of the music, the reading and preaching of Scriptures, and the prayers of the people. One of the most obvious fruits of such an approach is work toward liturgical theological and homiletic methods that work together rather than separately. In the case of the sermon, it would imply that the sermon is not a liturgical time-out but an integrated part of the larger whole of the ritual.

Further, it requires pastoral/theological congruence. Once it is determined what the intention of a community's Lord's Day service is, then liturgical theology can become a resource in assisting the community in accomplishing their ritual goal more effectively. If a community intends to offer thanks and praise to the Triune God, then the task of liturgical theology is to assess the Trinitarian language of the rite, how it is used, and how well it is understood by the people.[43]

Liturgical theologians are confronted by a global conversation about Christian worship, involving the plethora of free church and other non-traditional worship forms falling in the category of "worship," which pushes the limits of liturgical theology. Our challenge has been to find points of contact between what is traditionally known as liturgical theology and non-traditional, non-liturgical Christian rituals, which may or may not be worship per se. By inviting an analysis of services that focus in on the congruence of belief and practice, the place of God's story in worship, and the expectation for all present to offer themselves as living sacrifices, we might begin to create a methodology that honors the origins and intentions of these rites, putting them into dialogue with the ongoing conversation of liturgical theology in the broader church without necessarily holding those churches to all the liturgical forms that the liturgical traditions represent. It also encourages a pastoral and theological evaluation of services that are not intended to be worship services to assess them by their own intentions and standards, inviting conversation between these rituals and more traditional Christian liturgy. In the end, I hope to have proposed a work of liturgical theology, not something a lot like liturgical theology, and congruent with Alexander Schmemann's desire to "to explain how the Church expresses and fulfills herself in this act."[44]

---

43. For example, see Ruth, "Lex Amandi, Lex Orandi," 342–59.

44. Schmemann, *On Liturgical Theology*, 17.

The Impact of Alexander Schmemann on Protestant Liturgical Theology

Don Saliers

ALEXANDER SCHMEMANN, THE EXPATRIATE Estonian/Russian Orthodox priest and theologian, is rightly celebrated by liturgical theologians across Roman Catholic and Protestant traditions. No one can read very far into the literature of the past fifty years without encountering multiple references to his work. At the heart of his theology is a radical claim: "The purpose of worship is to constitute the church."[1] Such a claim sets a complex and demanding agenda for many of us. At the same time, Schmemann's claim raises substantial questions for traditions whose ecclesiology differs markedly from that of the Orthodox churches. Well before the Second Vatican Council, theologians were concerned with the relationship between theology, faith, and liturgical practices. However, the profound impact of the Council on most Protestant liturgical reforms, particularly stemming from the *Constitution on the Sacred Liturgy*, opened the door to many of Schmemann's central ideas. This essay emerges from my own engagement in the context of efforts at reform and renewal among diverse Protestant and Anglican traditions.

One passage in Schmemann's 1972 essay, "Liturgy and Theology" struck me early on with great force. As a young teacher of worship at Yale Divinity School, my own theological vocation seemed outlined in these words. He wrote:

---

1. Schmemann, *Introduction*, 19.

> Ultimately, the liturgical problem of our time is . . . a problem
> of restoring to liturgy its theological meaning, and to theology
> its liturgical dimension. Theology cannot recover its central
> place and function within the church without being rooted
> again in the very experience of the Church (in thanksgiving
> and supplication). . . .Theology must rediscover as its own "rule
> of faith" the Church's lex orandi, and the liturgy reveal itself
> again as the credendi.[2]

Here was a central problem stated succinctly by someone quite outside my tradition and my conventional sources and categories. That very year, I found myself at the Orthodox Center in Chambezy studying by experience the liturgies of Orthodox Easter for the first time.

Shortly after beginning to read more of Schmemann's writings, I joined with a number of Protestant and Catholic scholars in the newly formed North American Academy of Liturgy. Among the Protestants doing liturgical theology were Gordon Lathrop, for whom Schmemann also became an influential source, along with Presbyterians Arlo Duba at Princeton and Harold Daniels, who was already at work on the *Book of Common Worship*. Anglican Leonel Mitchell and others became part of a working group in Liturgical Theology for whom Schmemann was a significant figure. It was clear to me at that point that Schmemann was both a profound resource and a vigorous challenge to inherited Protestant views of the relationship between liturgy, piety, and theology.

Emerging Insights from Schmemann

From those early (and continuing) discussions and from my classroom use of other works—such as *Introduction to Liturgical Theology*, *For the Life of the World*, and *Of Water and the Spirit*—a persistent framing of crucial issues emerged. I, like others, found that the ancient formula of *lex orandi, lex credendi* provided a useful way of trying to state the relationship between liturgical prayer and theological doctrine. In some ways, it became an uncritical slogan in the early enthusiasm among Protestant theologians seeking to articulate how praying and believing are more than cause and effect. The surface implication was simply that the church's acts of worship proceed the formulation of theological doctrine. Understanding the formula this way overlooked the complex relationships between implicit and explicit theological claims in the reciprocity of Scripture, Eucharist, and Baptism, not to mention the role of the psalms in the formation of Christian prayer. A deeper

---

2. Schmemann, "Liturgy and Theology," 100.

"grammar" emerged as ecumenical and critical discussions of the formula developed in the 1980s and 1990s. Yet even the uncritical use of Prosper of Aquitaine's famous principle in fact allowed me and others to think about Christian liturgy as the ongoing prayer of the church as a primary source for theological reflection. As a consequence, the task of Christian theological reflection was seen to be impoverished when the liturgical assembly is not seriously included as a primary source for thought. In this sense, Schmemann lead us to understand Paul Ricouer's claim, "the symbol gives rise to thought," as crucial to all theological method. I could now ask: how would it be possible to discuss sacramental theology without reference to actual worshiping assemblies? This, of course, was an established approach in both Roman Catholic and Protestant "textbook" theologies.

Schmemann thus prompted me and others to distinguish the methods and sourcing of "liturgical theology" from a simple "theology of prayer" or a Protestant "theology of worship." Among the key notions that emerged was a distinction between "primary" and "secondary" theology. This distinction marked differences between the theology embedded in the actions and discourses of the living worshiping assembly and critical reflection that articulated "belief" explicitly in the form of doctrine or particular theological claims. The initial Protestant uses of this distinction, however, required bringing Schmemann into conversation with biblical and historical scholarship not present in his writings. David Fagerberg's *What Is Liturgical Theology?* represented a helpful compendium of the state of that discussion at the time.

The problem was an uncritical approach which drew the distinction too clearly. Gradually, historical awareness of how and why an overly simplified distinction between first and second order language was drawn—especially through the work of Maxwell Johnson and Paul Bradshaw. A stark contrast between the language of liturgy and the language of theological reflection on the liturgy would not answer the question Schmemann proposed. Furthermore, as the field of liturgical theology moved beyond the initial principles found in Schmemann and others, we began to take account of the cultural and social contexts as a crucial aspect in the work of liturgical theology. Protestant and Roman Catholic liturgical theology converged methodologically in taking with increasing seriousness the bearing of social and cultural contexts in formulating the complex reciprocity of biblical and liturgical forms of discourse. The work of figures such as Gordon Lathrop (Lutheran), David Power (Roman Catholic), and others offered a much closer examination of how the language and imagery of Scripture was already embedded in liturgical action in Christian assemblies. It could no longer be neatly separated, with "orandi" as prayer and "credendi" as doctrinal belief. More significantly, we were forced to ask questions about "performance practices" in specific Christian traditions, thus marking questions of aesthetics and social "situatedness" in reflecting theologically on liturgical practices. Still, Schmemann's fundamental point about the centrality of the worshiping assembly for Christian theology remained. Now, Protestant liturgical theologians had to specify the anatomy of liturgy in ways that Schmemann's more programmatic views would not have contained. This leads to the continuing critical appropriation of his work in current Protestant liturgical theology.

Influential Major Themes

What major themes in Schmemann's work continue to shape Protestant modes of liturgical theology? I propose four: 1) the eschatological character of Christian liturgy; 2) liturgical participation as theological reception; 3) theological critique of liturgical tradition; and 4) permanent tensions between Gospel and culture in the liturgical assembly.

Perhaps the most significant of Schmemann's themes to shape Protestant liturgical theology is his insistence on the eschatological character of Christian liturgy. The typical attitude toward the Eucharist or Lord's Supper prior to the liturgical reforms of the late twentieth century was focused on the memorial of Christ's passion as forgiveness of sins and assurance. The massive work of revising worship books among Lutherans, Methodists, Presbyterians, and Episcopalians began to rediscover the messianic joy of resurrected life in the Sacrament of the Table. A new accent on the essentially eschatological character of the meal—oriented toward the Kingdom of God—appeared both in revised texts and in theological commentaries. In nearly all revisions of the sacramental rites was a return to the early liturgical sources. This was the Protestant version of the famous *ressourcement* principle stemming from the *Constitution on the Sacred Liturgy*. This was clearly seen in Schmemann's conception of living Tradition.

In more systematic theology, Jürgen Moltmann, beginning with his *Theology of Hope*, provided a striking turn in Protestant constructive theology. Moltmann was aiming at a radical corrective and reconception of older forms of eschatology that had so dominated Protestant thought. No longer could we think of eschatology only as the doctrine of "last things"—final judgement, the end of the world, and eternal life. We began to reconceive eschatology as a *principle of thought*, indeed, as a fundamental way of doing theology. In my own case, I came to rethink all acts of prayer as eschatological cries. What is true of the Lord's Prayer, "your Kingdom come" was true of the whole economy of Christian liturgy and all its modalities. Christian eschatology invited us to reflect on the Kingdom of God in ways that were linked to piety and politics, to faith claims and the habitual structures of power in the world. This emphasized human participation in the present arrangements of power. Liturgical participation thus becomes a source of resistance to the "is" of the world in light of what is mediated of the "ought to be" of the Kingdom of God. Eschatology could no longer simply be confined to the end of time. Here was a clear connection with Schmemann's conception of the liturgical participation in the Kingdom, and the deep spiritual desire and longing for the Rule and Reign of God in the present age.

At the same time, Schmemann's work resonated with the Protestant disposition toward prophetic critique. There is much to be learned from Schmemann's critique of tradition. One of the recurring interests in Protestant liturgical reflection, and prominently in my own work, is the double question: Can Christian liturgy bear the seeds of its own self-critique? This implies the possibility that liturgy also may render judgement on social/cultural realities in which it is enacted. Schmemann clearly announces a strong critique of Orthodox tradition in his early work. He takes aim at a basic misunderstanding—to regard liturgy primarily as a matter of "cultural heritage" and national identity. To think of the continuity of tradition as essentially cultural self-expression is to deny the Gospel. For him, the Christian Gospel embodied in the full range of liturgical rites cannot not be the means for shoring up a sense of tradition in light of modernity. Rather, the Gospel remains a scandal since it addresses the fallen darkness of humanity. In this way, he encourages a prophetic critique of empty ritual in a time of secularistic ascendancy. While Protestant theologians differ on their assessments of "secularity" and the threat of secularism (a major accent in Schmemann), the invitation to a prophetic critique built into authentic liturgical participation is unmistakably there.

But there is also a surprise here. Schmemann opens room for both continuity and discontinuity of tradition. Surprisingly, for him, the real continuity is in the essential human existential situation of fallenness that remains the same from age to age. As he observes, "Is it not obvious indeed that man remains essentially the same? He faces the same eternal mysteries."[3] This while he emphasized, at least in principle, that the liturgical life can develop and unfold over time and culture. In this way, Schmemann promotes a radical revisioning of the question of time itself. The joyful participation in the Kingdom in the very structures of time and the liturgical year thus made a crucial linkage between liturgical participation and the reality of the divine promises. Even more, encountering Jesus Christ

3. See Schmemann, *Of Water and the Spirit*, esp. 150.

in Sacrament and Word was already a transaction between heaven and earth (to use Aidan Kavanagh's phrase). In this way, Schmemann helps to restore the appropriate tension between the "already" and the "not yet" which was more apparent in general Protestant theology, a theme traceable in part to the work of Albert Schweitzer's early twentieth-century portrait of Jesus. But Schmemann put this into the very idiom, patterns, and dynamism of the church's continuing worship life.

Participation as Theological Reception

Protestant theology has characteristically emphasized the centrality of the Word of God, and hence the indispensability of preaching and hearing. Reading, singing, and listening shaped the sense and sensibility of public worship. This was the indelible inheritance of the Reformation and the inherited "liturgical theology" of the Reformers. Attention was traditionally concentrated on verbal forms of participation. The ecumenical and liturgical movements were already broadening notions of participation to include a wider range of non-verbal and symbolic means. The iconic, gestural, and processive dimensions of worship have come to prominence in the experience and reflection among Protestant theologians in the past hundred years. The exposure to a wide variety of cultural traditions in Roman Catholic and Orthodox liturgical practice have exercised a deep influence. In many ways, one can argue that this—along with the reforms of worship books and sources of praxis—has caused a reassessment of what was already present or latent in Protestant worship traditions. Participation has never been solely a matter of hearing and scripture alone. The Lutheran and Anglican traditions have rediscovered the "eye" and the whole range of the senses mediated by singing and the central actions of baptismal and meal rites. The rise of Pentecostal traditions, while certainly not "liturgical" in the standard sense, have also contributed to Protestant liturgical theology's awareness of how the physical body receives word, prayer, and sacrament.

Here, the work of liturgical theologian Gordon Lathrop and others have opened the richness of symbol, metaphor, analogy, and the larger ecology of worship. Lathrop's trilogy of *Holy Things*, *Holy People*, and *Holy Ground*[4] is a remarkable achievement in this regard. While not without Protestant critics, these volumes stake out the territory for a resolute liturgical theological program. In several ways, this work not only honors the impulses in Schmemann's proposals about participation but also takes into account

---

4. See Lathrop, *Holy Things*; *Holy People*; and *Holy Ground*. The work of Alexander Schmemann echoes throughout these volumes.

a much more concrete and much more eccleisally and culturally "located" methodology than his. My work in *Worship As Theology: Foretaste of Glory Divine*[5] emerged in large measure in conversation with Schmemann, Lathrop, David Power, Nathan Mitchell, and others. The earlier preoccupation with texts, historical origins, and the centrality of the Word is now clearly a multiple disciplinary enterprise.

It can be said that Protestant and Roman Catholic liturgical theology have embraced the fundamental idea that the participation of worshiping assembles is a primary means of "theological reception." This implies that method and substance in theological thinking has to be reoriented to a primary locus in the worshiping assembly. This was a crucial point in Schmemann's original conception of theological method, referred to above: to restore to liturgy its theological depth and to restore the liturgical dimension to the work of theology.

Critique of Liturgical Tradition

Appreciation and continuing critical responses to Schmemann are marked by admiration, ambivalence, and ambiguity. To stand in any particular tradition of worship is to be shaped by a particular history of practice. It is also to raise questions about the faithfulness and adequacy of that tradition in light of changing social/culture environments over time. The impulse to reform liturgical practice and theology comes about when questions about faithfulness and adequacy emerge. Influenced by Schmemann's own appreciation and critique of tradition, I recently reflected on the present state of liturgical reform and renewal:

> Theological foundations for reform emerge when the churches confront basic contradictions and misunderstandings that develop over time in actual liturgical practice. Some result from cultural accretions that obscure the unity of Word and Sacrament. . . . Loss of connection with the earliest sources of liturgical life and the rich diversity of prayer forms is another weakness that requires recovery and new forms of imagination. These are results of discerning the "gap" between what is actually practiced and the . . . messianic promise found in the appropriation of Scripture and Tradition.[6]

---

5. Saliers, *Worship As Theology*. The title bears the marks of the rediscovery of eschatological thinking and the role of the non-verbal languages that marks contemporary Protestant liturgical theology.

6. See Saliers, "Theological Foundations of Liturgical Reform," 112.

Schmemann voiced his displeasure with misunderstandings of Orthodoxy just at this point. His was not an attack on ecclesial Tradition. Rather, he attacked both the secularist loss of genuine faith and the way in which Tradition itself was regarded as a finite cultural ceremonial. For him, the loss of the eschatological joy of full participation in the church's liturgy was a fundamental sin. In that sense, his critique was both internal to the actual loss of true liturgical piety but also a critique of the cultural captivity of the church's tradition itself. These issues have emerged among Protestant liturgical theologians as well. While ambiguity and ambivalence mark the task of liturgical theology, Protestant liturgical theologians face questions arising from quite different ecclesiologies. The Protestant tendency to mark discontinuity and irruption differs from a stress on continuity embedded in, with, and through the specific structures and iconographic-textual archeology of what is practiced. Schmemann has a far less developed sense of specifying how social/cultural forces erode faithful participation. On the other hand, Protestant liturgical theology begins with the disruption of continuity and seeks to find a deeper unity among diverse rite and traditions.

But the enduring legacy of Schmemann on Protestant liturgical theologians is his insistence on the worshipping assembly's participation in the resurrected life of Christ and on the permanent glory that keeps reconstituting the church's life in the world. This, of course, is a function of maintaining that in faithful liturgy, the assembly ascends with Christ to the very life of the Rule and Reign of God. While prophetic critique is possible, it emerges from a very different conception of how liturgy actually constitutes the church. Protestant theology contends that liturgy and ethical engagement are much more interpenetrating and symbiotically related. Participation in the Kingdom of God requires continual engagement with the principalities and power of the world as it is presently constituted.

Schmemann's legacy may also be put this way: the grace and glory of human acts of worship as a continuing gift of the Holy Spirit. All theology is reoriented toward liturgical praxis—what has been called the "source and summit" of the Christian life.

The prophetic tensions created by the Word of scripture in the liturgy keep pointing toward the eschatological joy of the resurrected life. While less developed in Schmemann's work, clearly there can be no abstract eschatology. Authentic Christian worship is indeed "for the life of the world." Contemporary Protestant liturgical theology has received this as crucial to the intrinsic relationship between liturgy, theology, and ethics that express faithful participation. This means that liturgical theology must share some of Schmemann's critique of superficial liberationist notions—meaning those ideas of human liberation that settle for bourgeois values instead of the full incarnation, passion, death, resurrection, and ascension of the Christ.

I propose that liturgical theology must always struggle to relate the mystery of Jesus Christ's passion and resurrection to the concreteness of historical forces. Thus, to participate in the liturgy of Jesus Christ, crucified and risen, requires the signs of the Kingdom to be marked in the ongoing intercessory force of the assembly's praxis. To worship in the name of Christ without anguish of the poor, engagement with the exiles, the outsiders, those crushed by the forces of present political and economic history is to ignore historical events and circumstances. This does indict the churches' failure of nerve to take human history seriously. Liturgical participation should be filled with joy. At the same time, Protestant liturgical reflection should take seriously a key point in Miguel de Unamuno's startling book, *The Tragic Sense of Life*:

> Those who say that they believe in God and yet neither love nor fear [God], do not in fact believe in [God] but in those who have taught them that God exists. . . .Those who believe that they believe in God, but without any passion in their heart, without anguish of mind, without uncertainty, without an element of despair even in their consolation, believe only in the God-Idea, not in God Himself.[7]

I do not know whether Fr. Schmemann ever read Unamuno, but one senses in his late journal writings, as Bruce Morrill has pointed out, an element of the elegiac that runs alongside the theme of eschatological joy. This contrast of joy and suffering, of doxology and lament, of ecstatic beauty and sobriety about the world is present in liturgical life as well. I think Schmemann knew something of this; Protestant liturgical theology seeks, at its best, to unfold this permanent tension in life and liturgy.

---

7. Unamuno, *Tragic Sense of Life*, 193.

PART 3

Schmemann and Liturgical Theology

Toward an Understanding of Pastoral Liturgical Theology

Joyce Ann Zimmerman, C.PP.S.

A number of themes repeatedly appear in Alexander Schmemann's works, for example, time, world, salvation, kingdom, Church, Eucharist, eschatology, and pneumatology. None, however, compares to the overarching importance of the relationship of celebrating liturgy with living what we celebrate. Certainly, concern for this pairing comes from Father Schmemann's teacher's heart. As dean and professor of liturgical theology at St. Vladimir's Orthodox Theological Seminary, he would hear many questions from his students ranging from "how so" to "why so." Father Schmemann was thoroughly pastoral.[1]

In his tome *Pastoral Liturgy*, Fr. Josef Jungmann, SJ, devotes the whole of part III to the "fundamentals of Liturgy and Kerygma."[2] Here, he slants pastoral as "pastoral care," not simply limiting himself to practical issues affecting those celebrating liturgy. More importantly, he is concerned with the wider issue of a life lived from liturgy: "Our whole life shall be a glorifying of God—in the calmness of labor, in the selfless fulfillment of duty; often it will be through a lonely and unnoticed life of devotion to duty. But on Sundays, above all, it should all flow together in the holy assembly."[3] Previous to this statement, Jungmann raises the question of whether Christians are living

1. Hence we do not find a systematic expose in Schmemann's works. There is also much repetition in his writings which serves to reinforce his major concerns.

2. The first two, more-lengthy parts of this work deal with the historical development of liturgy and its concomitant issues and challenges.

3. Jungmann, *Pastoral Liturgy*, 345.

liturgy and their faith consciously or unconsciously: "Conscious Christianity is present, then, when a person does not merely possess the treasure in the field in fact, but also knows that he possesses it and would be prepared to give his whole inheritance to win it or to keep it."[4]

Something is at stake in liturgy and Christian living. Both Jungmann and Schmemann decry a kind of Christianity practiced as mere habit, whether that is attending liturgy, making good moral choices, or keeping the rules. For Jungmann, being Christian is a conscious choice to follow Jesus Christ, which is fed by the liturgy and draws those who are baptized back to it. Liturgy—and particularly Eucharist—is central to baptismal living. As Schmemann puts it, "For mere 'going to church,' mere attendance, is not enough. True celebration is always a living participation."[5] Participation means so much more than posture, responses, listening, and so on. Participation means appropriation; that is, making what happens at liturgy our own in such a way that we can live what we celebrate.[6] Liturgy is where followers of Christ encounter him, are transformed more perfectly into being members of his Body (being transformed into more perfect images of Christ), and choose to live as he lived.

Our initiation into the Church's life and her liturgical life happens at baptism and chrismation/confirmation. Sometimes baptism and chrismation are relegated simply to the ritual(s), without any real sense that they are far more than ritual expression. As sacraments of the Church, they are living signs of a living reality. They are the life of the Church:

> The meaning of all this for us today is, first, that the whole life of the Church is, in a way, the explication and the manifestation of baptism, and second, that baptism forms the real content, the "existential" root of what we now call "religious education." The latter is not an abstract "knowledge about God" but the revelation of the wonderful things that have "happened" and happen to us in the divine gift of the new life.[7]

Liturgy is a privileged time for us to encounter God and God's kingdom, an encounter that enables us to remember and live God's presence in all the various circumstances of daily life.

4. Jungmann, *Pastoral Liturgy*, 330.

5. Schmemann, *Liturgy and Life*, 86.

6. I am grateful to my colleague Dr. Jennifer L. Lord who reminded me that, in Schmemann's context, to "live what we celebrate" is more than a personal appropriation of liturgy; it means that we live/celebrate that larger vision of God's kingdom, God's ongoing work of redeeming the world. This is what we make present in liturgy.

7. Schmemann, *For the Life of the World*, 69.

Schmemann's theological enterprise is, at root, pastoral liturgical theology. Liturgy is to be lived—period. However, much more ought to be said if we are to grasp fully the power of this simple statement: liturgy is to be lived. To live the liturgy is to live God's kingdom. We are to live our human part in the whole of creation which has been redeemed in Christ. We turn now to teasing out a "thick description"[8] of pastoral liturgical theology, then look to a way to relate liturgy and life, and finally consider some issues and challenges that must be faced if liturgy is to be lived faithfully and exuberantly.

Pastoral Liturgical Theology[9]

A good place to begin is with Schmemann's understanding of liturgical theology. He opens his *Introduction to Liturgical Theology* with the important point that liturgical theology "has appeared comparatively recently within the system of theological disciplines."[10] Before the great strides in understanding liturgy brought about by the Liturgical Movement of the last century, the term "liturgy" was largely unknown or misunderstood, and studies centered on preaching and rubrics. The Liturgical Movement generated both content and method. Its content was gleaned largely by returning to patristic sources, long neglected in the Church. Going "back to the sources," before historical accretions distorted the original intent of liturgy, was a major theme of the Second Vatican Council's agenda of *ressourcement*. The fourth and fifth-century mystagogues give us especially rich insights toward a fresh understanding of the initiation sacraments. The method of the Liturgical Movement not only opened up for us the value of symbol and typology but also taught us that the liturgical texts themselves are a source of theology. The mystagogues begin with the rite—the text and its experience—and explain from there, largely through the genre of homily.

Schmemann initiates his discussion with a simple enough statement: "As its name indicates, liturgical theology is the elucidation of the meaning

---

8. Cultural anthropologist Clifford Geertz uses this term to mean using many different details, impressions, interpretations, and contexts to come to a richer understanding by seeing all the possible meanings of cultural phenomena, such as rituals. Through thick description, meaning can be more accurately conveyed to someone outside of the culture or context. Thick description is opposed to "thin description," which is limited only to facts without the aid of context. See Geertz, "Thick Description," 3–30.

9. To my knowledge, Schmemann never uses the phrase "pastoral liturgical theology," but I think his work is permeated with this understanding of the phrase as I develop it here.

10. Schmemann, *Introduction*, 9.

of worship."[11] While theology "is above all explanation,"[12] the issue here is its starting point. A tendency has been to begin with doctrine or theology and impose it, so to speak, on the meaning of liturgy. Schmemann accepted fifth-century Prosper of Aquitaine's principle *legem credendi lex statuat supplicandi* (usually abbreviated *Lex orandi, lex credendi*: the law of praying is the law of believing) as a methodological mainstay. The starting point for doing liturgical theology is the liturgy itself, not doctrines or explanations about it: "What is needed is not so much the intellectual apprehension of worship as its apprehension through experience and prayer."[13] So when Schmemann understands liturgical theology as the "elucidation of the meaning of worship," he is saying we begin with the celebration itself, with the texts, with the people doing the celebrating: "In the early Church, in the writings of the Fathers, sacraments, inasmuch as they are given any systematic interpretation, are always explained in the context of their actual *liturgical* celebration, the explanation being, in fact, an exegesis of the liturgy itself, in all its ritual complexity and concreteness."[14] Liturgical theology is not a theology *of* liturgy but a theology that begins with the liturgy itself—it is a *liturgical* theology. The use of "liturgical" here as an adjective is critical: it is the liturgy that gives rise to its theology. Liturgy is *theologia prima*, first theology.[15]

For Schmemann, the "purpose of worship is to constitute the Church. . . . Its purpose is always to express the Church as the unity of that Body whose Head is Christ. . . . Its purpose is that we should . . . serve God."[16] In these words, Schmemann describes the Church as the Body of Christ united with its Head (made visible when one presides *in persona Christi capitis*), and points to the mission of the Church: to serve God, which, in turn, points toward living what has been celebrated, to being sent forth to "announce the Gospel of the Lord" or to "glorify the Lord by [one's] life."[17] For Schmemann, liturgical "services are not one of the 'aspects' of the Church; they express its very essence, are its breath, its heart-beat, its constant self-revelation."[18] An adequate or complete (i.e., holistic) under-

---

11. Schmemann, *Introduction*, 14.

12. Schmemann, *Introduction*, 14.

13. Schmemann, *Introduction*, 19. This is simply another way to speak of mystagogy.

14. Schmemann, *For the Life of the World*, 137.

15. On the concept of *theologia prima*, see Fagerberg, *Theologia Prima*.

16. Schmemann, *Introduction*, 19–20.

17. Two of the four dismissal formulae of the 2010 *Roman Missal*. The relationship of liturgy and life is taken up in the next section of this essay.

18. Schmemann, *Liturgy and Life*, 12.

standing of liturgy derives from the people and the celebration. This leads to the next issue, the requirement to broaden the notion of "text" beyond printed page and even beyond ritual enactment.

Schmemann's untimely death in 1983 precluded his capitalizing on the linguistic methodologies and textual hermeneutics that were just beginning to gain notice during his ministry and academic career. It is true that he liberally quotes from liturgical texts throughout his writings. However, it would be a mistake to think that text is limited to a printed page. All human action—including ritual—is fleeting, but this human action leaves traces or marks that can be recovered as documents of life.[19] Texts are not dead documents but living embodiments of human activity. Liturgical texts, then, are more than words and rubrics. They communicate to and from the worshipping community Gospel values, Gospel living, and self-giving service. Further, since Christian liturgy derives from Christ and his saving mystery, "the basis of all Christian worship is the Incarnation, [and] its true content is always the Cross and the Resurrection."[20] The relationship between liturgy and life is inextricable.

Now we have the tools in hand to propose a "thick description" of "pastoral liturgical theology." Just as "liturgical" is used as an adjective, so is "pastoral," which adds a qualifier to "liturgical." On the one hand, the very etymology of pastoral suggests leadership: the Latin *pastor* means herd, particularly shepherd. So we have two sides: leader and those led. Liturgically speaking, the pastor is Christ (the ordained priest is his visible presence), the herd is the Church, the Body of Christ gathered with the Head.

Before we pursue this line of thought any further, it is necessary to set aside some popular notions of "pastoral" and "pastoral liturgy." In a number of places, Schmemann rightly decries understanding pastoral liturgy as liturgy accommodated to people in its music, imposition of themes on liturgy, adjusting texts and rubrics so they are more understandable, and so forth.[21]

---

19. My doctoral dissertation and much of my subsequent work has attempted to tease out the meaning of liturgical texts using French Philosopher Paul Ricoeur's (1913–2005) textual hermeneutics. See Zimmerman, *Liturgy as Language of Faith*, and Zimmerman, *Liturgy as Living Faith*. For an overview of hermeneutical theory, critical and post-critical methods, and their implications for liturgical theology, see Zimmerman, *Liturgy and Hermeneutics*.

20. Schmemann, *For the Life of the World*, 122. This content—the paschal mystery—is addressed fully in the next section of this essay.

21. Schmemann criticizes a narrow, historical approach to understanding liturgy, whereby liturgists "have nothing to say to the liturgical experiments of every description that are carried out with the aim of bringing the services 'closer' to the 'needs,' 'ideas' and even 'demands' of the contemporary world, or, simply put, dissolving them into contemporary life" (Schmemann, *Eucharist*, 197–98).

Pastoral does not imply accommodation but instead it points to the assembly's own experience of liturgy as contributing to its meaning. Neither is a deeper understanding of pastoral liturgy directed to solving pastoral problems with the liturgy, that is, with pleasing people, with educating people about the liturgy, or with figuring out how to "entertain" people at liturgy so they happily keep coming. Although it is not wise to ignore all of these issues, when we wish to describe pastoral liturgical theology, we are moving beyond these practical matters to deeper considerations.

Schmemann's agenda is to *do* theology, beginning with the liturgy. By adding "pastoral" to the phrase "liturgical theology," we propose that the meaning of liturgy cannot be separated from the people who celebrate. Liturgy does not unfold in an unchangeable vacuum, but rather in the assembly gathered with the Risen One, where encounter with Christ is key. The closest Schmemann comes to a "definition" of pastoral liturgical theology is found in his discussions of "piety" or the "religious sense": "This religious sense can be defined as liturgical piety. This is the psychological acceptance of the cult, its experience within the religious mind, its refraction within the consciousness of the believer."[22] There is, of course, a danger of distortion whereby popular piety misinterprets symbols or rites. The point is, though, that people's participation in and appropriation of liturgy determines at least some of its meaning.

It is helpful to distinguish between the "surface structure" and "deep structure" of a text. Surface structure is what is at hand and discernable: words, postures, music, architecture, accoutrements, clothing, art, structural flow, movement, etc. The deep structure is the enduring meaning of a text, which can only be discerned through the surface structure. A thick description of pastoral liturgical theology would include as much of the at-hand surface structure as possible; the more comprehensive the examination of the surface structure is, the closer we come to discerning the deep structure. Although the inanimate elements of the liturgical surface structure are important, the *use* of them by the gathered assembly is most helpful for discerning the deep structure of liturgy. Pastoral liturgical theology is most complete when a mystagogical approach is the root methodology. Mystagogy unites text, experience, and memory.

Pastoral liturgical theology is an explanation/understanding (a theology) of liturgy that begins with the liturgical text (understood in its hermeneutical sense as making at-hand an enduring trace of human action) which is filtered through the celebrating assembly's experience. This experience is not simply a "good feeling" or even an "a-ha" moment. This pastoral

22. Schmemann, *Introduction*, 77.

experience is a transformative liturgical encounter with the Risen Christ, enabled by the Holy Spirit, and which draws us into the mystery of the eternal praise of the Father by the heavenly court. The adjective "pastoral" added to "liturgical theology" ensures that liturgy is not a passive event on the part of the assembly members but a participatory act. At liturgy, the assembled Body of Christ is invited to make a conscious surrender to the movement of the ritual action, opened to receiving God's transforming power, and propelled beyond the ritual action to live what has been celebrated. In other words, liturgy and life cannot be two different domains.

Liturgy and Life

As mentioned in the opening paragraph of this essay, one of Schmemann's most prevalent themes is that of living what we celebrate: liturgy and life cannot be separated. The Christian "worldview" is grounded in liturgy and thus flows from it. This worldview is expressed in liturgical spirituality, a way of living. The "approach to the world and to man's life in it . . . stems from the liturgical experience."[23]

Anyone who celebrates liturgy regularly knows that what takes place at liturgy has something to do with everyday living. But there is a problem with this statement which may be laid out in the following manner:

> One way to focus a liturgical quest for meaning is to ask a seminal question such as: What is the relationship between celebrating liturgy on Sunday and living as a Christian the rest of the week? . . . Liturgy and life are indeed related—even inextricably so. They also share a prevailing caveat: *demonstrating* the relationship between liturgy and life does not address *why* it is so. Often we have argued historically: it *has always been so*. We have argued logically: it *must* be so. But can we argue ontologically: it *is* so?[24]

Schmemann does not address the ontological question but demonstrates effectively the historical, liturgical, and pastoral reasons for asserting this pairing. To help us understand more adequately what is really at stake in pastoral liturgical theology, we must delve more deeply into an ontological grasp of the relationship between liturgy and life.

23. Schmemann, *For the Life of the Word*, 7.
24. Zimmerman, *Liturgy as Living Faith*, vii.

To quote Schmemann again: "If the basis of all Christian worship is the Incarnation, its true content is always the cross and Resurrection."[25] It is this "content" that interests us here. The words "cross" and "Resurrection" are a good synoptic way of speaking of the saving mystery of Christ. Paul expounds on this in his baptismal theology:

> Do you not know that all of us who have been baptized into Christ Jesus were baptized into his death? Therefore, we have been buried with him by baptism into death, so that, just as Christ was raised from the dead by the glory of the Father, so we too might walk in newness of life. For if we have been united with him in a death like his, we will certainly be united with him in a resurrection like his. (Rom 6:3–5 NRSV)

The saving mystery of Christ, however, is richer and more all-encompassing than what happened historically on that first Good Friday and Easter. From his kenotic "yes" to the Incarnation and becoming like us in all things except sin (Heb 4:15), to his teaching and preaching, to his obedience to the Father in all things, to his dying and rising, to his ascension and sending of the Spirit, to his commissioning his disciples to continue his saving ministry, to his promised Second Coming—all this is counted as his saving mission. All this is the paschal mystery. Into all this are we baptized.

The term "paschal mystery" is a relatively new theological term, but its meaning was celebrated and lived from the very earliest time of the Church.

> We find neither in Paul nor in the mystagogues any systematic explanation of the Paschal Mystery as such. In fact, the term itself is not used. We do find a comprehensive disclosure of the meaning of God's Mystery for us. We find an appreciation for the totality of that mystery, linking liturgical celebration with Christian living, both being an expression of our surrender and entry into Christ's mystery. By that surrender we are incorporated into Christ's body, the Church, and are continually transformed into being ever more perfect images of God's grace.[26]

Shifting to our present day, the explicit connection between paschal mystery and liturgy is clearly put forth in *Sacrosanctum Concilium*, the Constitution on the Sacred Liturgy promulgated by the Second Vatican Council:

> The wonderful works of God among the people of the Old Testament were but a prelude to the work of Christ our Lord in redeeming mankind and giving perfect glory to God. He achieved

25. Schmemann, *For the Life of the World*, 122.

26. Zimmerman, "Liturgy Notes," 107.

his task principally by the paschal mystery of his blessed passion, resurrection from the dead, and glorious ascension, whereby "dying he destroyed our death, and rising, restored our life."[27]

While dying and rising are a good synoptic way of referring to the paschal mystery, other pairings help us emphasize different aspects of this saving mystery and open up its depth, for example, soteriology/eschatology or *kenosis/theosis*. All of these pairings are symbols or metaphors for grasping Christ's saving mystery, which is enacted in the liturgy—the same mystery that is enacted in Gospel living.[28] No one way of talking about the paschal mystery can capture all of its richness. There is always a residue of meaning in our language that remains, enticing us to delve deeper, reflect longer, and live more intentionally. Here is the salient ontological connection: *the content of liturgy is the content of Christian living.* To put it another way, what we celebrate in liturgy, namely, the paschal mystery, is what we live:

> [The] celebration of liturgy does more than change us or "affect" our lives (although it does do that!). The liturgical event itself is a mediating configuring of the whole of Christ's mystery (on its one side) and our refiguring of it in our daily living (on its other side). This rescues liturgy from a ritual that simply unfolds in chronological time (although it does do that) and opens it up to a point in time that mediates Christ's mystery and our lived Christian experience.[29]

To put this yet another way, *the deep structure of liturgy is identical to the deep structure of Christian living.*[30] These remarks move us from merely *demonstrating* the relationship of liturgy and life to engaging a post-critical, hermeneutical, ontological approach that enables us to *assert* (ontologically) this relationship.

This being said, we raise an important question: is liturgy complete if it is not lived? Or, to put it conversely, if liturgy is not lived, are we truly celebrating it? What these questions are getting at is that we contribute more to

27. *Sacrosanctum Concilium*, 3. For a seminal article on the paschal mystery in the documents of Vatican II, see Kemper, "Liturgy Notes," 46–51.

28. For further remarks on paschal mystery and soteriology and eschatology, see Zimmerman, *Liturgy as Living Faith*, 68–71.

29. Zimmerman, "Paschal Mystery," 311.

30. Deep structure is what something is which is not immediately at hand; surface (not to be confused with shallow or unimportant) structure is what is at hand, what is discernible through the senses. In a thick description of pastoral liturgical theology, what is put forth is surface structure (its pastoral aspects). Reflection and explanation (the work of theology) help us grasp the deep structure. See Zimmerman, *Liturgy as Living Faith*, viii and 137.

liturgy than simply being present. Liturgy celebrates who we are in Christ, why we are in Christ, and what we are in Christ. God's praises are eternally sung when we so identify ourselves with Christ that his mystery is our mystery and his life is our life. Nothing less than this is at stake in the celebration of liturgy and the living of the Gospel.

One of the more important liturgical advancements of Vatican II's liturgical renewal is to emphasize the place of Scripture in liturgy: "Sacred scripture is of the greatest importance in the celebration of the liturgy. . . . Hence, in order to achieve the restoration, progress, and adaptation of the sacred liturgy, it is essential to promote that warm and lively appreciation of sacred scripture to which the venerable tradition of Eastern and Western rites gives testimony."[31] The revised Roman Lectionary now includes a three-year cycle of readings with Old Testament selections most often being the first reading on Sundays and solemnities. By stressing the importance of the word and opening up more Scripture during liturgy, the Council Fathers highlight that the proclamation of the word is not merely a prelude to the Liturgy of the Sacrament. *Sacrosanctum Concilium*, speaking of the Eucharistic rite, goes on to say that the "two parts which in a sense go to make up the Mass, viz., the liturgy of the word and the eucharistic liturgy, are so closely connected with each other that they form but one single act of worship."[32] Clearly, the Council Fathers intended to emphasize the close relationship of these two parts of sacramental celebrations. However, they gave no more detail as to why these parts are "closely connected" except to say that from Scripture do "actions and signs derive their meaning."[33]

Schmemann makes the point that:

> The divine liturgy is a single, though also "multifaceted," sacred rite, a single sacrament in which all its "parts," their entire sequence and structure, their coordination with each other, the necessity of each for all and all for each, manifests to us the inexhaustible, eternal, universal, and truly divine meaning of what has been said and what is being accomplished.[34]

What is critical in this passage is his mention of "sequence and structure." We have reflected on the paschal mystery as the *content* of liturgy, and we have considered paschal mystery from the purview of metaphors such as dying/rising and *kenosis/theosis*. Ricoeur would speak of a dialectic: two

31. *Sacrosanctum Concilium*, 24. See also 51.

32. *Sacrosanctum Concilium*, 56. All of the revised rites of the Roman Catholic sacraments include a Liturgy of the Word.

33. *Sacrosanctum Concilium*, 24.

34. Schmemann, *Eucharist*, 160–61.

poles of opposites that stand in creative tension with each other, a tension that opens up a world of possibilities, of newness. The two poles are never resolved in a synthesis, never disappear.

A structural analysis of the Eucharistic rite (indeed, of all sacramental rites) would lead us to see the Liturgy of the Word and the Liturgy of the Eucharist as two dialectical poles that enact the paschal mystery. Hence:

> as the ritual proceeds from the Liturgy of the Word to the Liturgy of the Eucharist, the rhythm of that dynamic moves from a soteriological toward an eschatological moment. The "stuff" of our everyday lives . . . is challenged by the prophetic confrontation with our Ideal self, the Lord Jesus Christ. We are confronted with the "not yet" of our existence: We are still weak humanity always in need of embracing the grace of salvation. This soteriological moment flows into an eschatological moment that discloses the full riches of what it means to be Body of Christ. . . . The dis-ease of our own unfinished selves finds rest in the messianic fullness of the Banquet of the Lord."[35]

What is suggested here is that Word and Sacrament are in the same dialectical tension with each other as is evident in our hermeneutical explanation of the paschal mystery. We encounter the word in a soteriological/already/ kenotic moment during which we are challenged to do more than *hear* the word: "Through liturgy we enter into communion with the Word of God, learn to know His will, remember the death and resurrection of Christ, and receive the gifts of the Holy Spirit, indispensable for our Christian life and action in this world."[36] The Liturgy of the Word is a prophetic moment during which we are called to live more perfectly our baptismal identity as the Body of Christ (images of Christ) and our commitment to a covenantal relationship with God. It calls forth from us a surrender of ourselves.

In dialectical tension with this prophetic word is the Liturgy of the Eucharist. This is an eschatological/not yet/theotic moment during which we stand at the Messianic Table and share in the most glorious of Divine Gifts: the very Body and Blood of the Risen Christ. For Schmemann, the "whole newness, the uniqueness of the Christian *leitourgia*, was in its eschatological nature as the presence here and now of the future *parousia*, as the epiphany of that which is to come, as communion with the 'world to

---

35. Zimmerman, *Liturgy as Living Faith*, 111.

36. Schmemann, *Liturgy and Life*, 13. There is a fortuitous, equivalent use of "Word" in this passage. The word can be Scripture, but it is also *the* Word, the second Person of the Most Holy Trinity. Particularly in the proclamation of the gospel is Christ actually present, challenging us to a greater conformity to him and his saving mystery.

come."[37] The Liturgy of the Eucharist (indeed, the whole liturgical celebration) is the "symbol of the kingdom par excellence" because it is there that we meet and commune with the Risen Lord in the here and now, "at his table in his kingdom."[38]

In its very structure, the liturgy embodies the dialectical rhythm of the paschal mystery. This is the same mystery into which we are baptized; for which we are nourished at the Table of the Lord; and to which we are called to live each day anew with deeper faith, surer hope, and kinder charity. At Eucharist, we celebrate the paschal mystery. In our daily living, we witness to it as responding to our baptismal call, our ministry. Schmemann asks a very pertinent question: "If Christians neglect their *ministry*, to which all, from the first to last, are appointed, then who will ring out the good news of the kingdom of God and introduce people to the new life?"[39]

Adding "pastoral" to "liturgical theology" opens up the necessity for grasping that liturgy is only of the people when it transforms them; liturgy is most fruitful when it propels us beyond the cultic occasion to live the saving mystery being celebrated; liturgy is more fully grasped when its "sequence and structure" become a rhythm played out in all we do. The work of pastoral liturgical theology is to recover the Church as the Body of Christ (image of Christ), the actualization of soteriological challenge and eschatological fulfillment, of the Risen Christ's *kenosis* and *theosis* embraced by each of us in all we do.

Issues and Challenges

All too often, people understand "Church" to be "church"—building, prayer activity, fountain of moral exhortation—largely something external to ourselves. Our baptismal theology tells us otherwise. Church is the Body of Christ gathered with its Head, the Risen Christ. Church is the assembly of the baptized celebrating Christ's saving mystery and being sent forth to live that mystery. Church is our participation in and actualization of Christ's saving mystery. Church is the "sacrament of the Kingdom—not because she possesses divinely instituted acts called 'sacraments,' but because first of all she is the possibility given to man to see in and through this world the 'world to come,' to see and to 'live' it in Christ."[40] An erosion of our self-understanding as Church robs liturgy of its content and purpose: "Having

37. Schmemann, *Eucharist*, 43.

38. Schmemann, *Eucharist*, 43.

39. Schmemann, *Eucharist*, 55.

40. Schmemann, *For the Life of the World*, 113.

ceased to be the expression of the Church, worship has also ceased to be the expression of the Church in relation to the world."[41] Recovering a self-understanding of ourselves first and foremost as Church is the condition for celebrating liturgy most fruitfully and living it most effectively.

A second issue and challenge: overcoming dualism. The Church has had a long history of dualism, very much grounded in Greek philosophical anthropology. Schmemann is concerned with dispelling the dualism between this world and the next, between matter and form, between natural and supernatural, between material and spiritual, between our time and God's time, and between our striving for salvation now and its eschatological realization. The advances of modern philosophy, the turn to linguistics, and post-critical hermeneutical methods give us the tools for moving beyond dualism. The consequence of the Incarnation is that by taking on human flesh, by marrying divinity with humanity, Jesus Christ showed us the way to live in this world while already enjoying the fruits of salvation and the world to come. The contrasts we experience in our daily living are opportunities to embrace a rhythm of life that leaves us with an experience of wholeness and completion rather than fragmentation and limitation.

A third issue and challenge: Liturgy and, particularly, the Eucharist, has for too long in the Church been directed to individual sanctification rather than to unity of faith and growth and members of the Body of Christ.[42] Corresponding with this has been an undue emphasis on sinfulness and little appreciation for God's gift of grace and salvation. The Church still has a long way to go to grasp that Jesus Christ has opened the door to salvation. Our life is less a struggle to "be saved" than living in the now the new Life Jesus has gained for us. And this Life is not something only in the future; it is God's gift to us now as we strive to be faithful to liturgical living. Members of the Church all too often do not appreciate themselves as being holy. The Scriptural injunction of the holiness code found in chapters 19 to 26 in the Book of Leviticus—"For I am the LORD your God . . . be holy, for I am holy" (Lev 11:44–45)—reminds us that not only are we called to be holy, but with our identity with Christ, we actually share in divine holiness. Liturgy invites us to the holiness that discloses God's Life given to us.

One final issue and challenge: We often limit our experience and expression of faith in terms of individual feelings and spiritual needs.[43] We sense this solipsistic approach to faith in statements such as, "I don't get anything out of liturgy," or when we judge the value and fruitfulness of

41. Schmemann, *Introduction*, 25.

42. See Schmemann, *Eucharist*, 141–42.

43. See Schmemann, 43–44. See also, Schmemann, *Introduction*, 77.

liturgy by whether we like and are moved by, for example, the music or homily. While good feelings at liturgy are not to be dismissed, they are not an adequate criterion for judging liturgy or faith. Both are actions, are verbs. Faith is less an adherence to doctrine than it is conformity of our will to God's will, our lively trust in a God who is merciful and kind. Hebrews offers us this description: "Now faith is the assurance of things hoped for, the conviction of things not seen" (Heb 11:1). The "things" of which this passage speaks are the eschatological fulfillment toward which we journey and are already sharing. Liturgy invites from us faith in that it challenges us to surrender ourselves to the "sequence and structure," to the rhythm and movement of the liturgy that carries us into the very Life of God. It is not a matter of *having* faith but of *celebrating* faith. Faith enables our participation in the kingdom of God, enables our cooperating with Jesus Christ in the furthering of the kingdom of God, and enables our commitment to faithful Gospel living. As Schmemann summarizes: "Thus, the kingdom of God is the content of the Christian faith—the goal, the meaning, and content of the Christian life. According to the unanimous witness of all scripture and tradition, it is the knowledge of God, love for him, unity with him, and life in him. The kingdom of God is unity with God, the source of all life, indeed life itself."[44] Faith directs us to God. Faith is the condition for *kenosis* and *theosis*. Faith is living the paschal mystery.

Concluding Remarks

Pastoral liturgy is ultimately about actualizing in the lives of the members of the Body of Christ the content of liturgy: the paschal mystery. Pastoral liturgy summons us to place liturgy at the very center of our lives. During liturgy, we experience the rhythm of our passing over from this life to the next Life, from being saved to already participating in eschatological fulfillment, from being weak and sinful creatures to being forgiven and loved Body of Christ. To conclude with Schmemann's words:

> It is only when we give up freely, totally, unconditionally, the self-sufficiency of our life, when we put all its meaning in Christ, that the "newness of life"—which means a new possession of the world—is given us. The world then truly becomes the sacrament of Christ's presence, the growth of the Kingdom and of life eternal.[45]

To that, we all happily make a resounding AMEN!

44. Schmemann, *Eucharist*, 40.
45. Schmemann, *For the Life of the World*, 74.

Liturgy Bursting Forth into the World

David W. Fagerberg

Fr. Robert Taft once remarked that Schmemann seems to have a long shelf life. That phrase normally means a long period of time: that a product is still fresh decades later. I am going to add an adaptation to it and say his shelf is both long and lengthy. It continues to impact generations of students, even though he died in 1983, and it continues to reach across divides, bringing Orthodox thought to citizens of the West, both Catholic and Protestant. Why this is the case might be revealed in the interplay of these collected essays, so I will only highlight what I think are two factors. First, when Schmemann presented the traditional union of liturgy and theology to the modern world, it was received as revolutionary. This involved more than setting the two subjects side-by-side; it involved more than treating the former as inspiration for the latter or the latter as a way into the former. He connected the two in an organic way when he used the phrase "liturgical theology."[1] Second, it was Schmemann's constant concern to connect liturgy with life.

One can hear both these themes in two revealing descriptions he gives of liturgical theology. On two different occasions, he writes that liturgical theology consists of unifying the otherwise isolated elements of liturgy, theology, and piety. In the first instance, he imagines someone requesting from him a final word:

1. This was understood by Aidan Kavanagh, and because he tried to explain it, the outlook is sometimes referred to as the Schmemann-Kavanagh school. I added my own apologetic voice of explanation when I first encountered it in graduate school, and am honored to be associated with it.

Finally one may ask: but what do you propose, what do you want? To this I will answer without much hope, I confess, of being heard and understood: we need liturgical theology, viewed not as a theology of worship and not as a reduction of theology to liturgy but as a slow and patient bringing together of that which was for too long a time and because of many factors broken and isolated—liturgy, theology, and piety, their reintegration within one fundamental vision. In this sense, liturgical theology is an illegitimate child of a broken family. It exists, or maybe I should say it ought to exist, only because theology ceased to seek in the *lex orandi* its source and food, because liturgy ceased to be conducive to theology.[2]

In the second, he worries about what happens when each is separated from the other. Liturgy without theology and piety becomes an irrelevant ceremony, although it may be intriguingly mysterious; theology without liturgy and piety becomes an intellectual exercise, although it may be helpful for specialized cases; and piety without liturgy and theology loses its living content, although it may be personally comforting.

The goal of liturgical theology, as its very name indicates, is to overcome the fateful divorce between theology, liturgy, and piety—a divorce which, as we have already tried to show elsewhere, has had disastrous consequences for theology as well as for liturgy and piety. It deprived liturgy of its proper understanding by the people who began to see in it beautiful and mysterious ceremonies in which, while attending them, they take no real part. It deprived theology of its living source and made it into an intellectual exercise for intellectuals. It deprived piety of its living content and term of reference.[3]

What I hope to explore here is the third of those problems: how liturgy might be the ground of spiritual piety if only it will burst its confines and find its way out of the temple into our lives.

Schmemann thinks that liturgy should become a living source for every moment of the Christian's life, not just for the duration of the liturgy's sacramental celebration. The heavenly light that shines in the liturgy should illuminate the mundane where we make our decisions, activate our values, decipher our obligations, encounter our neighbor, struggle with evil, commit to the Kingdom, repent of our sins, and exercise the gifts of charity and

---

2. Schmemann, *Liturgy and Tradition*, 46.

3. Schmemann, *Of Water and the Spirit*, 12. The reference he makes to having tried to show this elsewhere is to his book, Schmemann, *Introduction to Liturgical Theology*.

hope and faith given to us at the inauguration of our liturgical life in the renewing waters of baptism. Our liturgical-sacramental life exists *for the life of the world*, to use the title of perhaps his most famous book.[4]

We will go about our business in four steps. First, we must establish exactly what Schmemann means by *leitourgia*, for we will there discover that liturgy is pointed outward, not inward. Second, we must realistically admit the world's response when it is confronted with liturgy. Third, only if we make it past these hurdles can we discover liturgy's power when it floods our life. And fourth, we can find the connection between liturgy and life that overcomes the state of affairs called secularism.

On *leitourgia*

The word "liturgy" is customarily used to mean the ritual enactment of a Church service in ceremonial form; the prescribed set of forms for conducting public religious worship. Schmemann instead frequently uses the Greek word *leitourgia* precisely to establish a little distance from this terminology of ritual ceremony. Utilizing the Greek word might startle us into remembering "that the uniqueness, the radical novelty of the new Christian *leitourgia* was here, in this 'entrance' into the Kingdom which for 'this world' is still 'to come,' but of which the Church is truly the sacrament: the beginning, the anticipation, and the 'parousia.'"[5] This is the result of what Schmemann refers to as cultic antinomy: we use cultic forms to enter into something that transcends the cult itself. The inside (*leitourgia*) is bigger than the outside that contains it (liturgy). The Christian liturgy may appear to be one species in the genus of religious activity, but that is only in appearance. "If Christian worship is '*leitourgia*' it cannot be simply reduced to, or expressed in, terms of 'cult.' The ancient world knew a plethora of cultic religions or 'cults'—in which worship or cultic acts were

4. Schmemann, *For the Life of the World*. The existence of the book is an example of his shelf being both long and lengthy. Rare is the volume that continues to be read half a century later, escaping the flux of changing taste. A recent article by William C. Mills reveals—by archival research—that the book originated as a 1963 address to a Protestant ecumenical event. "The book began as a series of lectures to be delivered to the 19th Quadrennial Ecumenical Student Conference in Athens, Ohio, whose theme in 1963 was 'For the Life of the World,' which treated broadly of the question of mission and the relationship between Church and world, between liturgy and life. The conferences, organized under the auspices of the National Student Christian Federation and the World Student Christian Federation, brought together thousands of Protestant, Orthodox, and Catholic Christians for intense days of study, debate, demonstration, and prayer" (Mills, "Alexander Schmemann's for the Life of the World," 199–228).

5. Schmemann, "Prayer, Liturgy, and Renewal," 11.

the only real content of religion, an 'end in itself.' But the Christian cult is 'leitourgia' and this means that it is functional in its essence, has a goal to achieve which transcends the categories of cult as such."[6]

We can learn something about this essential functionality by thinking first of the leitourgia of Israel. Schmemann observes that the Septuagint used the word because it meant a public service performed on behalf of the community and for its benefit: "It implied the same idea of service, applied now to the chosen people of God, whose specific 'leitourgia' is to fulfill God's design in history, to prepare the 'way of the Lord.'"[7] The Church then used the word of her own activity for the same reason—she is the manifestation and presence of the new eon, of the kingdom of God:

> In a sense, the Church is indeed a liturgical institution, i.e., an institution whose "leitourgia" is to fulfill itself as the Body of Christ and a new creation. Christian cult is, therefore, a radically new cult, unprecedented in both the Old Testament and paganism, and the deficiency of a certain theology, as well as of a certain liturgical piety, is that they not only overlook the radical newness of Christian "leitourgia" but rather define and experience it again in the old cultic categories.[8]

Leitourgia has to do with mission or service, and the Church's leitourgia serves the world by its mission of proclaiming, witnessing, and celebrating the Kingdom. As Israel's leitourgia was prophetic preparation for the coming of the Messiah, the Church's leitourgia is to be the mystical body of that Messiah in sacramental preparation for the arrival of a Kingdom that has already begun to dawn. This cult is sacramental, not man-made, and it enables the supernatural ministry of the Church in the world. The presence of this Mystery is especially symbolized, sacramentalized, instantiated, concretized, enacted, ritualized, transacted, and celebrated (done) in the Divine Liturgy, the Eucharist, but not only there. The leitourgia is bigger than liturgy alone.

> In the early Church, however—and I have stressed it elsewhere—even the term leitourgia was not, as it is today, a mere synonym of cult. It was applied indeed to all those ministries and offices within the Church in which she manifested and fulfilled her nature and vocation; it had primarily ecclesiological and not cultic connotations. And the very fact that subsequently it was identified

---

6. Schmemann, Liturgy and Tradition, 79.

7. Schmemann, Liturgy and Tradition, 79.

8. Schmemann, Liturgy and Tradition, 79.

especially with "Divine Liturgy," the central act of Christian cult, reveals above all the peculiar character, the uniqueness of that cult itself, of its place and function within the Church. From the very beginning, this unique function was precisely to "make the Church what she is"—the witness and the participant of the saving event of Christ, of the new life in the Holy Spirit, of the presence in "this world" of the Kingdom to come.[9]

Trading *leitourgia* for liturgy is a reductionistic move of which Schmemann disapproves.

The eschatological character of the Church was little by little obscured when theology and piety were squeezed out of *leitourgia* (mission) and confined to liturgy (cultic ceremony): "The *leitourgia*—a corporate procession and passage of the Church toward her fulfillment, the sacrament of the Kingdom of God—was thus reduced to cultic dimension and categories among which those of obligation, efficiency, and validity acquired a central, if not exclusive, position."[10] When this happened, liturgy still remained at the heart and center of the Church's life, to be sure, but perhaps not for the best of reasons.[11] People who are enamored of liturgy for its own sake can lose the connection between the three inseparable realities of the Christian faith: the world, the Church, the Kingdom. This is not an argument that the Church could do without liturgy. It is only an argument that the liturgy must be founded upon her *leitourgia*, otherwise liturgical piety will become non-ecclesiological and non-eschatological.

The *leitourgia* should be the corporate passage of the Church toward her fulfillment, and a Christian is someone swept up into this corporate thoroughfare (the *Qahal Yahweh*, the *Ecclesia tou Theou*). The Christian moves through the world with an orientation toward the east, the eschaton, the light of the Kingdom. All of life can become liturgical because all of life is an effort toward and an experience of the Kingdom of God. The uniqueness of Christian *leitourgia* stems "from the faith in the Incarnation, from the great and all-embracing mystery of the 'Logos made flesh.'"[12] The mission of the Logos made flesh is redemption of the world, and that is the mission (*leitourgia*) given to the Church. Her mission is to make this eschatological truth, beauty, and goodness into a personal and political substance. This is the calling of the Church and it is the calling of each individual member of the Church: "One can rightly describe the Church

9. Schmemann, *Church, World, Mission*, 91.

10. Schmemann, "Prayer, Liturgy, and Renewal," 12.

11. Schmemann, *Introduction*, 25.

12. Schmemann, "Worship in a Secular Age," 6–7.

as an eschatological reality, for its essential function is to manifest and to actualize in this world the eschaton, the ultimate reality of salvation and redemption. In and through the Church the Kingdom of God is made already present, is communicated to men."[13]

To be interested in the liturgy, then, has a very different meaning for Schmemann: "One may be deeply attached to the 'ancient and colorful rites' of Byzantium or Russia, see in them precious relics of a cherished past, be a liturgical 'conservative'; and, at the same time, completely fail to see in them, in the totality of the Church's *leitourgia*, an all-embracing vision of life, a power meant to judge, inform and transform the whole of existence, a 'philosophy of life' shaping and challenging all our ideas, attitudes and actions."[14] This hardly leads to the conclusion that we should not be careful about liturgy. It only leads to the conclusion that what goes on inside the temple walls is something with a power (*dunamis*) designed to explode from there into our daily life. The liturgy is the sacramental formation of the Church; the Church is the sacrament of Christ offered to the world for its redemption; and a sacrament is both sign and instrument. The liturgy signifies and effects the Church's vocational identity.

> For it is precisely in and through her liturgy—this being the latter's specific and unique "function"—that the Church is informed of her cosmical and eschatological vocation, receives the power to fulfill it and thus truly becomes "what she is"—the sacrament, in Christ, of the new creation; the sacrament, in Christ, of the Kingdom. . . . And thus, is precisely the "*leitourgia*" of the Church's cult, the function which makes it the source and indeed the very possibility of theology.[15]

The primary reason Schmemann has for reading the liturgy in action is to develop the skill to "rediscover the oldest of all languages of the Church: that of her rites, the rhythm in the ordo of her *leitourgia*."[16]

Leitourgia is different from liturgy in the same way that the Church is different from the Jesus Club, and for the same reason: it comes from God and not from ourselves. *Leitourgia* is the mission given to the corporate Church at Pentecost and to the individual Christian at baptism. "The Church, the sacrament of Christ, is not a 'religious' society of converts, an organization to satisfy the 'religious' needs of man."[17] Failing this, the ac-

13. Schmemann, *Church, World, Mission*, 211–12.
14. Schmemann, *Church, World, Mission*, 88.
15. Schmemann, *Church, World, Mission*, 92.
16. Schmemann, *Church, World, Mission*, 98.
17. Schmemann, *Church, World, Mission*, 216.

tivity of the Jesus Club turns in upon itself and liturgy becomes religious narcissism. Alas, this is the state of affairs for many:

> The overwhelming majority of Orthodox people have no interest in the meaning of worship. . . . The believer loves the ceremonies, symbols, the whole atmosphere of the church building, this familiar and precious nourishment for his soul, but this love does not long for understanding, because the purpose of cult is thought of precisely as the bestowal of a spiritual experience, spiritual food.[18]

The Church has become a "cultic society," existing for the sake of the cult. When that happens, its membership cannot understand that worship places the Church before the face of the world and manifests her purpose there. Schmemann would like to correct this and so explain *leitourgia's* turn to the world. But what is the world's response?

The World's Response

Genesis says that the earth was without form and void when the Spirit of God moved upon the face of the waters. We could adapt this and say the world is without form, void, and will be formed by either Christ or the antichrist. In itself, the world is only the raw material of potentiality—that "in which and by which" we live, in Schmemann's words.[19] In this neutral sense, the world is good, but incomplete. It is cosmos (instead of chaos) because it comes from the hand of a creatively ordering God, but it still has the potential to become either sacramental or idolatrous, depending on how we treat it. Before the liturgy can flow into this world, as we tried to describe in the last section, the world will have to let down its defenses. That is why the Church is still militant in this age.

Schmemann is very realistic about this—as realistic as Scripture. The same gospel that says God so loved the world that he gave his only Son for it (John 3:16) says that Jesus' disciples do not belong to the world (John 17:16), that the world hates them (John 15:19) and, in turn, they must hate their life in this world (John 12:23). Jesus asked his Father to keep them from the evil one (John 17:15) while they wait for the judgment of this world, at which time the spirit that rules this world will be driven out (John 12:30). There is a fundamental antinomy at work here.

18. Schmemann, *Introduction*, 24–25.
19. Schmemann, *Church, World, Mission*, 216.

> It is strange, indeed, that in our present preoccupation with the
> world we seem to ignore the fundamental antinomy tradition-
> ally implied in the Christian usage of that term. We seem to
> forget that in the New Testament and in the whole Christian
> tradition, the "world" is the object of two apparently contradict-
> ing attitudes: an emphatic acceptance, a *yes*, but also an equally
> emphatic rejection, a *no*. . . . The whole point precisely is that the
> New Testament and the Christian tradition allow no choice and
> no reduction. They accept and reject the world simultaneously.[20]

This understanding is twofold, not dualistic. The former means that a single
reality requires more than one understanding, while the latter supposes a
doubling of creation, as if matter has a foreign place in the world of spirit.
The problem does not lie, as the dualist thinks, in a conflict between spirit
and matter. The problem does lie, as the ascetic knows, in a hostility between
God and man, a struggle between obedience and disobedience, a focusing
on the temporal to the exclusion of the eternal. The world becomes worldly
when it is taken without reference to God. Our original crisis is one of division, not dualism. Our problem does not lie in enjoying two realities of
spirit and matter, it lies in breaking the unity of one reality into twin arenas
of spirit and matter, religion and world, sacred and profane:

> Man was created as a priest: the world was created as the matter
> of a sacrament. But sin came, breaking this unity: this was no
> mere issue of broken rules alone, but rather the loss of a vision,
> the abandonment of a sacrament. Fallen man saw the world as
> one thing, secular and profane, and religion as something en-
> tirely separate, private, remote, and "spiritual." The sacramental
> sense of the world was lost. Man forgot the priesthood which
> was the purpose and meaning of his life. He came to see himself
> as a dying organism in a cold, alien universe.[21]

The problem does not lie in having bodies; the problem lies in not using our
bodies for our priesthood. This shift in identity changed man and woman
from priest into consumers, which is how Schmemann defines the effect of
original sin. "The priest is first and foremost the sacrificer. . . . And so he is
the man who can freely transform that dependence: he is the man who can
say *thank you*. . . . I've always understood the fall (or what is called 'Original

20. Schmemann, "Prayer, Liturgy, and Renewal," 8. The same point is made in
Schmemann, *Eucharist*, with similar language: "The Church's self-fulfillment in the Eucharist 'explains the antinomical character of that attitude, the correlation with the unit
of an emphatic *yes* to the world with an equally emphatic *no*" (Schmemann, *Eucharist*,
82).

21. Schmemann, "World As Sacrament," 223.

Sin') as the loss of man's desire to be a priest; or perhaps you might say the desire he has *not* to be a priest but a consumer."[22]

And when man and woman lost the desire to be a priest, they began to take the world differently. A distorted relationship with God yields a distorted relationship to the world. When life was no longer accepted at the hand of the Father, Adam and Eve tried to find life from the world of nature. Except the world of nature cannot provide it:

> The natural dependence of man upon the world was intended to be transformed constantly into communion with God in whom is all life. Man was to be the priest of a eucharist, offering the world to God. . . . The world is meaningful only when it is the "sacrament" of God's presence. Things treated merely as things in themselves destroy themselves because only in God have they any life. The world of nature, cut off from the source of life, is a dying world. For one who thinks food in itself is the source of life, eating is communion with the dying world, it is communion with death. Food itself is dead, it is life that has died and it must be kept in refrigerators like a corpse.[23]

Broken unity. Gone blind. Forgotten priesthood. Tolerating death. This is our situation.

So when we speak about a problem in the world, we are really speaking about *our* problem with the world. The Church's *leitourgia* (mission) to the world requires dying to self and ministering life to a death-dealing world. Schmemann says this world has condemned itself by rejecting and condemning Christ: "no one, therefore, can enter the kingdom without in a real sense dying to the world, i.e., rejecting it in its self-sufficiency."[24]

> In this world, Christ was rejected. . . . He was the heartbeat of the world and the world killed him. But in that murder, the world itself died. It lost its last chance to become the paradise God created it to be. We can go on developing new and better material things. We can build a more humane society which may even keep us from annihilating each other. But when Christ, the true life of the world, was rejected, it was the beginning of the end.[25]

Schmemann does not think of Church and world as two objects side-by-side, like two books on the shelf or two shirts in the closet. The Church

22. Schmemann, *Liturgy and Tradition*, 132.
23. Schmemann, *For the Life of the World*, 17.
24. Schmemann, "Ecclesiological Notes," 36.
25. Schmemann, *For the Life of the World*, 23.

does not run parallel to the world, leaving us to wonder which contestant will fall exhausted before reaching the eschatological finish line. No, rather, the world is where the Church lives, her very own environment. It is the matter on which eschatological form should be working, which is why the Church is trying to renew the world. So their relationship is complex, not simple; or in Schmemann's words, their relationship is antinomous. Here is a lengthy passage from Schmemann's *Journals* describing that antinomy:

> Here is, for me, *the whole meaning of liturgical theology.* The Liturgy: the joining, revelation, actualization of the historicity of Christianity (remembrance) and of its transcendence over that historicity.
>
> Hence, the link of the Church with the world, the Church *for the world,* but as its beginning and its end, as the affirmation that the world is *for the Church,* since the Church is the presence of the kingdom of God.
>
> Here is the eternal antinomy of Christianity and the essence of all contemporary discussions about Christianity. The task of theology is to be faithful to the antinomy, which disappears in the experience of the Church as *pascha:* a *continuous* (not only historical) passage of the world to the Kingdom. All the time one must leave the world and all the time one must remain it.[26]

The essence of Christianity is discovering the antinomy that the kingdom of God is both the goal of history and is already now among us. The latter is what we celebrate in *leitourgia,* the former keeps us from being complacent with cult. Christianity is historical, yet Christianity also has transcendence over that historicity. The relationship between Church and world is antinomous because it flows both directions: the Church is for the world, and the world is for the Church. All the time one must leave the world, and all the time one must remain in it.

The World As Liturgy

Only when we are on the other side of this conversion, denying ourselves in order to yield to God's saving economy, do we find *leitourgia* flooding the world. The world that killed itself by putting Christ to death must be raised by faith in that same Christ. Now liturgy breaks its cultic boundaries to become *leitourgia.* Now the mission which Christ worked on behalf of the family of Adam and Eve is placed in our hands, on our lips, in our lives, and

26. Schmemann, *Journals,* 234.

his liturgical activity before the Father sacramentally manifests itself in us in our world. Liturgy has burst its bounds.

What is the question that liturgy answers? It is: what is the Kingdom of God, and how does one experience it now? Every time the Church gathers on the eighth day to proclaim Christ's death and confess his resurrection, she is immersed in the new eon of the Spirit, and although, for the world, the Kingdom is still to come, by the Church, this Kingdom can already be experienced since she is commissioned to be sacrament of it in the world. The Church can therefore accurately evaluate the world, although the world cannot adequately appreciate the Church:

> The liturgy, especially the Eucharist, was precisely the *passage* of the Church from this world into heaven, the act by which and in which she fulfilled herself becoming "that which she is": entrance, ascension, communion. But, and this is the most important point, it was precisely this eschatological, i.e., Kingdom-centered and Kingdom-oriented character of the liturgy that made it—in the experience and the understanding of the early Church—the source of the Church's evaluation of the world, the root and the motivation of her mission to the world. It is because Christians—in the *passage* and *ascension* to heaven—knew the Kingdom and partook of its "joy and peace in the Holy Spirit" that they could truly be its *witness* in and to the world.[27]

A liturgicalized person (if I may coin a term) is a person who goes through this eschatological passage and becomes its witness and agent, i.e., a sacrament of the Kingdom. Now everything is liturgy. Now we can conduct our liturgy not only in the sacred but also in the profane. The Eucharist is not escape from the world; rather, "it is the arrival at a vantage point from which we can see more deeply into the reality of the world."[28] And from that vantage point, we see existence in the light of Mount Tabor. By our passage out of this alienation, the world suffering that alienation is saved. The whole world. The Church is "new life and redeems therefore the whole life, the total being of man. And this whole life of man is precisely the world in which and by which he lives. Through man, the Church saves and redeems the world. One can say that 'this world' is saved and redeemed every time a man responds to the divine gift, accepts it and lives by it. . . . The Kingdom is yet *to come*, and the Church is not *of* this world. And yet, this kingdom to come is already present, and the Church is fulfilled *in* this world."[29]

27. Schmemann, "Prayer, Liturgy, and Renewal," 11.

28. Schmemann, *For the Life of the World*, 26–27.

29. Schmemann, *Church, World, Mission*, 216.

Schmemann expresses this in various ways, but as time is running short, I will confine myself to combining two of his themes wherein this idea can be found: our cosmic priesthood and a Eucharistic world.

Our cosmic priesthood has been restored to us. As we saw above, man and woman were meant to be the priest of a cosmic Eucharist that offers the world to God, but they forfeited their liturgical career: "The first consumer was Adam himself. He chose not to be priest but to approach the world as consumer: to 'eat' of it, to use and to dominate it for himself, to benefit from it but not to offer, not to sacrifice, not to have it for God and in God."[30] The waters of baptism, when accompanied by conversion and faith, flip that upside down. Or rather, right side up. God makes us natural again:

> To be *priest* is, from a profound point of view, the most natural thing in the world. Man was created priest of the world, the one who offers the world to God in a sacrifice of love and praise and who, through this eternal eucharist, bestows the divine love upon the world. Priesthood, in this sense, is the very essence of manhood, man's creative relation to the "womanhood" of the created world. And Christ is the one true Priest because he is the one true and perfect man. He is the new Adam, the restoration of that which Adam failed to be. Adam failed to be the priest of the world, and because of this failure the world ceased to be the sacrament of the divine love and presence, and became "nature."[31]

We are human, so we hold the world in our hands in a different way than any other creature. The angels don't have bodies, the animals don't have spirit. The angels cannot engage matter, the animals do not know how to lift matter on high. (That is why losing our priesthood is described as losing our humanity and lapsing into animality.) But if restored to the state intended for Adam and Eve, we might again stand aright and offer the holy oblation in peace. The only way for that to come about is for Christ to become second Adam, and to replace the stolen fruit grasped by the hands of Adam and Eve. Standing once again in innocent nakedness in the garden of Eden, we will now hold in our hands not the fruit of the tree of knowledge but the fruit of the wood of the cross: Christ's own body and blood. In Eucharistic anamnesis, we recover our forgotten memory that real life is Eucharist.

> We know that we have lost this eucharistic life, and finally we know that in Christ, the new Adam, the perfect man, this eucharistic life was restored to man. For He Himself was the perfect Eucharist.... "To take in our hands the whole world as if it were

30. Schmemann, *Of Water and the Spirit*, 96.

31. Schmemann, *For the Life of the World*, 92–93.

an apple!" said a Russian poet. It is our Eucharist. It is the movement that Adam failed to perform, and that in Christ has become the very life of man: a movement of adoration and praise in which all joy and suffering, all beauty and all frustration, all hunger and all satisfaction are referred to their ultimate end and become finally *meaningful*. Yes, to be sure, it is a *sacrifice*: but sacrifice is the most natural act of man, the very essence of his life. Man is a sacrificial being, because he finds his life in love, and love is sacrificial.[32]

Sin is living a non-eucharistic life in a non-eucharistic world.[33] Salvation is the opposite. Eucharist is the life of paradise and *leitourgia* is the passage and ascension into it because in the Divine Liturgy, we offer the totality of our life to God.

Liturgical vision lets us see the world as God sees it, and that is how Schmemann defines the priestly eye. "All rational, spiritual and other qualities of man, distinguishing him from other creatures, have their focus and ultimate fulfillment in this capacity to bless God, to know, so to speak, the meaning of the thirst and hunger that constitutes his life. '*Homo sapiens*', '*homo faber*'. . . . Yes, but, first of all, '*homo adorans*'. The first, the basic definition of man is that he is *the priest*."[34] We have come home at last. We know how to do the world at last. "At last"—eschaton. It has already begun. The Fall of Adam and Eve was their relinquishment of a liturgical career, but now a second Adam has come to do what the first Adam failed to do and to teach the second Eve (the Church) how to do it. Liturgical spirituality is living in the world as cosmic priest.

The End of Secularism

There are two outcomes of *leitourgia* bursting the walls of its cultic dam and flooding the fields of our life. First, we receive a new understanding of the world, a new cosmology. I suppose it would be as accurate to say that we receive a new cosmos since, for us, the world is now made anew. It is no longer death-dealing but life-giving. Second, we receive a new understanding of liturgy, a new liturgiology. It would not be accurate to say we receive a new liturgy since there is only one *leitourgia*, which flows from the throne of God and of the Lamb down the middle of the great street of the heavenly

---

32. Schmemann, *For the Life of the World*, 34–35.

33. Schmemann, *For the Life of the World*, 18.

34. Schmemann, *For the Life of the World*, 15.

Jerusalem to us (Rev 22:1–2). But if we were to call it a "new liturgy" it would be to confess that our experience of this liturgy is startlingly new.

> All of a sudden, the liturgy ceases to be a "venerable," "ancient," "colorful," and "beautiful" rite and becomes a terribly serious thing. All of a sudden, my whole life is questioned and everything in it is seen under this terrifying possibility: "To put the Son of God to an open shame." And this possibility is here because the liturgy reveals to me who I am, what I am given, it puts me face to face with the glory of the Kingdom and, therefore, reveals the exile and alienation from God of my whole life.[35]

The liturgy is not new, but it is new to me when I take it as the passageway into the Paschal Mystery instead of a species of religious cult. "The Church itself is a *leitourgia*, a ministry, a calling to act in this world after the fashion of Christ. . . . The liturgy, therefore, must not be approached and understood in 'liturgical' or 'cultic' terms alone."[36] Minus this eschatological function of Christian *leitourgia*, Schmemann says, the Church becomes but one institution among other human institutions.[37]

Failure to unify liturgy with the world is what Schmemann means by the word "secularism." He offers the unusual perspective that a secularist is *not* necessarily an unreligious person. To the contrary, the secularist may be quite religious: attached to his Church, regular in attendance, generous in contributions, a practitioner of prayer and piety. "But all this will not in the least alter the plain fact that his understanding of all these spheres: marriage, family, home, profession, leisure, and, ultimately, his religious 'obligations' themselves, will be derived not from the creed he confesses in church, not from the Incarnation, Death, Resurrection, and Glorification of Christ, the Son of God become Son of Man, but from philosophies of life."[38] Secularism is a lie—not about the existence of God (the secularist admits the existence of God) but about our true human state. If secularism is a heresy, it is an anthropological heresy and not a theological one: "Secularism, I submit, is above all in negation of worship. I stress:—not of God's existence, not of some kind of transcendence and therefore some kind of religion. If secularism in theological terms is a heresy, it is primarily a heresy about man. It is the negation of man as a worshiping being, as

---

35. Schmemann, "Problems of Orthodoxy in America II," 177.

36. Schmemann, *For the Life of the World*, 23.

37. Schmemann, "Prayer, Liturgy, and Renewal," 12.

38. Schmemann, "Problems of Orthodoxy in America III," 173.

homo adorans: the one for whom worship is the essential act which both 'posits' his humanity and fulfills it."[39]

Failure to unify liturgy and cosmos is secularism in action. "What is denied is simply the *continuity* between 'religion' and 'life,' the very function of worship as power of transformation, judgment, and change."[40] This is what is so tricky. Secularism's error does not fall on the front side of the Church-world equation, it falls on the back side. It is doing the world wrongly by reason of confining religion to a place that is out of this world.[41] It first posits and then disconnects two orders of existence, and "makes 'food,' 'love,' 'time,' 'matter,' [and] 'money' entities-in-themselves, incapable of transformation, closed to grace. . . . Therefore, secularism is very happy with the 'sacred symbolism' so often offered as Christian teaching because it leaves intact and unquestioned the self-sufficiency of the 'real life.'"[42] I think Schmemann is pointing out something that we do not like to admit to ourselves, namely, that we like protection from God. If we establish the ground rules, then we know exactly how much of our lives he intends to govern, and we can give that part of ourselves to him on Sunday morning and keep the rest of our lives for ourselves. This is trying to tame the Lion of Judah with our liturgical catnip.[43]

If secularism lets cult and world drift apart, then we can take up sides. One person will propose that we can do without the world if we get the cult right; a second person will propose that we can do without cult if we get the world right; the third person will propose that real, meaningful work is done in the world; while a fourth person will claim the world lacks significance and the only really important action is what we do in worship. I think Schmemann denies all of these choices as the false alternatives presented by the spiritualist and the activist discussed in *For the Life of the World*. They are flip sides of the same mistake: "The only purpose of this book has been to show, or rather to signify that the choice between these two reductions of Christianity—to religion and to secularism—is not the only choice, that, in fact, it is a false dilemma."[44]

On the one hand, the world should not close in on itself to the exclusion of God, unwilling to receive the transfigurative power of *leitourgia*.

39. Schmemann, *For the Life of the World*, 118.

40. Schmemann, *For the Life of the World*, 133.

41. I presume this is why Aidan Kavanagh repeated frequently in class that "liturgy is doing the world, the way the world was meant to be done."

42. Schmemann, "Problems Orthodoxy in America II," 177.

43. My thought in the last chapter of Fagerberg, *Theologia Prima*.

44. Schmemann, *For the Life of the World*, 112.

This conjures an absent God because it "leaves the world profane, i.e., precisely *secular*, in the deepest sense of this term: as totally incapable of any real communication with the Divine, of any real transformation and transfiguration."[45] On the other hand, liturgy should not spin in the air, the teeth of its cogs failing to engage anything else. Liturgy should exceed its bounds and engage every aspect of our life. This is liturgy rendering our piety theological as we live life under the reign of God (which is what it means for the Kingdom to come). When this occurs, liturgy will function as a challenge to my whole life, something that Schmemann greatly desires. Liturgical theology has failed if liturgy is "a center without periphery, a heart with no control of blood circulation, a fire with nothing to purify and to consume, because that life which had to be embraced by it, has been satisfied with itself and has chosen other lights to guide and to shape it."[46] He urges us to reconnect liturgy and life, reconnect liturgy with the world in which it has been planted, reconnect the liturgical heart with the circulatory system, and kindle a purifying fire in our secular life.

Our worldview would exclude secularism if only our whole life would be made God-like and become God-centered. Then there would be no sector of human activity unavailable to our deification. The wall that stands between liturgy and life would be done away with, and when that happens, we would bring the world with us to liturgy, and the liturgy with us to the world. The world would be taken up in oblation, and liturgy descend as power. I will let Schmemann summarize his conclusion:

> What I mean is the *power* of the liturgy, first, to impress on the soul of man the Orthodox vision of life and, second, to help him live in accordance with that vision. Or, to put it in simple terms, the influence of the liturgy on our ideas, decisions, behavior, evaluations—on the totality of our life. This was, for centuries and centuries, the real function of the liturgy in the Orthodox Church: to immerse the man in the spiritual reality, beauty, and depth of the Kingdom of God and to *change* his mind and his heart. By revealing and manifesting the "bridal chamber adorned," the liturgy was revealing to man his exile and alienation from God and thus was bringing them to repentance, to the desire to return to God and do his commandments. . . . [The Orthodox man of the past] knew he was a sinner, and in the best part of himself, he had a nostalgia for the "peace and joy" of the Kingdom; he referred his life to it and judged it by Christian standards. He knew, and he knew it by and through the power

45. Schmemann, "Secularism," 133.
46. Schmemann, "Problems of Orthodoxy in America II," 175.

of worship, that God wants him to be a saint and that he is not a saint. Today, however, this power of worship has all but vanished. Worship is something one must attend an evening joy, it is a self evident "obligation" for the religious man, but it has lost all relevance for the real life.[47]

47. Schmemann, "Problems of Orthodoxy in America II," 165.

The Cosmic Scope of the Eucharist[1]

Porter C. Taylor

THROUGHOUT THE CORPUS OF his writing, Fr. Alexander Schmemann referred to the Eucharist often, with great passion and with a wide range of qualifiers and descriptors. Foremost among them is the title of his posthumously published book, *The Eucharist—Sacrament of the Kingdom*.[2] Indeed, every chapter in this work begins with "Sacrament of . . ." as Schmemann ties together sacramental and liturgical theology through his reflections on the sacrament of sacraments, the sacrament *par excellence*, the sacrament that is both source *and* summit of the Christian faith. Unfortunately, or perhaps inaccurately, *Eucharist* has not garnered the same amount of academic standing or notoriety as his other texts. This is likely based on Schmemann's admission that these writings were essentially done during the nooks and crannies of his life and are not substantially academic.[3] Despite this admission, it is *Eucharist*—and not *For the Life of the World*—that should be taken as Schmemann's definitive

---

1. This title is taken from a paper submitted during my graduate work at Fuller Theological Seminary. The directed study was focused exclusively on the Eucharist and I used Schmemann as my primary interlocutor. The original title was "The Cosmic Scope of the Eucharist: Why a Political View is Not Enough."

2. Schmemann, *Eucharist*.

3. "This book is neither a manual of liturgics nor a scholarly investigation. I wrote it during rare moments of leisure, in the midst of many interruptions. Now, putting together these chapters into one book, I do not pretend that they provide a complete or systematic study of the divine liturgy. Rather, this book represents a series of reflections on the Eucharist" (Schmemann, *Eucharist*, 9).

and most important work, for it represents the true embodiment and enactment of his (sacramental)-liturgical theology.[4]

While the Eucharist may be seen as the pinnacle of Christian worship, as the "source and summit" of Christian faith and life, it is too often misused and mistreated by well-meaning theologians—both vocational and lay—in an attempt to discern and appropriate the political, economic, or social dimensions of the sacrament. Schmemann saw a Eucharistic crisis in the Church and described it as, "Essentially . . . a lack of connection and cohesion between what is accomplished in the eucharist and how it is perceived, understood, and lived."[5] This essay, therefore, will be both an effort to highlight the significance of Schmemann's sacramental-liturgical work and to further it by using *Eucharist* as both our guide and teacher. To achieve this, we will first examine what Schmemann means when he defines the term "liturgical theology" as "the elucidation of the meaning of worship" and his suggested methodology. We will then turn to his understanding of the Eucharist as the sacrament *par excellence*, examining his three-fold understanding of the Eucharist's eschatological, soteriological, and ecclesiological implications. Finally, and most importantly, we will read his sacramental-liturgical theology through this new lens and venture deeper into the cosmic scope of the Eucharist.

Liturgical Theology

Schmemann's lasting and long-reaching influence over the field of liturgical theology during the last half-century cannot be questioned. This is easily demonstrated by the sheer number of references to Schmemann and his work by liturgical scholars, especially over the last twenty years.[6] Schmemann cuts a rather polemical figure within the field, though. Quite

4. I am indebted to Bruce Morrill for his guidance in using the term "sacramental-liturgical theology." For more, see his essay in this book and his plenary address at the Catholic Theological Society of America (Morrill, "Sacramental-Liturgical Theology Since Vatican II"). *For the Life of the World* is an important book, and it represents the departure point for many Protestants into Schmemann and liturgical theology. This volume represents such a reality—with essays from a variety of Christian traditions focusing primarily on *FTLOW* and very little said about *Eucharist*.

5. Schmemann, *Eucharist*, 9.

6. Bradshaw, "Difficulties in Doing Liturgical Theology"; Johnson, "Liturgy and Theology," 202–25; Morrill, *Anamnesis as Dangerous Memory*; Aune, "Liturgy and Theology 1," 46–68; Aune, "Liturgy and Theology 2," 141–69; Fagerberg, *Theologia Prima*; and Lathrop, *Holy Things*. I have only stumbled across one "primer" in the subject to date which failed to mention Schmemann even once. See Vincie, *Celebrating Divine Mystery*.

passionately, most *either* agree with him *or* vehemently disagree; it seems that all contemporary liturgical theologians are working in Schmemann's wake, either furthering or reacting to his teaching. In a post-Vatican II environment, which saw the growth of the Liturgical Renewal Movement ecumenically, Schmemann brought light to a subject that was in desperate need of a definition, identity, and goal.[7] As David Fagerberg reminds us, Schmemann was doing something new. He was not trying to pair liturgy and theology but to marry them in a way that created or gave birth to a third thing. Fagerberg writes:

> Liturgical theology is not yellow liturgy marbles mixed with blue theology marbles to make a jar full of yellow and blue marbles: liturgical theology is green marbles. What is new about Schmemann's definition was more than adding some additional marbles to the jar by outlining a new subject area to consider. Both men [Schmemann and Kavanagh] point to the conclusion that theology is liturgical and liturgy is theological.[8]

It is for this reason, the newness of his work, that both Robert Taft and Fagerberg have suggested that Schmemann has "a long shelf life." The newness of Schmemann's project has not yet grown old and scholars are still toiling in the soil that he tilled in the mid-twentieth century.

However, liturgical theology has not always been a featured course or subject of study in the church or seminaries. Schmemann points this out in the early pages of his *Introduction to Liturgical Theology* by saying liturgics courses offered in seminaries focused more on the "how" or the mechanics—often taught in canon law or pastoral settings—rather than the "what" of worship.[9] This, he suggests, occurs when liturgy and theology are divorced from one another[10]; that is, liturgy is relegated to secondary status when it is no longer seen as a viable *locus theologicus*. He writes: "A theology

7. Paul Bradshaw has pointed out that there is still little consistency when it comes to defining liturgical theology. See Bradshaw, "Difficulties in Doing Liturgical Theology."

8. Fagerberg, "What is the Subject Matter of Liturgical Theology?," 42.

9. "The study of liturgics, understood as liturgical theology, has appeared comparatively recently within the system of theological disciplines. What was called liturgics in the religious schools was usually a more or less detailed practical study of ecclesiastical rites, combined with certain symbolical explanations of ceremonies and ornaments. Liturgical study of this kind, known in the West as the study of 'rubrics,' answers the question HOW: how worship is to be carried out according to the rules; i.e., in accordance with the prescriptions of the rubrics and canons. But it does not answer the question WHAT: what is done in worship" (Schmemann, *Introduction to Liturgical Theology*, 9).

10. Schmemann adds a third member of the union in *Of Water and Spirit* and he suggests the divorce is between liturgy, theology, and piety. David Fagerberg has astutely labeled "piety" as "asceticism" in Fagerberg, *On Liturgical Asceticism*.

alienated from the Church, and a Church alienated from theology: such is the first dimension of today's crisis."[11] The divorce—for that is what it is—of liturgy and theology has effects more far-reaching than we can realize. Every field of theological inquiry and pastoral/ecclesial life is impaired by such a split. For instance, liturgy becomes a sterile, impersonal text to be studied for rules and guidelines while the doctrine of the Trinity has no reference point in the liturgy from which, or at least alongside which, it was birthed. It is the reversal of the divorce between liturgy and theology toward which Schmemann aims with his liturgical theology.

For Schmemann, liturgical theology is simply "the elucidation of the [theological] meaning of worship."[12] It would be easy to stop with this definition, and perhaps even include Schmemann's iteration of Prosper, deciding that Schmemann's is nothing more than a theology of/from worship,[13] but this would be neither fair nor accurate. While Schmemann did favor the use of *lex orandi est lex credendi*,[14] a phrasing which, on its own, requires a one-way interpretation of the relationship between liturgy and theology, his own comments are more nuanced. The answer to the divorce of liturgy, theology, and piety is simple: "Theology must rediscover as its own 'rule of faith' the Church's *lex orandi*, and the liturgy reveal itself again as the *lex credendi*."[15] The rule of faith is determined by the rule of prayer and, as such, the liturgy becomes the ontological condition for faith, doctrine, and theology. Schmemann expands on his definition when he writes, "Theology is above all explanation, 'the search for words appropriate to the nature of God.' . . . Therefore the task of liturgical theology consists in giving a theological basis to the explanation of worship and the whole liturgical tradition of the Church."[16] Liturgical theology is concerned with worship *and* the whole liturgical tradition; it is an all-encompassing endeavor seeking to understand and translate theologically that which is done liturgically.

Schmemann goes further in outlining the liturgical and theological nature of the Church's life when he writes: "The Church's life has always

11. Schmemann, *Church, World, Mission*, 130.

12. Schmemann, *Introduction*, 9.

13. Maxwell Johnson suggests Schmemann's is a "theology of liturgy" based on his interpretation of Prosper as "*lex orandi est lex credenda*" (Johnson, "Liturgy and Theology," 204).

14. Novak, "Revaluing Prosper of Aquintaine in Contemporary Liturgical Theology." Novak's article on Prosper is immensely helpful. While it cannot be used to alter Schmemann's understanding of *orandi*, it is worth noting that Prosper had in mind the *lex supplicandi* of the whole Church and not just the liturgical text.

15. Schmemann, *Church, World, Mission*, 146.

16. Schmemann, *Introduction*, 17.

been rooted in the *lex credendi*, the rule of faith, theology in the deepest sense of the word; and in the *lex orandi*, her rule of worship, the λειτουργία, which always 'makes her what she is': the Body of Christ and the Temple of the Holy Spirit."[17] Liturgical theology is therefore concerned with the theological meaning of worship within the context of the Church gathered. That is, participating in the Divine Liturgy affects something within the individual and the whole Body, thereby making her (the Church) into an already existing reality: the Body of Christ. This is part of the "what" of liturgical theology.

Liturgical theology is not solely concerned with rubrics, rules, and regulations—though these are important—but with what happens during and through worship as seen in text, vestments, gestures, rites, church buildings, and more. Properly understood, liturgical theology seeks to elucidate the meaning of worship through both form and function.[18] Similarly, liturgical theology should not be understood as the 'mining' of liturgy for embedded theological principles. Such an act would be appropriately labeled as "theology from liturgy/worship" and ought to be recognized as a poor substitute for liturgical theology.

Therefore, for Schmemann, liturgy is the primary and most complete source of theology for the Church:

> To affirm that liturgy is the source *par excellence* of theology does not mean, as some seem to think, a reduction of theology to liturgy, its transformation into "liturgical theology." . . . All theology, indeed, ought to be "liturgical," yet not in the sense of having liturgy as its unique "object" of study, but in that of having its ultimate term of reference in the faith of the Church, as manifested and communicated in the liturgy, in that catholic vision and experience which now, in its alienation from liturgy, it lacks.[19]

Such a view does not advocate from slapping the term "liturgical" onto theology but rather insists that the enactment of the liturgy does something theologically which must be taken seriously and seen as essential to the life and faith of the Church. Kavanagh certainly agrees with Schmemann, though he states it in a different way, suggesting that liturgy is the

17. Schmemann, *Church, World, Mission*, 132.

18. Paul Meyendorff produced a brief introductory paper on liturgical theology in the 1990's in which he argues that liturgical theology can be understood according to biological terms. Anatomy is the study of the body's form and physiology is the study of the body's function. Liturgical theology is both the study of worship's anatomy and physiology (form and function). See Meyendorff, "What Is Liturgical Theology?"

19. Schmemann, *Church, World, Mission*, 140.

"ontological foundation" of theology. It is in the outworking of this theo-logical meaning, the avenue by which it is determined and deciphered, that gives substance to Schmemann's claim.

Methodology

Central to Schmemann's understanding of liturgical theology is his concept of the "liturgical coefficient." This idea is foundational to his methodology, and yet almost all scholarly reviews and critiques of Schmemann's work fail to mention the concept, whether directly or indirectly. Scholars (such as Aune and Marshall) are so concerned with his rendering of Prosper or his acceptance of Hippolytus as the author of the *Apostolic Traditions* that his definition and methodology of liturgical theology receive little to no treatment. As Eugene Schlesinger points out in this volume, the fruit of Schmemann's work ought not to be thrown out because his appropriation of certain historical texts was misguided and/or wrong.

Schmemann provides a working definition for the liturgical coefficient in his *Introduction*:

> Worship simply cannot be equated either with texts or with forms of worship. It is a whole, within which everything, the words of prayer, lections, chanting, ceremonies, the relationship of all these things in a "sequence" or "order" and, finally, what can be defined as the "liturgical coefficient" of each of these ele-ments (i.e., that significance which, apart from its own immedi-ate content, each acquires as a result of its place in the general sequence or order of worship), only all this together defines the meaning of the whole and is therefore the proper subject of study and theological evaluation.[20]

The liturgical coefficient is nothing more or less than the understanding that each and every liturgical element, maneuver, gesture, and action in the *ordo* has both inherent meaning and also additional meaning gained based on its relation to every other element in the liturgy. For example, the placement of the Lord's Prayer within the Eucharistic liturgy will slightly alter its meaning if it is located within the Eucharistic prayer proper or at the beginning of the Liturgy alongside the Decalogue. So too, the epiclesis has inherent meaning when prayed over the elements (bread and wine or water for baptism) but would mean something entirely different if used during the absolution or the

---

20. Schmemann, *Introduction*, 19.

Collect for Purity.[21] This becomes a question of both *form and function*. As the form changes slightly, so too does the function of specific elements.

The liturgical coefficient radically changes the way one approaches the liturgy as subject matter to be studied because it places certain boundaries around it, protecting it [the liturgy] from those very efforts to pluck from it theological truths regardless of internal form and external function. Gordon Lathrop's significant work on the ordo and the idea of Baustiene fit nicely within this context—so too does Dix's shape of the Eucharist—because they acknowledge that there is a basic structure (form) of the liturgy that has been utilized and observed consistently for centuries.[22] A study of form and a search for an ecumenical ordo provides a strong foundation for liturgical theological inquiry as they represent an important piece of the methodological puzzle. Lathrop's own work bears witness to this reality as he takes the ordo and his concept of juxtaposition—derived from Schmemann's coefficient—as a driving factor in elucidating the meaning of worship.

Through the lens of the liturgical coefficient liturgy is seen as one cohesive whole rather than simply the sum of its parts. The whole must be understood before individual parts are examined. Furthermore, individual parts cannot nor should not be ripped out of their liturgical context. According to the liturgical coefficient, is not basic addition but rather exponential multiplication. Echoing Schmemann, it is as if the individuals (each liturgical element) become so much more than they are individually.

Too often, the study of individual elements or the whole *ordo* is limited to a historical analysis. Paul Bradshaw rightly suggested that "liturgical theology rests upon bad history, or no history at all."[23] Aune pushes the issue further in his *Worship* essays when he suggests that the way forward for liturgical theology is to become both more "historical and theological."[24] Contrary to these claims, however, while Schmemann may have left certain historical holes in his research or even subscribed to now-debunked thinking,[25] embedded deep within his methodology is an intimate connec-

21. The author is an Anglican priest, and although the references to specific liturgical elements are Anglican, the same can be said of any liturgy when the liturgical coefficient is applied as an interpretive key.

22. Note the use of the word "consistently" rather than "unanimously" here. I am not advocating for a universal liturgy nor am I suggesting that the *ordo* has been the same in all times and places. The suggestion here is that there has been a form of consistency and not uniformity.

23. Bradshaw, "Difficulties in Doing Liturgical Theology," 181.

24. Aune, "Liturgy and Theology 1."

25. The authorship of the *Apostolic Traditions* per se. See Eugene R. Schlesinger's essay in this volume for a fresh perspective on reading Schmemann despite these shortcomings.

tion between historical research and theological reflection/understanding. In fact, the two go hand in hand:

> After historical analysis, there must come a theological synthesis—and this is the second and major part of liturgical theology. The theological synthesis is the elucidation of the rule of prayer as the rule of faith, it is the theological interpretation of the rule of prayer.[26]

Here we encounter the joining of modern liturgical studies and theology of/from liturgy into one contiguous whole. Schmemann is committed to the historical analysis of liturgical texts, rites, and actions, but it is not his sole concern. Liturgical theology must take historical research and liturgical history seriously *and then* move toward a theological elucidation or interpretation of the rite in order to be considered as liturgical theology proper. Aune's article highlights the needless separation of liturgical history and liturgical theology under the umbrella of liturgical studies. Here I think we have cart before horse: liturgical theology should be the umbrella under which studies, history, etc. are housed. Historical research without theological reflection is but an exercise—important though it may be—in liturgical history. Theological reflection on the liturgy without the aid of historical analysis is always incomplete because liturgical history helps understand form and interpret function. Schmemann sums it up nicely in *The Eucharist* by writing: "I consider the lowering of the liturgy to a *history* of the worship services, which replaced the earlier imprisonment of theological scholasticism, to be wrong and harmful."[27]

Liturgical theology is neither the scouring of liturgical texts in order to discover theological meanings or implications to bolster pre-conceived notions nor is it the study of liturgy from or for purely historical perspectives. For Schmemann, liturgical theology is the remarriage of liturgy and theology (and piety), the practice and celebration of Church when she becomes "that which she already is" and she experiences her call and vocation.

> From the establishment and interpretation of the basic structures of worship to an explanation of every possible element, and then to an orderly theological synthesis of all this data—such is the *method* which liturgical theology uses to carry out its task, to translate what is expressed by the language of worship—its structures, its ceremonies, its texts and its whole "spirit"—into

---

26. Schmemann, *Introduction*, 21.
27. Schmemann, *Eucharist*, 197.

the language of theology, to make the liturgical experience of the Church again one of the life-giving sources of the knowledge of God.[28]

The Eucharist, therefore, ought not to be seen as the moment of consecration or even limited to the Eucharistic prayer proper but as the whole of the liturgy from the gathering of God's people as the *ecclesia* to her dismissal back out into the world.[29] Worship as a whole is the subject matter of liturgical theology. There are significant theological meanings to the gestures, actions, vestments, and liturgical surroundings to be considered when making claims of a liturgical theological nature. Schmemann warns the reader on this point to beware of the temptation to resort to mere, crude symbolism when talking about these elements. He points specifically to the Gospel procession and the attached theological explanation of Jesus going into the world to preach. The Gospel procession does in fact have meaning beyond its pragmatic function, but it is not a meaning one can assign *ex nihlo*. Making the sign of the cross is appropriate and meaningful at certain junctures and totally senseless at others. This falls within the scope of liturgical theology as well. All that is done in liturgical worship, written and unwritten, said audibly and performed physically, is in the line of vision here. Let us begin to *do* liturgical theology rather than simply talking about it.

Eucharist—Sacrament of the Kingdom

The Eucharist is by far the most complete examination of the whole Divine Liturgy in Schmemann's corpus. If *Introduction to Liturgical Theology* is to be seen as simply the definition of terms and outlining of liturgical-theological methodology, and if *For the Life of the World* is a practical theological outworking of liturgical mission and ministry, then *The Eucharist* is the embodiment of the liturgical coefficient and liturgical theology proper. *The Eucharist* represents the *doing* of liturgical theology instead of theological discussion (*Introduction*) or application (*FTLOW*). To this text we must now turn to see Schmemann's liturgical theology on display and to assess the cosmic scope of the Eucharist.

---

28. Schmemann, *Introduction*. Emphasis added.

29. "For I see the entire task at hand in demonstrating as fully as possible that the divine liturgy is a single, though also 'multifaceted,' sacred rite, a single sacrament, in which all its 'parts,' their entire sequence and structure, their coordination with each other, the necessity of each for all and all for each, manifests to us the inexhaustible, eternal, universal and truly divine meaning of what has been and what is being accomplished" (Schmemann, *Eucharist*, 160–61).

As the title suggests, the entire book is structured around the explication and elucidation of the Eucharist because, for Schmemann, everything begins and ends with the Eucharist: "Any liturgical theology not having the Eucharist as the foundation of its whole structure is basically defective."[30] His examination of the Eucharist follows the logical progression as outlined in his methodology: the rite is seen as a whole, each element is examined in chronological order, and particular attention is given to the location of each element and its inherent and inherited meaning based on its relation to other elements.

Schmemann's understanding of a sacrament is noteworthy at this point because every chapter in *The Eucharist* is titled after the sacrament of one thing or another: "For a 'sacrament', as we have seen, implies necessarily the idea of transformation, refers to the ultimate event of Christ's death and resurrection, and is always a sacrament of the Kingdom."[31] This sentence undergirds all of Schmemann's sacramental thought and writing. Sacraments imply transformation, refer to the Paschal Mystery, and have the Kingdom as *telos*. Ultimately, Schmemann will argue for a three-fold understanding of the Eucharist: eschatological, ecclesiological, and cosmical. He expounds on this in detail:

> From the very beginning, this unique function was precisely to "make the Church what she is": the witness and the participant of the saving *event* of Christ, of the new life in the Holy Spirit, of the presence in "this world" of the Kingdom to come. . . . What is important for us at this point is the relationship between this cosmical and eschatological nature of the Church and her λειτουργία. For it is precisely in and through her liturgy—this being the latter's specific and unique "function"—that the Church is *informed* of her cosmical and eschatological vocation, *receives* the power to fulfill it and thus truly *becomes* "what she is": the sacrament, in Christ, of the new creation; the sacrament, in Christ, of the Kingdom.[32]

Schmemann's thesis of the Eucharist is summed up in this quote. He will spend the entirety of *The Eucharist* outlining each liturgical element and its logical progression from *synaxis* to dismissal in an attempt to argue that the Eucharist actualizes the Church as that which she already is, invites her into the saving event of Jesus, and calls her to a vocation of embodying the already established but not yet fully realized Kingdom. I will examine

30. Schmemann, *Introduction*, 24.
31. Schmemann, *FTLOW*, 81.
32. Schmemann, *FTLOW*, 136–37.

these three elements in brief before turning toward the cosmical vocation of which he writes.

The call to worship is made by the Holy Spirit and the answer is the *synaxis* of the *ecclesia*. It is assumed, perhaps, that the urge or intention to attend church is a decision made by the individual. This first step is essential: God's word goes forth into his creation and it does not return empty. God moves and his people respond. Here, we also see a difference between *synaxis* and *ecclesia*: the *synaxis* becomes the *ecclesia* once gathered in the name of the triune God. Not every gathering is the Church and not every local expression of the Church is gathered. She *already is* the Church, but in gathering she becomes it once more; the faithful join together and become something collectively greater than they are individually. Ecclesiology rests upon the regular gathering of God's people for word and worship, prayer and praise, feast and fast. Jean Jacques von Allmen shares this sentiment when he suggests that it is in "worship . . . where the life of the Church comes into being."[33]

However, God's people do not simply gather for fellowship or something arbitrary. The business of gathering as *ecclesia* is singularly focused: worship of the triune God. The church participates in this worship through her words, her cries, her pauses, her offerings, and through the plethora of "Amens" she offers throughout the liturgy. Throughout the *ordo*, the church is an active participant in the Divine Liturgy.[34] Every prayer—save those prayed silently or privately by the priest—concludes with a collective, "Amen." The *amen* prayed by the people is far more than a stylistic flourish; it carries great meaning. To say "Amen" is to say, "Yes, this is so, and let it be so."[35] It is the affirmation and proclamation of the people bearing witness to God's divine action. It is the testimony of the Church to God's presence in their midst and his faithfulness to his covenant. From the opening acclamation of the Kingdom until dismissal, and certainly with the Eucharistic prayer proper in between, the gathered faithful are constantly affirming "Amen." Yes Lord, may it be so. The Amen does not simply close the prayer: *it seals the prayer*. Indeed, the participation and proclamation of the people

---

33. It is in the sphere of worship, the sphere par excellence, where the life of the Church comes into being, that the fact of the Church first emerges. It is there that it gives proof of itself, there where it is focused, and where we are led when we truly seek it, and it is from that point that it goes out into the world to exercise its mission" (von Allmen, *Worship*, 43–44). The connection and similarities between Schmemann and von Allmen require further exploration.

34. Even the titular "Divine Liturgy" bears further witness to the belief that God is present and active in the worship of his Church. The Church participates in the heavenly and eternal liturgy through his worship.

35. Schmemann, *Eucharist*, 48.

is always a hope-filled response to the divine work. Remember that Schmemann saw the participation of the Church in the liturgy as her participation in the "saving act of God"—i.e., the Church does not initiate salvation nor does she initiate worship: she always responds.

Throughout the liturgy, the Church bears witness to the saving acts of God as recorded in Scripture and therefore becomes an agent of proclamation, a sacrament of the Kingdom as she represents Christ in the world. She hears her very vocation expressed through liturgical word and action: confession, proclamation, offering, thanksgiving, body broken and blood poured, distribution of gifts, and an invitation to come to the feast. Liturgy, by this reasoning, forms *ecclesia* through *synaxis*, and then arms and equips her with the necessary tools and training for Kingdom living. Her vocation is revealed through liturgical action and she is similarly dismissed in order to act it out.

There is a profound eschatological dimension to the celebration of the Eucharist. Just as every Eucharist is a remembrance of Jesus' life, death, resurrection, and ascension; just as it is a dangerous memory of Passover and Last Supper; just as it is the enactment of sacrifice in the present now, so, too, is the Eucharist the declaration of hope for future fulfillment. The Kingdom of God, in its glorious splendor and fullness, fully realized and fully present, is the hope of Eucharistic joy and celebration. Without such hope, there would be no point in celebrating the Eucharist, at least not in any sense beyond a memorial of past actions. "The event which is 'actualized' in the Eucharist is an event of the past when viewed within the categories of time, but by virtue of its eschatological, determining, completing significance, it is also an event which is taking place eternally."[36] The power of the Eucharist, the reason that we celebrate zealously on a weekly basis, is that it is the culmination of past grace and future joy in one present act, it is the convergence of past, present, and future in one otherworldly, *Kairos*-type moment before the throne of the King of kings and Lord of lords.

Traditional liturgies commence worship with a two-fold blessing: blessed be God and blessed be his Kingdom. From the outset, the object and subject of worship is made plain: God and his kingdom. Why do we bless the kingdom? "It means that we acknowledge and confess it to be our highest and ultimate value, the object of our desire, our love, and our hope. It means that we proclaim it to be the goal of the sacrament—of pilgrimage, ascension, entrance."[37] The link between the Kingdom of God and the Eucharist is the primary focus of Schmemann's book because the Kingdom

36. Schmemann, *Introduction*, 72.
37. Schmemann, *Eucharist*, 47.

of God, for Schmemann, is also the goal of the Christian life: "But God has saved the world. He saved it in that he again revealed its *goal*: the kingdom of God; its *life*: to be the path to the kingdom; its *meaning*: to be in communion with God, and, in him, with all creation."[38] This communion with God and all of creation begins to reveal the cosmical dimension of the Eucharist because, as a sacrament of the Kingdom, we are citizens of God's kingdom now realized on earth, humans called to a specific vocation.

The cosmical dimension of the Eucharist has to do with the vocation offered by God to Adam and Eve in the Garden and now restored through Christ and understood in the liturgy. In his discussion of "The Sacrament of Thanksgiving," Schmemann asserts:

> Thus, each time [the thanksgiving] is raised up the *salvation of the world is complete*. All is fulfilled, all is granted. Man again stands where God placed him, restored to his vocation: to offer to God a "reasonable service," to know God, thank and to worship him "in spirit and in truth," and through this knowledge and thanksgiving to transform the world itself into communion in the life that "was in the beginning with God" (John 1:2), with God the Father, as was manifested to us.[39]

The vocation is restored: to praise God, direct the praise of creation back to Creator, and invite others to join in communion. Adam and Eve were created as the first priests and rulers over creation, and while the Fall may have drastically altered our ability to commune with God, the vocation is still the same. The Eucharist as the Sacrament of the Kingdom and sacrament of sacraments is the place where God's stewards, priests, and rulers gather together and direct the praise[40] of creation back to Creator.

The most cosmical act, the purest, most right action of a human being is this: thanksgiving to God. The Eucharist is nothing more and nothing less than giving thanks to our Creator with the understanding that this is "meet and right." The Eucharist proper begins with the sursum corda and then with the declaration that it is "meet and right" to give God thanks and praise. This is what it means to be human! This is what *homo adorans* and *homo liturgicus* looks like. Schmemann elaborates:

> After the darkness of sin, the fall and death, a man once again offers to God the pure, sinless, free, and perfect thanksgiving.

38. Schmemann, *Eucharist*, 61.

39. Schmemann, *Eucharist*, 181.

40. "Praise," in this instance, is an all-encompassing term, providing an umbrella for praise, petition, lament, confession, and more, because all presuppose that God is worthy of worship and all are forms of doxology.

A man is returned to that place that God had prepared for him when he created the world. He stands at the heights, before the throne of God; he stands in heaven, before the face of God himself, and freely, in the fullness of love and knowledge, uniting in himself the whole world, all creation, he offers thanksgiving; and in him, the whole world affirms and acknowledges this thanksgiving to be "meet and right."[41]

Schmemann is talking about the priestly actions of Jesus, and it is through the priesthood of Christ, through our participation in his life, death, resurrection, and glorious ascension, that the Church is able to make our thanksgiving before the throne of Almighty God.

Everything in this section has been tied directly to one word, laced throughout Schmemann's work: vocation. It is the church's (ecclesiology) eschatological and cosmical vocation that is expressed fully through her liturgy. Schmemann clearly states through *The Eucharist* that the church receives her call and is informed of her vocation through the liturgy; she becomes the Body of Christ and a sacrament of the Kingdom.

The Cosmic Scope of the Eucharist

Every eighth day, the faithful followers of Jesus gather together for worship, prayer, reading, exhortation, and ritual. The Eucharist begins with the *synaxis* or the assembled people. The people do not assemble of or on their own accord, rather they do so in response to the prompting of the Holy Spirit and the grace of the triune God. God always moves first.[42] The Church is gathered from the corners of the neighborhood, city, region, state, country, and world. While a single parish may only represent a small geographical area, the whole of God's Church is in worship on Sunday, joining voices in prayer, praise, lament, and thanksgiving. Worship begins as the procession of Cross, preacher, celebrant, and other ministers goes forth from nave to chancel. The voices of the faithful are joined up in song, and, with their voices, they do bring the entirety of their lives. The space that they inhabit during worship may be part of a liturgical time and space beyond the confines of this world, but they remain precisely who they are.

41. Schmemann, *Eucharist*, 170.

42. This should be a sufficient rebuttal to Aune's claim that Schmemann and Co. are concerned with a bottom-up approach to liturgical theology versus his own top-down agenda. Schmemann, Kavanagh, Fagerberg, and Lathrop are all clear that God moves and acts first and the participatory acts of the gathered Church are but a response! This is a false dichotomy.

Their relationships, fears, worries, anxieties, joys, triumphs, and more are present in worship with them.

Since the earliest years after Jesus' death, as outlined by both the *Didache* and Justin Martyr's *Apology*, the *ecclesia* has gathered for the reading of the Apostles' writings and an exhortation(s). Hebrews tells us that the word of God is living and active (Heb 4:12), and the prophet Isaiah records that God's word goes forth from his mouth and does not return empty (Isa 55:11). Scripture has been part of the Christian cult since even before the split with synagogue worship in the mid-first century,[43] and it was part of the Jewish cult long before that. Long has Israel read aloud the words of Torah and of YHWH in her worship. To read Scripture is to participate in something greater, in something larger, in something most *real*. God is present and moving as his Word is being read and then proclaimed kerygmatically. Scripture shapes, forms, molds, convicts, strengthens, enlightens, and much more. Or rather, the Holy Spirit does all of this through the Word of God just as the word poured forth from God's mouth and the Spirit hovered over the deep in Genesis 1. In our journey toward the Altar, everything is first and foremost an action of God before it is ever a responsive-action of the church.

The Word proclaimed and the story retold may be locally explicated and appropriated—such is the joy and work of liturgical preaching—but it is the story of the God who created the cosmos and loves his creation; it is the story of creation, fall, redemption, and consummation. The story is one of love, pain, loss, joy, hope, and triumph. It is the universal story, the one true story which undergirds the entirety of our existence and *the people of God are invited to join in!* This is not a story to be read and forgotten or to be seen and left as unaffected; it is the story of which we are part, into which we are called, and by which we proclaim God's love. The sermon or homily is the preacher's reflection upon the passage(s) and upon God's activity in the world; the Holy Spirit leads and guides the preacher as she prays, "Lord open my [our] lips, that my mouth shall proclaim your praise." Through the reading of God's word and the explication of it by the preacher, the story of God is re-told, and the people of God are invited to participate, to join a story already in motion, and to take part in the saving acts of God. The salvation narrative becomes tangibly present in the liturgy as God's people dangerously remember and proclaim all that he has done. This memory and proclamation is both personal and corporate; it is local, global, and cosmical

43. We see Jesus reading a passage from Isaiah in the synagogue in Luke 4—it was customary for Israel's Scriptures to be read aloud publicly as part of worship.

because it tells of God's redeeming acts for the whole of creation and beckons the church to participate in his ongoing work.

Prayers are offered for the church, the world, and those around us. The prayers prayed and the offering offered are the church's opportunity to present before her Creator all that he has created and to ask that he may bless it all. Schmemann discusses this when he writes:

> But already, from the very beginning, in these "common supplications" made "with one accord," in their joyous and triumphal antiphons, which proclaim and glorify the kingdom of God, we signify that the "assembly as the Church" is above all the joy of the regenerated and renewed creation, *the gathering of the world*, in contrast to its fall into sin and death.[44]

This is why Eucharist is "for the life of the world" in Schmemann's thought; for just as Christ willingly handed himself over to suffering and death, so too does the Church offer herself willingly for the life of the world. This is the very role of the priest—both the Priest and the priesthood of all believers: to direct the praise and worship of creation to the Creator. In our prayers for the world and those around us, we bring every relationship, every possession, and every interaction before the Throne and ask that they be blessed and sanctified.

The anaphora is the culmination of the move from Word to Altar. Schmemann described the movement of the Eucharist as a journey of ascent and return.[45] The ascent begins with the *synaxis* and reaches its climax with the lifting up of gifts and hearts (*Sursum corda, up hearts!*) and the participation of the *ecclesia* in the foretaste of the eschatological banquet. Here, the *ecclesia* ascends to the heavenly Throne Room and joins in the heavenly chorus with the thrice-holy hymn, joining voices with "the angels, archangels, and all the company of heaven who forever sing this hymn to proclaim the glory"[46] of the Holy Name. The people receive the Body and Blood of Jesus from Jesus, the great High Priest, as he presides over the Eucharist through the priest *in persona Christi*. Christ is ever-present, always active in the celebration. The people give thanks for their meal and, after being blessed, are dismissed to go out into the world as the Eucharistic people, sharing the love and news of God with all whom they meet. The Eucharist is seemingly incomplete if the *ecclesia* remains ascended. It is like Peter's words and Jesus' rebuke on Mt. Tabor: it is good for us to be here, but we cannot remain on the summit. One day, when God is all in all, we will see God clearly and we will be

---

44. Schmemann, *Eucharist*, 53.

45. Schmemann, *Eucharist*, 199.

46. Episcopal Church, *Book of Common Prayer*, s.v. "Eucharistic Prayer A."

ascended and glorified. Until that time, however, our ascent must always be met with a return: we must return to our homes, lives, neighbors, work, family, and everything else God has given us. Why? Because in returning, we are able to invite others, indeed all of creation, to join us in the praise and worship of Almighty God.

The climax of the *ordo* is also the climax of the Church's worship. The Eucharist is the pinnacle of the liturgy of time, of the *lex orandi*, of every action here on earth. In the Eucharist, we find the Church united as a whole, across both time and space, through prayers, the reading of Scripture, the exhortation, the sharing of peace, the offering of gifts, the offering of the elements, and the distribution of the consecration Bread and Wine, Body and Blood. In the Eucharist, we encounter the Church as she was always meant to be, as she one day will be before her Lord and Savior. The realization and fulfillment of the Church's nature is not something the Church does to herself. It is rather the response of the people of God to God.

The Eucharist, therefore, cannot nor should not be relegated to simplistic political, economic, or social readings. It is the giving of the thanks of the gathered church on behalf of the world and the whole of creation; it is the joining of the church militant with the church triumphant in the throne room of the Triune God as the "voices of angels and archangels and all the company of heaven sing, 'Holy, holy, holy Lord,'" it is the participation of the Church in the mission of God, it is the offering of self and gifts for the benefit of all around. In short, it is the embodiment of the cosmic vocation given by God to humanity in the Garden: steward creation and direct her praise to the Creator. Anything short of such a vision falls short of God's intentions for his creation.

Feasts: Participating in the Mystery

(Schmemann's Liturgical Theology as Guide for Sacramental Living)

Dwight W. Vogel, OSL

Sharing stories, food, and sign-acts are fundamental to the development of human communities. When these events of sharing embody the identity of a community in significant ways, such meaningful events are often called "feasts." Feasts have been important community experiences in diverse cultures throughout history, including Christian liturgical practice.

The liturgical theology of Alexander Schmemann provides a foundation for guiding sacramental living or, to use Schmemann's terminology, a "mysteriological piety."[1] I have found his treatment of feasts, brief and tantalizing in and of itself, to provide important clues about sacramental living, especially when placed in the larger context of his thought.

One of my favorite philosophers of language is Humpty Dumpty, who contends in *Alice in Wonderland* that words can mean whatever we want them to mean, so long as we "pay them enough."[2] The word "piety" carries baggage for me that it does not for Schmemann. I find "sacramental living" to be a more accurate and helpful phrase for what I want to say regarding Schmemann's thought. In this article, sacramental living is identical with mysteriological piety, so I will often put the two terms together, speaking of "sacramental living as mysteriogical piety."

---

1. Schmemann, *Introduction*, 177.
2. Caroll, *Through the Looking Glass*, 125.

Whichever term you prefer to use, we must recognize that Schmemann rejects a spirituality that operates without any reference to the world, seeking to escape the problems of the world by withdrawing into an experience that makes a person feel good, nor will he accept a highly individualistic spirituality without any reference to other persons, either individually or communally. He insists on the need to confront the world's problems (and our own) by understanding them in a different perspective, returning to "the truth, the righteousness, the joy of the Kingdom of God."[3]

Schmemann rejoices in the "genuine discovery" by the liturgical movement of the twentieth century that worship "eternally actualizes the nature of the Church as the Body of Christ" as that which "embraces, expresses, inspires, and defines the whole Church, her whole essential nature, her whole life."[4]

Bruce T. Morrill and Don E. Saliers find the heart of Schmemann's liturgical theology to be "the principle that Christian faith and truth are made incarnate and manifested in the liturgy."[5] Schmemann will not allow this to be a compartmentalized concern, safely kept in a pigeonhole marked "liturgical theology," where only those interested in it as a narrow academic concern may venture. No, we must see the whole fabric of the Church's *leitourgia* as an all-embracing vision of life, which judges, informs, and, most importantly, transforms the whole of existence, shaping and reconstructing all our ideas, attitudes, and actions.[6] This perspective, I suggest, moves from an intellectual inquiry into the nature of liturgy toward an understanding of living the liturgy in the totality of life. Schmemann notes that his main thesis is that "the experience of the Church is primarily the experience given and received in the Church's *leitourgia*."[7]

For over fifty years, the book we know as Schmemann's *For the Life of the World* has influenced students and professors, liturgical theologians and liturgical practitioners, clergy and laity. There, he insists that *leitourgia* is not to be restricted to the words of liturgies and the rubrics about how to properly perform the ceremonies. He returns to the original meaning of the Greek, where liturgy means "an action by which a group of people become something corporately which they had not been as a mere collection of individuals—a whole greater than the sum of its parts" and, in addition,

3. Schmemann, *Liturgy and Tradition*, 98–99.

4. Schmemann, *Introduction*, 14.

5. Morrill and Saliers, "Alexander Schmemann," 53.

6. Schmemann, *Liturgy and Tradition*, 98–100.

7. Schmemann, *Liturgy and Tradition*, 55.

"a function or 'ministry' of a [person] or a group on behalf of and in the interest of the whole community."[8]

He rejects both spiritualization and secularization as valid options, writing that "whether we 'spiritualize' our life or 'secularize' our religion, whether we invite [people] to a spiritual banquet or simply join them in the secular one, the real life of the world, for which we are told God gave his only begotten Son, remains hopelessly beyond our religious grasp."[9]

Schmemann rejects the dichotomy of spiritual as opposed to material, or sacred as opposed to profane. The food we eat and the world which we engage in order to live are both given by God and given as communion with God. We are hungry for food, but even more fundamentally, we are hungry for God.[10]

Blessing God is not a religious or cultic act but a way of life. The natural reaction of a humanity to whom God has given this "very good" creation, this "blessed and sanctified world," is to bless God in return, thanking God in our role as *homo adorans*, our priestly function. In the very act of blessing God, we unify the world so disjointed from the perspective of the fallen world but unified in the presence of the One in whom all is connected (Col 1:17). Receiving the world from God, we offer it back to God by filling the world with eucharist (thanksgiving), transforming what we receive from the world, separated and alienated from one another, the cosmos, and God, into communion—intimate relationship with God who is all in all (Eph 4:6).[11]

This is the fundamental experience of the liturgy in which we become "the sacrament, in Christ, of the new creation: the sacrament, in Christ, of the Kingdom."[12] The connection between feast and this kind of sacramental spirituality, understood by Schmemann as a mysteriological piety, is found in his writing regarding the Three Day Feast (the Triduum):

> If the word *mystery* can still have any meaning today, be experienced and not merely "explained," it is here, in this unique celebration which reveals and communicates before it "explains," which makes us witnesses and participants of one all-embracing

8. First written as a study guide for the National Student Christian Federation (1963), then published with the title *For the Life of the World: Sacraments and Orthodoxy* (1973).

9. Schmemann, *For the Life of the World*, 13.

10. Schmemann, *For the Life of the World*, 14.

11. Schmemann, *For the Life of the World*, 15.

12. Schmemann, *Liturgy and Tradition*, 57.

Event from which stems everything else: understanding and
power, knowledge end joy, contemplation and communion.[13]

The liturgical celebration of feasts is *kairos* time,[14] not in the sense of a holy
day instead of a profane one or the commemoration of a past event but
rather as a transformation of time, a time that fully belongs in this world
and yet transforms all times into times of *remembrance* and *expectation*,[15] a
theme to which we will return.

This insistence that a sacramental spirituality, a mysteriological piety,
not escape the human dimension but be embedded in it is found again in
Schmemann's exploration of feast, for he notes that Christianity accepted
the fundamentally human phenomenon of feast as a way of putting meaning into life. Feasts do free us from the regular rhythm of work and rest, but
Schmemann sees them not as being merely a break in our work schedule
but rather the fruit of that work. Without work, there would be no feast. The
feast is that toward which work moves and from which it flows.[16]

Feasts are organically related to natural cycles of seasonal time, for
example, springtime and harvest, or longer days or nights. Feasts function
within the whole framework of our life in the world, marking birth, puberty,
vocation, marriage, and death. A sacramental spirituality must be embedded in the ordinary, not a release from it.[17]

In addition to these universal characteristics, however, Schmemann
notes that there are additional dimensions of meaning for feasts in Christianity. Here, his insistence on the mysteriological component is clear. Christian feasts are enriched by their relation to our participation in the paschal
mystery, that is, by our incorporation into Christ's incarnation, life, death,
resurrection, and consummation. While a particular feast may focus on one
of these aspects, the context of the whole of the paschal mystery is always
present. So Schmemann insists that "it is precisely faith *as experience*, the
total and living experience of the Church" that is at stake. A sacramental
spirituality, a mysteriological piety is grounded in the faith by which the
Church lives, which is not assent to doctrine but a living relationship to "the
Life, Death, Resurrection and Glorification of Jesus Christ, His Ascension
. . . the descent of the Holy Spirit on the last and great day of Pentecost—
a relationship which makes her a constant 'witness' and 'participant' of

13. Schmemann, *Liturgy and Tradition*, 63.

14. Schmemann, *For the Life of the World*, 48.

15. Schmemann, *For the Life of the World*, 51–52.

16. Schmemann, *For the Life of the World*, 54. See also Schmemann, *Introduction*,
200–1.

17. Schmemann, *For the Life of the World*, 54.

these events, of their saving, redeeming, life-giving, and life-transforming reality."[18] When I first read this passage, I wrote "paschal mystery!!" in the margin. So, Joyce Ann Zimmerman concludes, the paschal mystery is more than Christ's mystery: "The very meaning of paschal mystery includes our own engagement in it."[19]

We have already noted that the Three Day Feast (the Triduum) is a unique celebration, revealing and communicating this mystery through our participation or, one might say, our immersion in it. However, the Three Day Feast is far from being the only experience we have of participating in this mystery. Because of its temporal connection with the day of Resurrection, the weekly eucharistic feast on the Lord's Day is another—but so is every weekday eucharistic feast. The Three Day Feast immerses us in experiencing the paschal mystery which, while centered in death-and-resurrection (as if they were one word), is broader and deeper than the events commemorated in that feast itself.

Schmemann's Orthodox tradition was not beset by an extreme focus of the eucharist on the death of Jesus. Participating in the eucharist is itself participating in the whole of the paschal mystery. To participate in the paschal mystery is not temporally limited to the feast itself. Just as we saw in Schmemann's treatment of feast, this experience is not separate from but rather integrated with patterns and practices of life. Thus, our daily experience is transformed into a meaningful perspective by our participation in the paschal mystery through *leitourgia*. Mere experiencing becomes an experiential awareness that enables the understanding and practice of life. So Schmemann writes that "it is in the Eucharist that the Church ceases to be 'institution, doctrine, system' and becomes Life, Vision, Salvation; it is in the Eucharist that the Word of God is fulfilled and the human mind made capable of expressing the mind of Christ."[20]

His explication of the liturgy of the Eucharistic feast as a journey or procession serves as a guide for sacramental living. It begins when we leave our homes to go to participate in the Eucharistic liturgy. That "procession" is already "sacramental act," for we are on our way, a way of transformation from our lives as individuals into "a new community with a new life," making present the One in whom all things were at their beginning and will be at their end. This is a real separation from the world. The attitudes and actions found in the headlines of the morning newspaper are not the foundation of sacramental living. A cautionary note: this does not mean that

18. Schmemann, *Liturgy and Tradition*, 54.
19. Zimmerman, "Paschal Mystery," 312.
20. Schmemann, *Liturgy and Tradition*, 85.

Schmemann's understanding of the Eucharist is escapist or world denying, although at this point it might seem so. Transformative living cannot take place without our "leaving behind" a focus on the old patterns and values of the world in which we live.[21]

We cannot understand this "leaving" without recognizing that to become temples of the Holy Spirit, we must ascend to heaven, where Christ ascended, leaving this world, joining with Christ in the liturgy as participants in the mystery of the world to come. This is not another world, however, different from the one created by God and given to us. It is this same world, "already perfected in Christ but not yet in us."[22]

The transformative power of the eucharistic feast is not to be found in a certain part of the service, let alone in certain sacred words. The eucharistic feast is a sacrament in its entirety; the whole liturgy, then, is a guide for sacramental living. The entrance rite is our actual entrance, our participation in the procession that leads to the Kingdom of God. It is the beginning of our ascension to the Throne of God.[23] That is very different from thinking that we decided it would be a good thing to meet with others who share our values to pray and praise God together. It already partakes of "mystery"— something I do not understand and cannot articulate but which is none the less real and in which I know I am participating.

We have left our usual way of thinking and doing and joined the procession to the Kingdom of God. The essence of this movement of the liturgical journey is the passage from "this world" to the heavenly sanctuary. We stand in the presence of the glorified Christ and are covered with his glory. Nothing will communicate this sphere but art. Schmemann turns to the words of Romano Guardini: "It is in the highest sense the life of a child, in which everything is picture, melody, and song. Such is the wonderful fact which the liturgy demonstrates: it unites act and reality in a supernatural childhood before God."[24]

Sight and sound, whether in nature or as the result of the creative genius of human beings, are important components of sacramental living. Mystery, whether of the presence of the glorified Christ or the eternal Transcendent One, is beyond language. Poets and mystics come the closest to being able to use them fruitfully. Our procession to the Kingdom of God is enabled by the arts—not as ends in themselves but in their iconic role as two-way doorways to the Divine.

21. Schmemann, *For the Life of the World*, 26–27.

22. Schmemann, *For the Life of the World*, 41.

23. Schmemann, *Liturgy and Tradition*, 82.

24. Guardini, *Church and the Catholic*, 180–81.

Schmemann's liturgical experience is of joining with the thrice holy hymn of the angels, coming to that "glorious and incomprehensible above and beyond of which we know only one thing: that it eternally resounds with the praise of divine glory and holiness. . . . 'Holy' is the word, the song, the 'reaction' as we enter heaven, standing before the heavenly glory of God."[25]

This is not a natural component of the everyday sacred, the sacrament of the ordinary, which we have discovered to our joy. The value of that discovery is less than it might be because it has taken place in a spiritual atmosphere that has confused the holiness of God with superficial words and songs that praise God but do not testify to the awesome nature of God. Even the word "awesome" has been cheapened by overuse. Praise words and songs often have more to do with our feelings than the glory of God. Sacramental living, a mysteriological piety, is grounded in our living what we sing: "We praise you, we bless you, we worship you, we glorify you, we give thanks to you for your great glory!"[26]

To speak of a "Service of Word and Sacrament"—as if they were two things—would make no sense to Schmemann, for he testifies to the Orthodox perspective that "the Word is as sacramental as the sacrament is evangelical." Just as sacrament is understood as a manifestation of the Word, so proclaiming the Word is a sacramental act of transformation, transforming human words into the Word of God, thus making manifest the Kingdom. The hearer receives that Word and is transformed into a temple of the Holy Spirit. The "Alleluia" sung before the Gospel is read is understood as a God-bearing act, a "joyful greeting of those who *see* the coming Lord, who *know* His presence, and who express their joy at this glorious *parousia*" (literally, "presence" or "arrival"). The Alleluia celebrates the affirmation: "Christ is here!" in the reading of the Gospel and, we might add, in those transformed through hearing it. For sacramental living, the glorification of God and the transformation of life are inextricably bound.[27]

For Schmemann, the offering of the gifts in the eucharistic feast must be understood in light of our having been created as celebrants of the sacrament of life and its transformation into life in God. Food is life; when we offer up elements of our food to God, what we offer is the totality of our lives and the world of which we are a part. In our function as *homo adorans*, real life is itself eucharist, "a movement of love and adoration toward God." There alone the meaning and value of everything is revealed and fulfilled. We must acknowledge that this eucharistic life has been lost, but in Christ

---

25. Schmemann, *For the Life of the World*, 31–32.

26. From "Gloria in excelsis."

27. Schmemann, *For the Life of the World*, 33.

it is restored to us, for Christ is Himself the perfect eucharist. We fully participate in this, *our* eucharist. We are sacrificial beings; sacrifice is natural to us for we find our life in love and love is sacrificial.[28] Understanding the meaning of the procession as the gifts are brought to the altar contributes to our understanding of sacramental living.

Schmemann's understanding of the nature of love as sacrifice flows into his insistence that the kiss of peace is one of the fundamental acts of the eucharistic liturgy. To be who the eucharistic community is called to be, it must reveal the divine love given us by God. Indeed, "the content of Christ's Eucharist is love," and only through love can we be participants in it. The problem is that we have lost this love. We are called to witness to that love, to re-present it, to make it present, for creating and transforming love is the principle of the eucharistic sacrament.[29]

With the eternal doxology, we join in the "holy, holy, holy Lord, heaven and earth are full of your glory!" For Schmemann, it is essential that we ascend to heaven in Christ to become aware that creation in its true nature is the glorification of God, "as the response to divine love in which alone creation becomes what God wants it to be: thanksgiving, eucharist, adoration."[30] It is only with this heavenly perspective, when we join with angels and archangels in the eternal doxology, that we are able to know the purpose of all that exists.[31]

Then, in the eucharistic feast, we are at "the paschal table of the Kingdom." What we have offered (our food, our life in the world, our very selves), we have offered in Christ, who has become our life. We have an experiential awareness of the amazing trans-action of God's economy, for it is "given back to us as the gift of new life." We had to ascend, to be "lifted up," to partake of the world to come. But Schmemann warns us not to think this is another world! It is our world, the same world, "already perfected in Christ but not yet in us."[32] And here he returns again to the meaning of feast as food:

> Since God has created the world as food for us and has given
> us food as means of communion with Him, of life in Him, the

---

28. Schmemann, *For the Life of the World*, 34–35. See also Schmemann, *Liturgy and Tradition*, 83.

29. Schmemann, *For the Life of the World*, 36–37.

30. Schmemann, *For the Life of the World*, 39.

31. Schmemann, "Liturgy and Eucharist," 83, and Schmemann, *For the Life of the World*, 39–40.

32. Schmemann, *For the Life of the World*, 41–42. See also Schmemann, *Liturgy and Tradition*, 83.

new food and the new life which we receive from God in His Kingdom is Christ Himself. He is our bread . . . and all our bread was but a symbol of Him, a symbol that had to become reality.[33]

In Orthodox understandings of this transformation, the Holy Spirit is clearly the agent. Thus, the moment of that transformation is not in the words of institution but in the *epiclesis*. This is not, Schmemann insists, to replace one causality and formula with another. It is because the eucharistic feast is eschatological. The Holy Spirit comes on Pentecost to manifest the world to come. The Holy Spirit is the one who takes us *beyond*.[34]

So the time comes to return to the world. We cannot stay on the mountain or in heaven with the angels. "We are sent back. . . . It is again the beginning, and things that were impossible to us are again revealed to us as Possible." The word Schmemann uses is "competent." God makes us competent to be witnesses of the Kingdom that is to come, fulfilling what God has done and continues to do, what Schmemann calls "the liturgy of mission."[35]

Our participation in the paschal mystery through *leitourgia* makes us who we are, that is, the Body of Christ and the Temple of the Holy Spirit.[36] That participation includes the experiential awareness that we are created, fallen, and redeemed. The words themselves are all too familiar; the meaning Schmemann pours into them is something else again. Rather than seeing the world as inherently evil, polluted by the very fact of its material existence, he insists on the goodness of the created order in our everyday experience: "To claim that we are God's creation is to affirm that God's voice is constantly speaking within us and saying to us 'And God saw everything that he had made and behold, it was very good.'"[37] It is the misuse of this goodness which is evil.

But sacramental living, a mysteriological piety, must also take into account that we are part of a world that is fallen. It is instructive that the story of the fall in Genesis has to do with food. It is the fruit of the only tree not offered as gift to humanity. Eating it was communion with itself alone and not with God. According to Schmemann, "it is the image of the world loved for itself, and eating it is the image of life understood as an end in itself."[38]

33. Schmemann, *For the Life of the World*, 43.

34. Schmemann, *For the Life of the World*, 44.

35. Schmemann, "Liturgy and Eucharist," 83, and Schmemann, *For the Life of the World*, 45–46.

36. Schmemann, *Liturgy and Tradition*, 52.

37. Schmemann, *Liturgy and Tradition*, 98.

38. Schmemann, *For the Life of the World*, 16.

Thus, the fall is our turning away from humanity's role as priest of a eucharistic feast which offers the world to God and, in this offering, receives the gift of life. When humanity lost this eucharistic life, it lost the power to transform life into Life. Ceasing to be priests of the world, humanity became the world's slave.[39]

These striking images correlate with our experiential awareness. We are caught in intersecting webs of systemic evil. Greed interpenetrates our existence. We would like to think we are victims—not perpetrators—of greed and oppression. Then we realize the difficulty of making any purchase of goods or services that are not infected with evil. A basic component of liturgy through the years has been confession of sin. Granted that the sins focused on may have been more personal and pelvic than systemic and organic, confession of sin was a reminder of the Fall. Contemporary "prayers of awareness" seek to remedy earlier myopias but no doubt manifest astigmatisms of our own. Lists of sins, whether personal or corporate, seemingly trivial or profound, only remind us of the deeper problem. We have ceased to be aware of the comprehensive immensity of the gifts of a good creation blessed by God and of our eucharistic role in offering all that we have and are back to God, not only for ourselves but on behalf of the whole creation. A sacramental spirituality as a mysteriological piety involves claiming and acting on our God-given calling to be priests, to live out *leitourgia*.

But the cycle is not yet complete: receiving the gift of creation, of our very lives, offering ourselves back to God in all our interconnectedness, the mystery of the economy of God is that we receive it back again, redeemed and transformed. Through the paschal mystery, from creation and incarnation to Spirit-gift and consummation, all is redeemed. This vision of the world as created, fallen, and redeemed is "an intuition we receive from God with gratitude and joy."[40]

Joy is an essential characteristic of sacramental living based on Schmemann's liturgical theology. He notes that "joy" is the word opening and closing the gospel story in Luke: "I bring you tidings of great joy" (Luke 2:10), "and they worshipped him and returned to Jerusalem with great joy" (Luke 24:52). This sense of a joy which cannot be taken away from us cannot be defined; indeed, in its presence, "all definitions are silent." When the experiential awareness of joy in its fullness is central to our understanding of our participation in the paschal mystery, we are able

---

39. Schmemann, *Liturgy and Tradition*, 17.

40. Schmemann, *Liturgy and Tradition*, 98–99. My expansion of the scope of the paschal mystery is indebted to the work of Joyce Ann Zimmerman.

to deal with "redemption as the plentitude, the victory, and the presence of God, who becomes all in all things."[41]

In this understanding of sacramental living as mysteriological piety, every feast day—indeed, every eucharistic feast—became an end in itself, "acquiring a depth, beauty and richness of content which . . . transmitted the inexhaustible 'joy of the Church.'"[42] Our participation in the glorification of God is paralleled by the gift of joy which is not something we achieve by seeking it, but comes as grace, the natural result of the life in the Spirit which comes through participation in the paschal mystery.

Bruce Morrill and Don Saliers note that Schmemann summarizes genuine Christian liturgy as cosmological (the world as sacramental), ecclesiological (the Church as manifestation of the Kingdom in this world), and eschatological (the kingdom that is to come), which together are the basis for "liturgy's transformative potential for the Church and Christians in society."[43] These dimensions provide the experiential awareness of "new life in new time existing within this old world and its time for the express purpose of its salvation and renewal."[44] This gift of grace through participating in the mystery is both an experiential awareness of the new creation and a vision of the coming Kingdom, and provides both the source and the continuing dynamic of life and faith.[45]

For Schmemann, liturgical feasts are our participation in the paschal mystery that makes sacramental living as mysteriological piety possible. This perspective provides new levels of meaning for my understanding of liturgical feasts as communal events that *re-member the past* as we are nourished by stories into which the community enters *(anamnesis)*, embodying the deep mysteries and rich symbols of the Tradition. For me, these feasts also *celebrate the present*, generating, celebrating, and embodying the community's identity. Our sense of the deep significance of our community's identity is birthed even as we celebrate together. This significance is not something "out there," separate from us. It is part of our being, our thinking, our doing. These feasts express, sustain, and empower the community's way of being in the world, manifesting a "large table," which is inclusive and expansive, rather than a private and exclusive one. In addition, I believe they *shape the future*. In feasts, we envision a future hope that transforms how we act in the present *(prolepsis)*. They enable us to see beyond the immediate

41. Schmemann, *Liturgy and Tradition*, 99.

42. Schmemann, *Introduction*, 177.

43. Morrill and Saliers "Alexander Schmemann," 53.

44. Schmemann, *Introduction*, 216.

45. Schmemann, *Liturgy and Tradition*, 58.

situation and call us to act in preparation for that future. They celebrate not only who we are but also who we are becoming.[46]

Having surveyed Schmemann's understanding of the significance of our participation in the paschal mystery in the eucharistic feast, how are we to understand sacramental living as mysteriological piety?

We recognize that it is based on our experiential awareness. I just returned from a community meal in my retirement community. If I had turned on a tiny, inexpensive recorder, the microphone would have picked up a cacophony of undifferentiated sounds from the intersection of tableware and plates and the countless conversations going on. Some might say that is the sound that is "really there." But that's not what I hear. I become experientially aware of the conversation at my table and, within that, of the person with whom I am conversing. When an announcement is given over the sound system, a filter automatically goes up. Is it the prayer? Is it an announcement about an activity in which I am interested? Is it an announcement of an event in which I have little interest or cannot attend? I am not making a conscious choice, but it is a choice none-the-less, developed out of habits of awareness that grow out of what I have chosen to attend to in the past or something new that catches my "attention" as worthy of awareness.

Sacramental living as mysteriological piety results from patterns of awareness which become habits of attentiveness that enable us to live our lives in relation with others who share similar patterns of awareness. When I tell the story of moving into this community, I usually say, "We hung our first picture on Ash Wednesday and we hung the last one on Easter Sunday." It is not that I didn't know the day and date of the secular calendar. It is just that my patterns of thought organize time in a way that is common to those of us for whom the liturgical calendar is the most natural way of keeping time. And that has implications for how we understand the patterns of time. What patterns of awareness, what habits of attention do I cultivate in solidarity with others in the procession that follows the Way of Jesus?

Sacramental living as mysteriological piety is world affirming, not world denying. It is communal not individualistic, holistic not compartmentalized. The path of this procession of participating in the mystery is not sacred as opposed to secular or profane, not spiritual as opposed to material. Creation, given by God for our good, is good. Our procession is thus deeply rooted in attending to a sense that the world and all that is in it is potentially sacramental for those with eyes to see and ears to hear.

The key mark of our humanity is that we are *homo adorans*, called to be priests offering ourselves and our world up to God through the sacrifice of

46. See Vogel, *Lukan Book of Feasts*.

love which we share with Christ. Blessing God is not just something we do but a way of life, grounded in the paschal mystery understood comprehensively: centered in our experience of the Three Day Feast, reaching out through every feast day, and made known in every eucharistic feast we share.

We are people on a journey, a procession of transformation into a new community with a new way of life. Ascending to stand with the glorified Christ, we share with the angels the glorification of God, and that experience gives us a new perspective on our lives and the life of the world. In the "Alleluia," we affirm that Christ is here for us and with us at every present moment, even as the Holy Spirit takes us beyond, sent out in the liturgy of mission to be witnesses to and agents of the Kingdom that is to come. As those created good for good who have marred that image, we receive the grace that all is redeemed in the Kingdom that is to come. Remembering the past, glorifying God in the present, shaping the future as we are shaped by the Holy Spirit for it, we are marked with the gift of joy.

This is not a rational construal, a logical outline defining our terms, but an experiential awareness that leads to patterns of attending to our participation in the paschal mystery. That participation is itself a feast in which the food we eat is incorporated into the Body of Christ, whose body we are. Finally, the purpose of this sacramental living does not have to do with developing some personal spirituality but rather to be the "sacrament" that is, the epiphany of the new creation.[47]

Through participating in the paschal mystery in liturgical feasts, we receive power to fulfill our cosmic and eschatological vocation to "become what we are, the sacrament in Christ of the new creation: the sacrament in Christ of the Kingdom." Participation in the mystery of this new life in the Holy Spirit makes the world of the Kingdom that is to come present in this world.[48] Sacramental living as a participation in the paschal mystery witnesses to joy given to the Church for the life of the world.

47. Schmemann, *Liturgy and Tradition*, 57.

48. Schmemann, *Liturgy and Tradition*, 56–57.

Time and Eschatology, the Week and Shabbat

The Differentiated Unity of Schmemann's Ordo
and the Jewish Sabbath

Kimberly Belcher

"All philosophy, all religion is ultimately an attempt to solve the 'problem of time,'" wrote Alexander Schmemann in "The Time of Mission," the third chapter of *For the Life of the World*, in 1963.[1] It is no accident that in this seminal work, Schmemann places time second only to the Eucharist in his outline of Christian liturgical theology, only then to continue with theologies of the other sacramental rites. For if the 1960s, for Schmemann, constituted a time of crisis for Christian theology, that was uniquely evident in its crisis of time.[2]

Schmemann's treatment of time sometimes seems frighteningly prescient:

> One of the main purposes of progress was to reduce occupation, to "liberate time" for an activity more worthy of man. But the very opposite took place: never, even in the darkest ages, did occupation have such a crushing, hopeless, all-embracing character as in our days of the flowering of technology and of all kinds of "conveniences." . . . There is no time . . . there is only work, when everything is confused, lost in boredom, absurdity,

---

1. Schmemann, *For the Life of the World*, 47.

2. Morrill, *Anamnesis as Dangerous Memory*, 78–83. My reading of Schmemann is much indebted to this and other works by Morrill.

monotony, and there is "relaxation," the physical vent-hole, necessary to the organism, in order to be able to continue its work.[3]

Yet if Schmemann's "devastation of time"[4] has since been exacerbated by cell
phones, social media, telecommuting, and the expansion of the precariat,[5]
the form of secularization that impinges on that time has changed. In "Worship in a Secular Age" (1972), Schmemann defined secularism as "above
all, a *negation of worship.*"[6] He did not mean primarily that worship was
unpopular, that people were prioritizing secular pursuits above worship
commitments, or even that worship was confined to private spaces outside
the purview of the state. Rather, he had to bear in mind the Soviet state's
eradication of Christian time (particularly Sunday liturgy and the liturgical
calendar) by coercive propaganda and physical force.

The "deep divorce" between the Christian worldview and contemporary
culture and society formed, for Schmemann, "a self-evident assumption" that
unified contemporary theology.[7] In 1963, 1972, and even at the time of his
death, in 1983, the logical end point of that divorce was exemplified by the
USSR. The upheaval of the Soviet satellite states in 1989, as well as succeeding
events, has altered the pressures exerted on liturgical time.

Increasingly, it is the internalized pressures of late modern life, rather
than external force, that prevent human and social bodies from experiencing the ecclesiological and eschatological revelations of liturgical time. For
Schmemann, the cyclical aspect of "natural"—that is, unredeemed—time
suggests cosmic completeness and joy, while the linear aspect, tending as
it does towards one's own death, provokes anxiety about the meaningless-
ness of life.[8] Today, as the "work-week" spills outward into domestic and
festal space and time, with "relaxation" instead of leisure filling in smaller
and smaller interstices in Western working people's experience, the cosmic
completion of cyclical time, too, may be losing ground.

In his context, against the horizon of a state-sanctioned erasure of liturgical time, Schmemann envisioned the ordo of the liturgy and the task
of liturgical theology as the articulation of an intrinsic and essential connection between the Eucharist and "the liturgy of time."[9] This connection
is first of all a contrast: "The Eucharist is the actualization of one, single,

3. Schmemann, "Divine Worship and Time," 99.

4. Schmemann, "Divine Worship and Time," 99.

5. See Standing, *Precariat.*

6. Schmemann, *For the Life of the World*, 118.

7. Schmemann, *Liturgy and Tradition*, 90.

8. See Kaethler, "Eucharistic Anthropology," 61–62.

9. Schmemann, *Introduction*, 43.

unrepeatable event, and the essence of the Sacrament consists first of all in the possibility of the conquest of time. . . . No matter when the Liturgy is celebrated . . . it is essentially independent of the day or hour."[10] If the Eucharist is timeless, the non-sacramental liturgies of the ordo are time-full: "Here, time is not only the external and natural framework but in a sense also the very object of worship, the principle defining its content."[11]

These two liturgical structures, the timeless and the time-keeping, or the sacramental and the non-sacramental, are the *ordo*. This meant, for Schmemann, both that they are equally fundamental to liturgical experience and that they are equally ancient.[12] In other words, they combine to form a layer of liturgy that is continuous, despite the number of historical alterations in the form of each: they are the unchanged and unchangeable structure of the liturgy. They do not transmit a "message about" Christian doctrine but rather give cosmic time an incarnational shape.[13]

To say that the Christian pattern of cosmic time is incarnational is to point towards its eschatology: in the incarnation, the eschaton has come into the mundane. Better, "eschaton" delineates a space when the eternal will have come into fruition in the world that keeps time. The incarnation is the first fruits and the revelation of that coming reality; the Eucharist, taking its place in the pattern of structured Christian time, participates in the eschaton within history.

The relationship between the Eucharist and the liturgy of time, then, demonstrates the proper relationship between the church and the world:

> Just as the Church, though "not of this world," is present in this world for its salvation, so also the Sacrament of the Lord's Day, the Sacrament of the new aeon is joined with time in order that time itself might become the time of the church, the time of salvation. It is precisely this fulfillment of time by the "Eschaton," by that which overcomes time and is above it and bears witness to its finitude and limitedness, which constitutes the sanctification of time.[14]

The Eucharist is not set apart from mundane time, rendering it holy; rather, it occupies its proper place in that time, making all time holy. The firm location of the Eucharist on Sunday marks "the transformation of time, not of

---

10. Schmemann, *Introduction*, 43.
11. Schmemann, *Introduction*, 43.
12. Schmemann, *Introduction*, 89.
13. Morrill, *Anamnesis as Dangerous Memory*, 87–88.
14. Schmemann, *Introduction*, 80.

calendar."[15] Sunday was *"one of the days . . .* the first of the week, fully belong-
ing to this world,"[16] and yet, "through the eucharistic ascension," revealed
"the Day of the Lord . . . in all its glory and transforming power as the *end* of
this world, as the *beginning* of the world to come."[17] This paradox demanded
that the Lord's Day be distinct from the Sabbath; at the same time, Christian
eschatology demands that Sunday be experienced not as a holy day set apart
but as a day both set apart and wholly ordinary.[18]

In *The Eucharist,* Schmemann describes the eschatological significance of new, Christian time as being both *"remembrance and
expectation."*[19] In the later, posthumous essay, "Liturgy and Eschatology,"
he describes the experience instead as a tension between *promise* and *possession:* "The Kingdom is not only something promised, it is something
of which we can taste here and now. And so in all our preaching we are
bearing witness, *martyria,* not simply to our faith but to our possession
of that in which we believe."[20] This is an important distinction: whereas
both remembrance and expectation can, in principle, take place in merely
cognitive assent, the possession of the Christian faith is something that
describes a state of being, not a state of mind. Moreover, it is appropriately
beyond human work and potentially even beyond human knowledge. One
can possess—or better, be possessed by—what one desires without being
aware of it. Indeed, desiring holiness is a consequence of being possessed
by it, though not fully possessed, not yet.

Christian time, then, is not an escape from the everyday, but a transformation of the ordinary: *"By itself,* time is nothing but a line of telegraph
poles strung out into the distance and at some point, along the way, is our
death,"[21] and yet, within "the experience of the Church, as the New Aeon
and an anticipation of the Kingdom of the age to come . . . time [becomes]
a history within which this Kingdom must grow and 'be fulfilled' in the
faith and practice of men."[22] Christian time is the proleptic possession of the
Christian eschaton (that is, Christ), not a matter of knowledge of what is to
come but a matter of experience that arouses ever-greater desire. It is liturgy,

15. Schmemann, *Eucharist,* 51.

16. Schmemann, *Eucharist,* 51.

17. Schmemann, *Eucharist,* 51–52.

18. See Morrill, *Anamnesis as Dangerous Memory,* 103.

19. Schmemann, *Eucharist,* 52.

20. Schmemann, *Liturgy and Tradition,* 94.

21. Schmemann, *For the Life of the World,* 47. Emphasis added.

22. Schmemann, *Introduction,* 88.

wherein the church receives its very identity, experientially, from God in Christ, that transforms time.

The relationship of the church to the world is communicated to worshippers through the experience of time that is inseparable from the *ordo*: "we live in a kind of rhythm—leaving, abandoning, denying the world, and yet, at the same time, always returning to it; living in time by that which is beyond time; living by that *which is not yet come, but which we already know and possess*."[23] This eschatological vision transforms time: on the one hand, desire points to the frailty and brokenness of creation, including time; on the other, possession speaks to the origin of creation and its redemption outside of human beings.

Time, the holy, and the jewishness of the ordo

It was through the eschatological character of the *ordo* that Schmemann was able to discern the dependence of the Christian on the Jewish liturgy of time. His critique of "mysteriological" liturgical theology and piety (from which he partially exculpates Odo Casel[24]) is motivated less by the historical evidence in favor of early public liturgies of time than by a different understanding of "the holy." Against the *mysterium tremendum et fascinans*, Schmemann sets the *sobor*, which situates the difference between the holy and the world within a greater unity.

Schmemann's understanding of holiness and *sobor* is most clearly expressed in his treatment of liturgical space. "In its best Byzantine or Russian incarnation, the temple is experienced and perceived as *sobor*, as the gathering together of heaven and earth and all creation in Christ—which constitutes the essence and purpose of the church."[25] It is a misapprehension of the nature of liturgical space in contemporary Orthodox liturgical piety that suggests that the sanctuary, beyond the iconostasis, is "a particularly 'holy' place with its own brand of 'sanctity,' as if to emphasize the 'profane' category to which the laity standing outside it belong."[26]

The temptation of the strict delineation between sacred and profane is an ongoing oversimplification of Christian truth. Whereas in human religion, both space and time are used to construct the interrelationship between the holy and the mundane, perhaps sacred time is more significant for the Christian ritual experience of the holy than sacred space.

23. Schmemann, *Liturgy and Tradition*, 95. Emphasis added.
24. Schmemann, *Introduction*, 82.
25. Schmemann, *Eucharist*, 19.
26. Schmemann, *Eucharist*, 20.

Schmemann's concern about Orthodox sanctuary piety, for example, is parallel to his insistence that Sunday ("Resurrection" in Russian[27]) is not the Sabbath day of rest but rather the first day of the week, the first day of the new creation. Both concern the character of the holy, which, in Christianity, does not spring from "the dichotomy of the sacred and the profane, but the 'sacramental' potentiality of creation in its totality, as well as in each of its elements. Yet anyone who is acquainted with our liturgical piety . . . knows equally well that it is the first meaning which triumphs here to the virtual exclusion of the second one."[28]

As Schmemann points out in "Worship in a Secular Age," liturgical piety that fiercely divides the sacred from the mundane (focusing, as he puts it, on "sacrality" instead of "sacramentality") contributes to secularity, even as it apparently reacts against it: "For it leaves the world profane, i.e., precisely *secular*, in the deepest sense of this term."[29] For the *saecula* to be leavened by the *saecula saeculorum*, there must be an underlying unity—that of creation fallen and waiting for redemption—that mitigates and resolves the distinction of liturgical practice. As Schmemann sees it, the holiness of "the religions" is a matter of difference; for Christians, holiness is an experience of differentiated unity.[30]

"Differentiated unity" is sure to raise the specter of the Trinity, yet Schmemann rightly instead emphasizes the Christian liturgy as dependent on the Jewish construction of time. The threat of secularism, as Schmemann experienced it in the mid-twentieth century, together with the gradual, post-war repudiation of anti-Semitism, exposed the continuity between Jewish and Christian liturgical time and eschatology. In defense of his position (*contra* Gregory Dix) that the basic liturgy of Christian time was an element of primitive Christian practice, Schmemann turned to its origin in Jewish liturgical time.

"Christianity was for [the earliest Christians]—as 'Hebrews after the flesh'—not a new religion to which they were converted through a rejection of the old (as pagans were converted later on) but the fulfilment and ultimate perfection of the one true religion, of that one sacred history of

27. Schmemann, *Celebration of Faith*, 2:25.

28. Schmemann, *For the Life of the World*, 132. In this particular paragraph, Schmemann is discussing liturgical piety with regard to Epiphany and holy water.

29. Schmemann, *For the Life of the World*, 132

30. I wonder whether this reading of "the religions" relies on the most unsubtle piety within the world religions, much like the types of Orthodox piety Schmemann is critiquing in "Worship in a Secular Age"; however, the question of the diversity of understandings of the holy outside Jewish and Christian thought is beyond the scope of this essay.

the Covenant between God and His people."³¹ The history of the covenant, first of all, altered the linear experience of time. In a covenant cosmology, time cannot be merely telegraph poles marking the way to death; it becomes a gap—but also a bridge—between the historical performance of the covenant agreement and the contemporary community of the covenant. Hence, the ritual performance of memory becomes a concern—not ritual practice as an entry into mythological time but rather into an event of the past that both becomes present and reinterprets the present.

Memory and the commemorative performance of covenant history, however, is not the dominant concern in Schmemann's treatment of the Jewish origin of Christian time; rather, it is the eschatological participation in the promised and possessed future that is primary. Participation in the covenant event is oriented towards that future. It is the future that universalizes the covenant, making it coextensive in some way with creation, which allows the human community today to participate in the covenant of the past.

Time, eschatology, and contemporary Jewish liturgical theology

Schmemann discovers the eschatological ramifications of the ordo through analysis of the historical connection of early Christian and early rabbinic Jewish worship. It is informative (and beginning to seem necessary) to turn to contemporary Jewish worship to discover elements of the worldview that informed the earliest development of Christianity that have been lost over time through historical accident, prejudice, or misunderstanding. As a Roman Catholic scholar, then, I want to delve briefly into some contemporary studies of Jewish liturgical time and eschatology before returning to the problem of Schmemann's ordo and the new generation with its new secularity. I make no claim to be exhaustive, but even a brief survey can be suggestive and corrective.

Emma O'Donnell discovers this in her ethnographic study of contemporary Jewish and Catholic-monastic experiences of time. Citing Franz Rosenzweig, for example, she argues that "prayer is capable of entering into the domain of the future. . . . '[Prayer] must hasten the future, must turn eternity into the nighest, the Today.'"³² One of O'Donnell's subjects, a Jewish woman named Hannah in the text, encapsulates the duality of memory and anticipation: "There's a sense of justification of the hope [for the future] be-

31. Schmemann, *Introduction*, 59–60.

32. O'Donnell, *Remembering the Future*, 118. Quotation from Rosenzweig, *Star of Redemption*, 289.

cause of the past. . . . I remember God's salvation in the past because it gives me hope that God will save me in the future."[33] In other words, these two condition one another: hope occurs because of one's participation in the communal memory (notably through liturgical practice), but at the same time, the communal memory is cultivated out of hope for the future.

Shabbat is the origin Hannah identifies for her anticipatory liturgical spirituality, particularly the *birkat ha-Mazon* or blessing after the Shabbat meal.[34] Certainly, the Shabbat liturgies, both of the synagogue and the home, are deeply eschatological. Consider, for example, the *L'khah Dodi* hymn that personifies the Sabbath, greeting it and looking towards the future. Lawrence Hoffman calls it "probably the best-loved composition in all of Jewish liturgy,"[35] with its repeated refrain (addressed to the people of Israel), "Go forth my love to meet the bride / Shabbat's reception has arrived!"[36] This exultant greeting, while expressing, at one level, the marriage of Israel and the Shabbat, also points toward a meeting "on a grander scale with *Binah* (known as *Shabbat Hagadol*, the Great Sabbath) in the world to come. Hence, Shabbat is a foretaste of the world to come, *Shabbat Hagadol*."[37]

Like Schmemann with "the Eucharist on the Lord's Day," O'Donnell points to the primacy of the Sabbath in Jewish liturgical time:

> As both a memorial of the past and an anticipation of the world to come, the celebration of Shabbat practices the "eschatological memory" . . . historical time is situated within a celebration of cyclical time, on the seventh day of each week. The cyclical holiday of Shabbat thus connects historical time to cyclical time, celebrating primordial history within a weekly cycle.[38]

For Orthodoxy, Judaism, and my own tradition of Roman Catholic worship, there is a constructive tension between the annual cycle, in which events are commemorated in their historical and thematic specificity, and the weekly cycle, in which the whole of covenant history is celebrated in its aggregate wholeness. It is against the annual cycle that the weekly cycle can be

33. O'Donnell, *Remembering the Future*, 54.

34. O'Donnell, *Remembering the Future*, 55.

35. Hoffman, *My People's Prayer Book*, 8:119. On the same page, translator Joel Hoffman also offers his tribute to "the almost unbelievable beauty of *L'khah Dodi*, in my mind the most perfect poem of our liturgy."

36. Hoffman, *My People's Prayer Book*, 8:115.

37. There are several other levels of symbolic signification in the text as well, which I leave out of the discussion here for the sake of comprehension. See Kimenman, "Kabbalah," 8:129.

38. O'Donnell, *Remembering the Future*, 99.

experienced as completion; in fact, it is likely that Schmemann's experience of cyclical time as satisfying and complete is influenced by this liturgical experience. It is whole for him because it is holy.

For Schmemann, the unequivocal distinction of "the holy" from "the profane" was deeply problematic. Rather, the *sobor*, where heaven and earth gathered together, expressed the true Christian cosmology. I hazard that the setting aside of sacred *times*, particularly times of differing degrees of holiness—even on independent and therefore competing calendars—is an especially powerful way to express and mitigate the human need for ritual distinctions. It allows for a time designated to encounter the holy, accommodating the needs of human limitations without limiting the Holy One to a set time or space.

Again, a comparison with Jewish liturgical theology is illuminating. In *Beyond the Text*, Hoffman holds similar concerns about the pervasive and invisible influence of "the numinous" on Reform Judaism that Schmemann feels about mysteriological piety in Orthodoxy. Like Schmemann, he is arguing for a broader methodological study of liturgical texts and practices, attentive to their cultural context and "inner logic"—not only doing liturgical theology but "liturgical anthropology," or, more to the point, anthropology in the service of historically-informed liturgical theology. In other words, Hoffman's approach to the Jewish liturgy is an extension of method, community, and time, which can shed additional light on the eschatology of Christian time.[39]

In the second chapter of *Beyond the Text*, Hoffman attends to the ritual of *havdalah* ("separation") that puts an end to the Sabbath time. Like Schmemann, he is not only interested in the origins of a practice but also in its underlying logic, which often governs its historical development.[40] For *havdalah*, Hoffman finds its anthropological structure and its purpose as central to understanding its liturgical theology. "*Havdalah* is the ritualized reminder of the Jewish system of categorization" which "is recited at precisely that time when the oppositions it contains are in danger of confusion."[41]

Hoffman observes that in the historical origin of the *havdalah*, as also in the contemporary secular environment, the Biblical Jewish worldview, which divides the world into holy and profane, competes with an alternate set of categories. The moment at which it is performed, at the close of the Sabbath, when holy time is passing away and ordinary time is returning, is a

---

39. Hoffman, *Beyond the Text*.

40. Unlike Schmemann, for Hoffman it is also possible, in principle, for historical liturgical development to be capricious and arbitrary. Hoffman, *Beyond the Text*, 41–42.

41. Hoffman, *Beyond the Text*, 39, 42.

time that threatens distinctions central to the identity of the Jewish people: "When the holy people left its holy time to mix with non-holy peoples in non-holy days, they reminded themselves of the essential dichotomy that underlies the Jewish experience of reality. And, since that time fell also at the moment when day became night, the secondary distinction, that of light and darkness, was included."[42]

If the *havdalah* acts as an inscription of characteristic difference, however, there are certain elements of Hoffman's analysis that also suggest a tension between *inscribing* the difference and *challenging* it. One is the use of the *berekah* form, one is the ritual recognition of *differing* degrees of holy time, and one is the addition of Elijah.

To take Elijah first, Hoffman notes that the *havdalah* reinscribes the characteristic distinction of Judaism and the supplementary distinction between light and darkness, when the categories were indistinct. It is recited at sunset, when light and darkness are mixed, and at the end of the holy time, when the holy time and the holy people are passing into ordinary time and mixing with the other nations. This, he argues, provokes an anxiety about the categories, a sense of danger which, in turn, promotes the assimilation of the Elijah piety of medieval Judaism and the magical or quasi-magical ritual additions, as well as the requests for "good luck."[43] Elijah, as a holy wild man, tends to be associated with liminal periods, as in this case of liminality between light and dark, between the holy and the profane. Although Elijah's presence is a response to the threat of category mixing, he is also a proof of the joy of liminality. "He is almost not of this world, having no fixed abode, no friends, no predictability; when he dies, he flies up to heaven in a flaming chariot."[44] Elijah is not a stable reinscriber of boundaries but embodies *communitas*, "the polar opposite of social structure . . . *havdalah* time, the ideal occasion to expect Elijah, who comes in disguise, berates the mighty, moves freely back and forth from heaven to earth and even the Garden of Eden, where, we will recall, he sits under the Tree of Life recording Israel's good deeds."[45]

There is an oddity here: the Sabbath is the holy time, but it is the end of the Sabbath, when the holy comes crashing back into the ordinary, when the eschatological figure appears. Whereas the *L'khah Dodi* makes the Sabbath itself an eschatological figure, the *havdalah* shows that the

42. Hoffman, *Beyond the Text*, 41.
43. Hoffman, *Beyond the Text*, 42–45.
44. Hoffman, *Beyond the Text*, 44.
45. Hoffman, *Beyond the Text*, 45.

coming of ordinary time, too, is not only dangerous but also pregnant with divine potential.

Besides Elijah, there are other elements of the *havdalah* that suggest that the ritual categories are more than dichotomous. Hoffman points out that the synagogue *havdalah* text is different when the Sabbath is followed by a holy day. In such a case, the text reads, in part:

> You have bequeathed to us times of joy, holy festivals, and feasts for free will offerings. You have granted us the holiness of the Sabbath, the glory of the festival, and the festive offering due on the pilgrimage festival. Lord our God, You have divided holy from profane, light from darkness, Israel from [other] peoples, the seventh day from the six days of work. *You have distinguished between the holiness of the Sabbath and the holiness of a holy day.*[46]

The complexity of the festal calendar, which stems from the independence of the weekly cycle from the annual and monthly cycles, serves as a ritual reiteration that the distinction between the holy and the profane, while blessed, is not absolute. Rather, there are different degrees of holy time, and the transition from one to another, like the transition from sacred to profane time, provides an opportunity to recognize the cosmological paradigm.

The third characteristic I want to examine has the earliest origin, since it precedes Rabbi Jochanan's third-century rehearsal of the four traditional prayer categories (blessings, prayers, sanctifications, and separations). It is the influence of *berekah* form ("Blessed are You") on the other types of prayer discussed by Rabbi Jochanan. In the contemporary home *havdalah* that Hoffman studies in *Beyond the Text*, this influence results in the following sequence of prayers:

> Blessed are You, Adonai our God, ruler of the world, creator of the fruit of the vine.
>
> Blessed are You, Adonai our God, ruler of the world, creator of varied spices.
>
> Blessed are You, Adonai our God, ruler of the world, creator of the lights of fire.
>
> Blessed are You, Adonai our God, ruler of the world, who distinguishes between the holy and ordinary, between light and dark, between Israel and the nations, between the seventh day and the six days of work.

46. Hoffman, *Beyond the Text*, 23.

Blessed are You, Adonai our God, ruler of the world, who distinguishes between holy and ordinary.[47]

This sequence of prayers creates a literary tension—one that, I would argue, is both constructive and necessary—between the God-given distinctions and categories enshrined in liturgical life and the universal kingship of the creator of all. By associating the division of holy and ordinary with God's lordship over the fruit of the vine, over spices, and over fire (this last literary tension is augmented by the ritual fact that fires cannot be lighted during the holy time of Sabbaths or certain holy days), the contemporary *havdalah* both authorizes the distinction between holy and profane *and* recognizes that both the holy things and the profane things are the subjects of God, who is ultimate.[48]

This tension between the differentiation of the holy and the profane (a distinction given by God) and God's rulership of all is also echoed in the *L'khah Dodi*. Kimelman suggests that in the *L'khah Dodi*, the profane (Friday, before sunset, that is, before the Sabbath begins) is reinterpreted as "the unredeemed or not-yet-redeemed" which is brought together with the holy in marriage "under the canopy of the holy. [*L'khah Dodi*'s] redemptive vision is both utopian (looking toward the end of time) and restorative (recapitulating the perfection of Eden)."[49] So both at the beginning and at the end of Shabbat, the unity-in-distinction, or differentiated unity, is ritualized; these two points ritualize the complex truth that God has distinguished the holy from the profane but is ruler of all and will gather all together.

Schmemann, the Christian future, and liturgy in the present

The Jewish Sabbath liturgy, then, also enshrines the differentiated unity characteristic of Schmemann's ordo. The Christian pattern adopts the schema that treats the seventh day as a recapitulation of the created order but rehearses it differently. It is important to Schmemann that it is on the *eighth* day that Christians celebrate the Day of the Lord, which is an ordinary day of work but also a timeless foretaste of the eschatological future. As a result, the theological meaning—and, more importantly, I would argue, the ritual experience of Sabbath—has been diminished. There is a temptation for many of us to relegate the Eucharist to a strictly otherworldly experience, rather than *sobor*.

47. English translation from Hoffman, *My People's Prayer Book*.
48. Pilz, "Earth Is the Eternal's and the Fullness Thereof," 18–20.
49. Kimenman, "Kabbalah," 8:128.

Schmemann recognized the fact that the early Christian liturgy of time was not merely based on liturgical forms haphazardly, say, because they were the only models early Jewish Christians had available. Rather, from the first, Christian liturgy preserved Passover, Pentecost, and the Sabbath cycle "because she preserved that theology of time of which they were the expression."[50] What I have tried to add here is that it is often the nuances of liturgical practice that communicate subtle but essential matters such as the difference (but not dichotomy!) of the sacred and profane. The transitions in and out of holy time and space matter a great deal. Contradictions and competitions between different calendars can be a help as well as a hindrance. Black and white thinking needs to be confronted with the liturgical experience, over time, of a wide variety of participants.

These challenging experiences should come, must come, even from those whose experience of time and worship is outside of Christian idioms. Kimelman's treatment of the L'khah Dodi can provide an inspiring example. Commenting on stanza 16, "Spread out to the left and the right / Proclaiming the Holy One's might," he says, "As Israel brings about redemption . . . it spreads out to the left and right sides . . . encompassing the rest of the universe."[51] Like the Shabbat itself, this spatial metaphor is translated into a temporal ritualization: "Appropriately, the Sabbaths of Islam (Friday) and of Christianity (Sunday) are the first days to the right and to the left of the Sabbath of creation. In sum, the spatial sanctity of Eretz Yisrael will expand throughout the world; the temporary sanctity of Shabbat will radiate through the week."

Perhaps the largest question left is in what our eschatology really consists, and how far the unity of differences can carry us. By what are we possessed, and what, therefore, do we desire? At the beginning, I alluded to a change in the experience of secularism, a shift in the pressures that erase the experience of Christian (or, I may now expand, liturgical) time. The cultural backdrop,[52] the dominant cultural experience of time, has shifted. The secularism of our day is not the dominance of a desacralized competing calendar but the attempt to have the biological, psychological, and financial needs of an individual compete and determine the necessary cycles of work and rest. The end result of this system is not merely ritual impoverishment, it is the human diminishment of those who cannot afford the *havdalah* of holy and profane time. My work pays well enough that I can afford the leisure to pray, not only weekly, on Sunday, but even morning and evening. My

---

50 Schmemann, *Introduction*, 87.

51. Hoffman, *My People's Prayer Book*, 8:132.

52. For a discussion of this term, see Hoffman, *Beyond the Text*, 149–71.

neighbor's work pays so poorly that she spends Sunday looking for a third job—to make ends meet—while she cares for her mother-in-law, who has fallen sick, and her two children. For those of us who are Americans, what does it mean to preach a religious freedom that only extends to the leisure class? More broadly, how long will Christians tolerate a world in which the ordo is a privilege afforded only to those who are so full of relaxation that they are sometimes openly bored with the rest and restoration it reveals? Or can Shabbat show us hope for a Sabbath in which widows, orphans, the enslaved, and the powerless, too, experience real *communitas*? It is then, I think, that the vision of liturgical time, and thus of the Eucharist on the Lord's Day, will be compelling to my secular neighbors.

PART 4

Schmemann and Sacramental Theology

The Liturgical Is Political.

Bruce T. Morrill, S.J.

Introduction

THE LITURGICAL IS POLITICAL. This thesis statement is meant to be both
comprehensive and bold—characteristics whereby I hope to imitate (and
thereby honor) the work and person of Father Alexander Schmemann.
The thesis seeks to provoke or, for those readers who might find the assertion obvious, to generate critical inquiry into a topic—namely, the
relationship between sacraments and ethics, faith and (social) action,
mysticism and politics, liturgy and life—that has remained current from
the origins of the Liturgical Movement to the present. As a major contributor to that history of theological-pastoral reform and renewal, Fr.
Schmemann published a tight little corpus of writings that would lead
me to imagine him quickly taking issue with my succinct thesis. A couple
of trenchant statements among his most widely read textbooks can open
into a bit broader interrogation of his publications—especially his posthumously published journals—so as to advance the question from the
perspective of political theology.

Eruptions of the Political in Schmemann's Liturgical Theology

The question driving Schmemann's pastoral-theological vocation was articulated in his earliest book on sacraments and Orthodoxy, published in
1963, which he then slightly revised and expanded with two appendices in
1973, to produce a text that continues to attain a wide readership. The book
has for its very title his thesis that what the church exists for, what its "work"

(the Greek noun *ergo/ergon*, verb *leitourgo*) is for, is *For the Life of the World*. Throughout the text, Schmemann labors to demonstrate how the Christian faith, grounded in the paradoxically joy-instilling glory of the Cross, is for neither an escapist, gnostic mysticism to be practiced in this present life nor an individualistic eschatology, pining and preparing for each person's heavenly reward in the next:

> "Through the Cross joy came *into the whole world*"—and not just to some men as their personal and private joy. Once more, were Christianity pure "mysticism," pure "eschatology," there would be no need for feasts and celebrations. A holy soul would keep its secret feast apart from the world, to the extent that it could free itself from its time. But joy was given to the Church *for the world*—that the Church might be a witness to it and transform the world by joy. Such is the "function" of Christian feasts.[1]

That Schmemann puts the word "function" in scare quotes indicates that he likewise has little patience for those who see "activism" and "relevance" as the solution to the church's faltering viability in North Atlantic societies due, in no small part, to the purposelessness of its arcane liturgy. Those sorts of Christians in this late-modern time are getting it quite wrong in terms of how that life of service is to be empowered and pursued:

> Christianity begins to fall down as soon as the idea of our going up in Christ's ascension—the movement of sacrifice—begins to be replaced by His going down. And this is exactly where we are today; it is always a bringing Him down into ordinary life, and this we say will solve our social problems. The Church must go down to the ghettos, into the world in all its reality. But to save the world from social injustices, the need first of all is not so much to go down to its miseries, as to have a few witnesses in this world to the possible ascension.[2]

As I argued in my fuller analysis of Schmemann's thought two decades ago, a careful reading of this assertion discerns that he is not necessarily dismissing work for social justice as part of the church's mission; rather, he is subordinating that work to practice of the liturgy. Such an interpretation enables Schmemann's writings to contribute to the description and analysis of what political theologians generally call the mystical element of the Christian praxis of faith.[3]

---

1. Schmemann, *For the Life of the World*, 55.
2. Schmemann, *Liturgy and Tradition*, 135.
3. See Morrill, *Anamnesis as Dangerous Memory*, 124–25.

By the end of his life, however, Schmemann's rhetoric became more incendiary or, at best, hyperbolic. A passage at the very center of the preface to *The Eucharist*—his last, posthumously published book—arguably amounts to the apotheosis of Schmemann's effort to articulate the "crisis" he perceived in the liturgy and, thus, in the church:

> Meanwhile, it can be said without exaggeration that we live in a frightening and spiritually dangerous age. It is frightening not just because of its hatred, division, and bloodshed. It is frightening above all because it is characterized by a mounting rebellion against God and his kingdom. Not God, but man has become the measure of all things. Not faith, but ideology and utopian escapism are determining the spiritual state of the world. At a certain point, western Christianity accepted this point of view: almost at once, one or another "theology of liberation" was born. Issues relating to economics, politics, and psychology have replaced a Christian vision of the world at the service of God. Theologians, clergy, and other professional "religious" run busily around the world defending—from God?—this or that "right," however perverse, and all this in the name of peace, unity, and brotherhood. Yet in fact, the peace, unity, and brotherhood that they invoke are not the peace, unity, and brotherhood that has been brought to us by our Lord Jesus Christ.[4]

From a scholarly, theological point of view, Schmemann's gross generalization—indicting theologians, pastors, and professed (professional?) religious of malpractice and possible infidelity to God—is indefensible. His signed date to the preface is November 1983, by which time more than a decade's worth of nuanced, sophisticated North Atlantic political theology and South American liberation theology had reached publication in English. Study of even just a small sample of that literature would find both Roman Catholics and Protestants valorizing the irreducible role of prayer, Scripture, and liturgy in what Christianity has to offer critically in the struggles for humanity and the planet.[5]

Attention to scholarly texts, however, was not essential to Schmemann's methodology in his last book, as he himself explains in the opening sentences of the preface: "This book is neither a manual of liturgics nor a scholarly investigation. . . . Rather, this book represents a series of reflections on the eucharist. These reflections, however, do not come from

---

4. Schmemann, *Eucharist*, 9–10.

5. See, among others, Gutiérrez, *Theology of Liberation*, 143–61; Segundo, *Sacraments Today*, 53–67; and Soelle, *Suffering*, 75–78, 166–68.

scientific analysis but from my experience, limited though it may be."[6] He wrote that preface within a month of his death, at age 62, weakened by terminal cancer. Physical frailty, nonetheless, had not affected the content of the dozen thematic chapters; rather, as he recounts in that opening paragraph, he drafted them over several years "during rare moments of leisure, in the midst of many interruptions." That note is crucial for assessing fairly and engaging profitably not only this but all of Schmemann's writings. What Schmemann understatedly reports as "many interruptions" entailed a busy life of administrative, teaching, and pastoral duties at St. Vladimir's Seminary in Yonkers, treks to Manhattan to record a weekly sermon with Radio Free Europe for dissemination behind the Iron Curtain, plus frequent travel for speaking engagements in North America and abroad. Schmemann's professional theological vocation, therefore, primarily took the forms of teaching and service rather than academic-research scholarship. This assessment should by no means be taken as demeaning either his intellectual aptitude or his theological-traditional knowledge[7]; rather, it is a matter of identifying accurately how he utilized his time and energy, making him the particular sort of priest-professor that he was. I am arguing that out of that profession, the method of his theological writing took its form, with both its strengths and its weaknesses.

In his theological writing, Schmemann practiced what he professed. His fundamental argument about second-order theology (including liturgical theology) was that theology had to be done by those who actually participate in and reflect upon the church's liturgy (primary theology). It is through the celebration of the liturgy that the content for (and spirit of) academic and pastoral theology is revealed. Participation in the sacraments and other rites of the church thereby constitute "the ontological condition of theology."[8] The theologian—any theologian—must be immersed in the life of the church, for which the liturgy is the sacrament (the ritual-symbolic manifestation[9]) of the church's very mission in the world, witnessing to the hidden, yet ever-coming reign of God. That being the case for Schmemann, narrative is then arguably an implicit category of his theological method: the experience of that participation can only exist in one's memory by

6. Schmemann, *Eucharist*, 9.

7. As a young scholar, Schmemann excelled through his seminary and graduate education in Paris, benefiting from the formidable professors at St. Sergius (especially Afanassieff, as well as Bulgakov, Kern, and Florensky) as well as his Catholic professors Daniélou and Boyer. See Meyendorff, "Life Worth Living," 4–6.

8. Schmemann, "Theology and Liturgical Tradition," 18. See also, in the same volume, Schmemann, *Liturgy and Tradition*, 43–44.

9. See, Schmemann, "Sacrament and Symbol," 135–51.

means of (an internal, if you will[10]) narrative. Schmemann's argument is that ecclesially responsible theology is born of practice, which Schmemann consistently calls "experience."[11] That laudable assertion, however, requires a further methodological recognition: practice only becomes experience through narrative. There is, thus, what I would call a narrative dimension to all of Schmemann's writings. That characteristic of his method affords a further meeting point with political theology, a correlation that promises critical enhancement of, and even some correction to, what Schmemann sought to accomplish in his theological corpus.

Narrative's Constitutive Role in Theology, Liturgical and Political

Those well acquainted with Schmemann's monographs and collected essays on liturgical theology might, in considering my argument for the essential role of narrative therein, call to mind his occasional pithy (at times, biting) short accounts of liturgical malpractice. Innovative chapel services (and, in one case, a moratorium on chapel entirely) at Protestant seminaries particularly exorcized him.[12] He expressed disbelief at how the reform and renewal Vatican II intended was subverted by freewheeling local innovations in the liturgy, drawing the quest for the church's service to the modern world into the practice of the rites themselves.[13] Still, broader allusions to the pious customs and understandings among the Orthodox faithful—so driven by self-gratifying, subjective, spiritual-escapist, "religious" or "churchly" feelings[14]—comprised a steady backstory for what he was *arguing against*. These characterizations, however, would seem best (most generously) read as setting the stage for what he was in each instance *arguing for*. Schmemann's

10. Schmemann consistently writes of an "inner" knowledge or "from within." For just one example, see Schmemann, *Eucharist*, 144.

11. See, among many others, Schmemann, *Eucharist*, 133, 149. In my argument, I am taking a more positive and constitutive role for narrative than Schmemann, for whom "words" refers to (abstract) theories external to (liturgical) experience. I would press him on this, calling for a more sophisticated theory of experience.

12. See Schmemann, *Liturgy and Tradition*, 94; *For the Life of the World*, 125–26.

13. Schmemann pointedly characterized the church's concern for social justice (which term he put in scare quotes) as "hasty" and unprincipled. See *Liturgy and Tradition*, 46. Mocking the fundamental concept on which Pope John XXIII convoked the Second Vatican Council, Schmemann referred to those seeking reform in dialogue with modern society "the *aggiornamento* generation." See Schmemann, "Liturgical Theology," 139.

14. Schmemann, *Eucharist*, 144–46, 23–24, 30–31, 182. See also, among others, Schmemann, *For the Life of the World*, 48–49, 53, 82, 97–99, 108–9, 130–33, 150; *Liturgy and Tradition*, 92, 100; and "Liturgy and Theology," 57, 65.

primary narrative-theological sources lay not in the negative evidence of relevance-striving, social-justice-themed worship or the proliferation of popular Orthodox pious, "illustrative"[15] interpretations of various ritual units of the Divine Liturgy but rather in his positive experiences of what he carefully argued to be the normative, traditional practice (and "understanding") of the Orthodox rites. His arguments about liturgy's governing role in Christian life come from his practice, his own experience thereof. How else can one interpret the recurrent, eloquent odes to liturgy's power to transport its participants into life-giving, eschatological joy,[16] which he continuously insisted comprises the vision that should then guide how Christians perceive and act in the world? And act they must, he argues, for so that liturgical experience requires of them, sending each "back into the world *in joy and peace,* 'having seen the true light,' having partaken of the Holy Spirit, having been a witness of divine Love."[17]

But act how, both as individuals and as a church? "'It all depends' on thousands of factors—and, to be sure, all faculties of our human intelligence and wisdom, organization and planning, are to be constantly used."[18] The regrettable irony in that statement is that it leaves Schmemann's theology susceptible to one of the modern perversions he constantly condemns, namely, the utter separation of the "sacred" from the "secular." While it is true that liturgy, the primary locus of the Church's biblically based tradition, cannot prescribe social policies, still, it must be able to offer guidance, to provide definite points for fair discussion as the faithful debate among themselves and contribute to the commonwealth of the *polis.* For Schmemann, however, the broad divine vision of the liturgy enables participants to "recover the world as a meaningful field of Christian action," which seems to amount to strengthening hope (although he himself does not use the word). In the end, hope would seem to be what liturgy provides

---

15. See Schmemann, *Eucharist,* 44–46, 71.

16. Having cited Luke's gospel ending on a note of joy (Luke 24:52), Schmemann "worries" about theology and concludes: "There is in fact no theological definition of joy. . . . Yet only if this experience of the joy of the Kingdom in all its fullness is again placed at the center of theology, does it become possible for theology to deal once more with Creation . . . with the historic reality of the fight between the Kingdom of God and the kingdom of the prince of this world, and finally with redemption as the plentitude . . . the presence of God, who becomes all in all things. . . . [Liturgy's] function is to reveal to us the Kingdom of God. . . . It is this that theology strives to bring . . . to a 'post-Christian' world as the gift of healing, of redemption and of joy" (Schmemann "Liturgy and Tradition," 99–100). See also, among others, Schmemann, *For the Life of the World,* 53–60, 78–79, 103–5, 113, and Schmemann, *Eucharist,* 42, 53, 176, 209.

17. Schmemann, *For the Life of the World,* 113.

18. Schmemann, *For the Life of the World,* 113.

the faithful "in the darkness of *this world*," the blessed, empowering assurance that, despite it all, life—in the Christ who "has *already* 'filled all things with Himself'"—is worth the effort.[19] The thoughtful (both prayerful and learned) specificity with which he articulates the true meaning in a given element of a rite, or the sacramental reality of liturgy and the church as a whole, he does not match with careful description and analysis of how the churches (including the Orthodox) have been or are positively bringing the knowledge gained in liturgy to bear on the world. A further example may help demonstrate what I admit remains for me a troubling, theoretically evasive problem in Schmemann's work.

In his treatment of baptism, Schmemann gives a bleak prognosis for the infant "who, according to statistics, has a great likelihood some day of entering a mental institution, a penitentiary, or, at best, the maddening boredom of a universal suburbia." Facing this "'demonic' reality" during the baptismal rite, "the Church also knows that the gates of this hell have been broken and that another Power" has laid its claim on not only the individual baby but "on the totality of life, on the whole world."[20] Despite his effort to save his argument from the very individualism he condemns in modernity, Schmemann's recourse to the "totality" and the "whole" is exemplary of how, in the end, his liturgical theology balks at the hard challenge of constructively addressing the irreducibly social nature of the human being. To my reading of him, what the Church offers each individual participant in a given performance of a sacramental rite is a strengthening of the virtue of hope.

Having spent many hours now revisiting Schmemann's captivating work, I am left wondering whether there is even a viable ecclesiology, both practical and theoretical, in his theology.[21] The frustration for Schmemann himself comes to a head in his perhaps most explicitly political discussion of the church: ethnic nationalism. In his most direct, overt addressing of the political, blending the individual and corporate (ecclesial, societal), he indicts the convergence of Orthodox piety with ethnic nationalism that has continuously defeated the church's ability to witness to a fraternal unity that could enlighten ("transform") at least the Orthodox, if not other peoples. Those centuries-old, ethno-national, Orthodox mutual-excommunications make "a hypocritical lie" of every Orthodox ecumenical claim, as does the long-running, nearly universal reduction of the dominical command to love

19. Schmemann, *For the Life of the World*, 113.

20. Schmemann, *For the Life of the World*, 70.

21. I introduce this quandary acknowledging that Schmemann repeatedly summarized the genuine nature of liturgy as cosmological, eschatological, and *ecclesiological*. See Morrill, *Anamnesis as Dangerous Memory*, 89.

one's enemies (performed in the liturgy's Kiss of Peace) to the self-evident love of family and neighbors: "One's own people, one's own country—all those persons and things that we would usually love anyway, without Christ and the gospel."[22] These are narrations embedded in—and essential to— Schmemann's liturgical theology.

Such negative narrative elements, however, altogether tend to subvert his most fundamental claim: The liturgy then, in fact, does not simply prove capable of conveying what Schmemann has argued is its primordial, traditional vision, that is, it does not *in and of itself* have the power to transform people, even if "from within." Schmemann insists the fault lies not in the rites, as if they needed updating for relevance. Orthodoxy has not undergone anything like the post-Vatican II revision of the Mass and other rites. And yet, over the decades of his life-narrative, Schmemann could report no progress in the churches, no evidence of liturgy popularly affecting what he insists it should by its very nature be able to do. Individual piety gets it wrong, as does the clericalism of the ordained.[23]

Consider: the liturgy only exists in actual performance, with each of its participants, including the clergy, bringing their own experiences *to* their worship and tacitly crafting their own experience therein. That is why, for example, performative hermeneutical theories about the "worlds" *behind*, *of*, and *in front of* a text have proven useful to some liturgical theologians in their efforts to understand better the ongoing dynamic process whereby participation (engagement) in the liturgy (the performative text) affect all the worlds involved.[24] Schmemann's arguments, however, always operate in a resolutely unidirectional manner: a normative *understanding* and participation in each performance of a liturgical rite positively transforms the participant's perception of oneself and the world. Tellingly, Schmemann even specifies that every liturgical enactment is a singular, if not autonomous, moment, such that "Christian mission is always at its beginning."[25] One gets a sense it is about always starting over, returning refreshed "back into the world," but the world thereby ends up having nothing to contribute to the

22. Schmemann, *Eucharist*, 135. Schmemann's characterization of this rampant hypocrisy as a "lie" is especially striking, given Orthodox theology's strong reliance on the Johannine tradition, in which the devil is the consummate liar (John 8:22) and those who claim to love God but hate their fellow Christian are liars (1 John 4:20).

23. See Schmemann, *For the Life of the World*, 92, and Schmemann, *Eucharist*, 230–35.

24. See, for example, the several articles Margaret Mary Kelleher published in *Worship* during the 1980s and 1990s, as well as Zimmerman, *Liturgy as Language of Faith*, and Zimmerman, *Liturgy and Hermeneutics*.

25. Schmemann, *For the Life of the World*, 113.

liturgical "vision." Indeed, by the last paragraph of the chapter on mission, Schmemann turns even his "it all depends" away from the "thousand" complex worldly factors impinging upon a decision for action back to say it all "primarily" depends on "that new life" one experiences through participating in church.

There must be a further, fuller way, then, to enlist and work with narrative so as to provide a more adequate theoretical integration of liturgy and life in service to what Schmemann rightly identifies as the practical urgency of the problem. The "new" political theology that emerged in Germany in the late 1960s, garnering widespread consideration across the North Atlantic theological academy in the ensuing decades, has grappled with that very challenge, saying the problem lies with the church's subjects and institutions. The political (*politische*) entails both subjects, whom Schmemann critiques in terms of piety and ethno-nationalism, and institutions, including not only Schmemann's ecclesial concerns but also the economic, governmental, educational, cultural, and familial dimensions of human living. Following the lead of Johann Baptist Metz, political theology seeks to be not another niche category of theology (e.g., reflecting on politics); rather, it is a practical fundamental theology constructively attentive to current experiences and praxes of faith, "understanding itself as a corrective with respect to existing theological approaches, . . . preserving and carrying on their substance and intentions precisely in a critical-corrective relationship to them."[26] In so defining its mission, political theology bears a striking similarity to Schmemann's effort to advance liturgical theology as fundamental to all theology. Indeed, Metz explicitly insists that political theology seeks to keep all theology "bound to a praxis of faith that is dually constituted as mystical-political."[27] Contrary, on the other hand, to Schmemann's characterization of liberation-type theologies, political theology from its very inception was not "a liberal exercise in reductionism, replacing a properly theological concern with the mystery of God in favor of human moral imperatives," but rather, as Matthew Lamb recounts, it "insisted on the concrete importance of the transcendence of genuine faith for the redemptive healing and creative transformation of society."[28]

The positive corrective that political theology can bring to Schmemann's theology is to rescue it from being mired in what proves *practically* to be unproductive paradox, repeated descriptions of the experiential chasm between the (eschatological) truth the liturgy reveals and contemporary

26. Metz, *Faith in History and Society*, 30.

27. Metz, *Faith in History and Society*, 29.

28. Lamb, "Political Theology," 772–73.

believers' persistent inability to apprehend and act upon it. Lamb explains: "Paradox tends to juxtapose the genuine meanings and values of Christianity, on the one hand, and the many sins, failures, and ambiguities of concrete ecclesial and world history, on the other."[29] Needed instead is a genuinely dialectical, mystical-political theology, as Metz conceives it, wherein Christian faith is not a concept (a set of propositions to defend) but fundamentally a praxis of mysticism and politics. The dialectic is the tensive, productive movement between (prayerful) liturgical practices and (ethical) engagement in all aspects of society, such that these different activities can mutually inform and critically impact each other. I would therefore propose adding a fourth element—the political—to Schmemann's three-point analysis of the crisis of late-modern Christianity. The crisis is not only one of "the divorce" between theology, liturgy, and piety[30] but also of politics. After all, we the faithful—and not just the Christ revealed in liturgy—are incarnate, bodily, but therefore social, political. Politics, in fact, pervade those three elements of the contemporary crisis of the church, as Schmemann conceived them, however much he, for autobiographical and historical reasons, tended to ignore or even deny that reality in his efforts to protect liturgy and tradition from a corrupt (modern) age.

As a practical fundamental theology always working dialectically with the actual praxis of faith in historical context, political theology necessarily has recourse to narrative. Indeed, Metz posits narrative, along with memory and solidarity, as the fundamental categories out of which political theology functions.[31] An additional correlation with Schmemann's methodology thereby emerges, affording further means for political theology's exercising a "critical-corrective relationship" with his liturgical theology. The constructive possibilities have been enhanced since my first attempt at such a "dialogue" some twenty years ago by the subsequent publication of *The Journals of Father Alexander Schmemann 1973-1983*, which span the decade from the revised release of *For the Life of the World* to the completed draft of *The Eucharist*. *The Journals* comprise a treasure trove of narrative straining toward yet resisting the political as a fourth, critical-corrective element to augment Schmemann's analysis of the "theological and spiritual" crisis in the church, a "tragedy" that he at least once admitted "no liturgical reform can by itself and in itself solve."[32]

29. Lamb, "Political Theology," 777.

30. For description and analysis of this hallmark of Schmemann's theology (including multiple citations of his work), see Morrill, *Anamnesis as Dangerous Memory*, 77–87.

31. See Metz, *Faith in History and Society*, 167.

32. Schmemann, *Liturgy and Tradition*, 41.

The Journals: Narrative Theology of Liturgy, Life, and World

In his foreword to *The Journals*, an edited translation of eight notebooks that Schmemann's family discovered after his death, Serge Schmemann acknowledges how distressing his father's negative views of "various forms of spirituality, or the institutions of the Church, or the science of theology, or even of himself and his colleagues" might be to many readers. Although his father never explained what he intended to do with them, the entries (totaling 340 published pages) function as "more than a diary," with many portraying "his thoughts, his spiritual struggles . . . an inner debate," while "others are written as for publication," giving the "overall impression . . . that Father Alexander always intended some further use for [them]."[33] My initial reading of the volume gratifyingly confirmed the hermeneutical judgments I had made about Schmemann's thought in my analysis and constructive work with what had been available to me as of the 1990s.[34] They all the more support my present thesis for how intrinsic (essential) narrative is to his liturgical theology, how deeply embedded in his life-narrative were the pastoral-theological arguments propounded in his books and essays. While thorough citation of passages from *The Journals* would exceed the page-limit of this present essay, a summary of key themes may suffice for concluding with a constructive mystical-political proposal.

Having noted the often-conflicted character of these "highly personal" journals of "a priest and teacher of unwavering faith," Serge Schmemann explains that:

> what ultimately persuaded those closest to Father Alexander that they should be published is that however strong the doubts and pains, he always returns—even from the anguish of impending death—to joy; the joy of the beauty of an autumn day, the joy of friendships, the joy of the Liturgy, joy in the certainty of the Kingdom and the love of God.[35]

Thus, one immediately finds joy confirmed as the primary category in Schmemann's theology; his journals constantly reiterate the experience of joy within his first-order theology (liturgy and life). His son has made my analysis easier by having deftly identified the objects of his father's joy. First, there is the uplifting cosmic beauty of the natural world around him: the crisp air, frost, or snow in bright winter sunshine, solitary drives through

33. Schmemann, *Journals*, vii.
34. That reading was for my review of the book. See Morrill, "Review of *Journals*," 187–89.
35. Schmemann, *Journals*, vii.

open countryside, weeks on the Quebec lake where the family summered annually from the first year they arrived in America, and the list could go on. Joy would likewise well up in the socio-cultural world of humanity's creation: the apparel and demeanor of businesspeople on city streets, the view of Manhattan approached by bridge, cozy (a favorite adjective) family scenes in lighted windows while walking home through his wintry West-chester neighborhood, consoling returns to the Paris of his youth each New Years. The latter point to the "joy of friendships" but, above all, the companionship of family, his beloved wife and children, expanding to their spouses and the grandchildren: the profound happiness they brought him, Schmemann touchingly, repeatedly expresses.

Those sites of joy bespeak the sacramentality of the world, making the cosmic dimension of divine worship a natural inclination of human-ity that, as Schmemann taught (in his second-order theology), the church takes up into eschatological joy. Often does Schmemann recount his joy in participating in liturgy. Still, a pattern emerges across the hundreds of entries whereby the liturgical experiences seem perfect, in contrast to his disgust with popular and church culture, doubts about theology, and fa-tigue with school politics. Liturgy has a salving quality, renewing him after dispiriting conflicts and exhausting duties. While such a medicinal experi-ence (interpretation) of the sacramental rites has a certain resonance with patristic tradition, the danger of escapism lurks nonetheless. Evident in all the accounts of joy in natural and manmade beauty (in which he is always walking, driving, or sitting alone) is an individualistic quality or, in the case of family and friendship, an interpersonal one—characteristics likewise implicit in his accounts of liturgical joy. I risk overstatement here, but what does not run that risk is a questioning of the escapist quality to both types of sacramental experiences—natural and liturgical. Despite all his second-order theology's decrying of the separation of sacred and profane, as well as of the individualistic and "bourgeois," Schmemann's first-order theological experience betrays a troubling disjunction between the negative struggles in daily life and participation in the liturgy's symbolic ascension into the kingdom of God. One example must suffice.

An entry from November 1976 typifies Schmemann's exasperation with the state of the seminary and the wider church, as well as his means of relief:

> Troubled days because, since the beginning of the school year, I feel more acutely than ever the terrible confusion of the religious situation. On one hand, the book by Froissard,

a meeting with youth in the city last Sunday, the Liturgy—all are like drinks of "living water" that bring inner joy and satisfaction. On the other hand, a foolish conflict at the seminary, the denunciation by some students of other students' heresies (they do not kiss icons, etc.) and not enough piety, and more— a student who wishes to exorcise another, etc. A dull wave of pseudo-religiosity, the whole atmosphere saturated with self-affirmation . . . in everything one pushes "God" and "Orthodoxy." It seems that nobody around us is happy—happy with the happiness that should be flowing out of Liturgy, prayer, theology, etc. We all firmly proclaim that one cannot be happy without God. But then why is man so unhappy *with* God? . . . For years I have been asking myself this question. It seems that in the world there is no longer a peaceful, humble, joyful, and free standing before God, walking to Him; no more: "Serve the Lord with fear and rejoice in Him with trembling" . . . (Ps 2:11). So, I rejoice in every hour of solitude, of autumn sunshine on golden trees, of total calm and silence.[36]

Preoccupied with the immediate (political) trouble in the seminary, Schmemann's reflection elicits his long-running agony over how the mystical— "Liturgy, prayer, theology, etc."—proves incapable of instilling participants with a joy "flowing out" into their world. Schmemann's lived, first-order theology seems trapped in paradoxical mode, wherein the truth and meaning revealed in mystical experiences and the sins and failures of church and society are in a fruitless stand-off. Moreover, by so heavily repairing to solitude (granting due respect to introverted personalities), the narrative could reinforce, in the current earbud-media-device age, younger generations' disengagement from social institutions, civic and ecclesial.

Vision Adjustment: The Experience of Radical Contrast

Political theology seeks to correct the practical impotence of paradoxical (dualism-prone) thinking that juxtaposes ecclesially experienced truth from the world's fallen condition by pressing for a dialectical movement between the mystical and political, the liturgical and ethical. In his voluminous probing of the question from the late 1960s to early 1990s, Edward Schillebeeckx developed a theory germane to Schmemann's predicament: the radical contrast-experience. Starting not from the confidence of joy but the shock of suffering, Schillebeeckx posits a basic, "pre-religious,"

---

36. Schmemann, *Journals*, 134.

pan-human phenomenon, wherein people experience the painful contradiction in the single reality of their world, wherein evil, hatred, and suffering (chronic or episodic) threaten to crush beauty and meaning. Commenting on how there "even seems to be more joy and song among the oppressed than among the oppressors," Schillebeeckx asserts, "despite all their wretchedness, human beings are too proud to regard evil as being on an equal footing with good."[37] The experience of negative contrast is marked by the indignant "no" people declare in the face of an evil or oppressive situation. That negation nonetheless discloses a positive element to this radical experience, nurtured by fragments of goodness, love, and beauty, affirming an alternate, positive vision of what should be, what must be. This "open yes" is "a consensus with 'the unknown' . . . a better, other world, which in fact does not yet exist anywhere."[38] Out of that vision, people assess and act, creating further experience of the "yes."

To this universal, radical human experience, Christians bring their particular symbol and narrative: "The recognizable human face of this transcendence which has appeared among us in the man Jesus, confessed as Christ and Son of God."[39] The negative contrast elicits faith and hope, the experience of God's gracious invitation to join in the single history of salvation and liberation.[40] Here, a resonance emerges between political theology and Schmemann's liturgical theology: "We know about the fallen state of the world only because we know about its glorious creation and its salvation by Christ. The knowledge of the fallen world does not kill joy, which emanates in this world, always, constantly, as a bright sorrow." By thereby insisting that joy is "the *tonality* of Christianity that penetrates *everything*—faith and vision,"[41] Schmemann articulates a quality to Christian experience not unlike the "open yes" Schillebeeckx identifies in radical experiences of contrast. For both theologians, liturgy and mysticism nurture that openness,[42] but with this difference: Schillebeeckx corrects the idealistic "*everything*,"

37. Schillebeeckx, *Church*, 5. In his treatment of negative contrast-experiences, in this, his last major book, Schillebeeckx explains it as an effort "to radicalize" a concept he had repeatedly developed. See Schillebeekx, *God the Future of Man*, 90–97, and Schillebeekx, *Christ*, 813–17.

38. Schillebeeckx, *Church*, 6.

39. Schillebeeckx, *Church*, 6.

40. This argument is a constant throughout Schillebeeckx's work. See also Metz, *Faith in History and Society*, 109, 151–54, 193–94, and Metz, *Passion for God*, 37, 45.

41. Schmemann, *Journals*, 137.

42. Schillebeeckx affirms "that the original and authentic use of the word God is to be found in the context of worship" (Schillebeeckx, *Church*, 80). On prayer and worship, see also Schillebeeckx, *Church*, 64, 73, and Schillebeeckx, *Christ*, 40–42, 810–12, 830–34.

redirecting faith's vision to actual, specific history, to current realities of suffering and redemption. Therein lies a different knowledge of the world. Mystical-ethical praxis dialectically creates a different experience of church. Schmemann's seems to be knowledge *about* the world, that is, a descriptive awareness of the world's "fallen" character that nonetheless does not engage it as a site of practical-theological work (an *ergon*). For political (and liberation) theology, the content of faith is likewise cognitive, but it is a critical knowledge "peculiar to the story of 'pathic' praxis, above all the 'pathic' power of stories of the suffering of quite specific men and women."[43] In such praxis, Christians come experientially to know Christ, imitating the Jesus whose contrast-experience was an intimate love of God (as his Abba) empowering but also informed by his prophetic message and practical love for sinful, suffering humanity.[44]

From their largely anemic North Atlantic liturgical-communal situations, political theologians have turned to the church's emerging center of gravity, observing how poor Christian communities in the Southern Hemisphere are *making* a world, how faith is not only remembering (essential as that is) but also acting (not only interpersonally but also politically).[45] Schillebeeckx is typical in reporting a fervent, joyful, empowering faith, hope, and love in Latin American Eucharistic celebrations, "the mystical stirring of their social and political urge for liberation."[46] To assert one history of salvation and liberation (outlandish, impossible, perhaps even threatening, until one sees how the poor are able to do it) is to read history with a practical and critical intent. With changed vision, Jon Sobrino explains, comes the hard but life-giving work of conversion, an invitation to share in the values and priorities of the poor base communities: "Resistance, simplicity, joy in life's basic elements, openness to the mystery of God . . . grassroots economics, community organization, health care, housing, human rights, education, culture . . . ecological consciousness . . . care of nature and Mother Earth in ways far superior to the ways of the West."[47]

Schmemann concludes his chapter on mission in *For the Life of the World*: "A Christian is one who, wherever he looks, finds Christ and rejoices in Him."[48] In the end, however, such an affirmation avoids the converting,

43. Schillebeeckx, *Church*, 177.

44. See Schillebeeckx, *Church*, 179–82. For a review of Metz on this theme, with multiple citations, see Morrill, *Anamnesis as Dangerous Memory*, 34–40.

45. See Metz, *Passion for God*, 42–47.

46. Schillebeeckx, *Church*, 180. See also works by Metz, Sölle, and others.

47. Sobrino, *No Salvation Outside the Poor*, 62. On conversion, see Sobrino, *No Salvation Outside the Poor*, 58–60, 66.

48. Schmemann, *For the Life of the World*, 113.

evangelical question of *where* one is looking and *with whom*. The pastoral-academic theologian does well to interrogate whether one is constantly in one's comfort zone that, ironically (paradoxically, tragically), proves uncomfortable to a painful degree:

> While walking to Vespers yesterday, I asked myself, "Then what do I want? What is my life: If everything is unnecessary and fussy, then what; sit at home, in comfort, with money, write a little, watch television?" I am well on my way to doing just that. . . . I don't know; these thoughts were quite real. I should ask myself: "What does Christ want from me? Am I doing, at least partially, what He wants?"[49]

As is so regularly the human case, Schmemann is able to perceive the problem more clearly through encounter with those who are "other." From his journal entry upon giving the commencement speech at a Chicago-area seminary:

> An Episcopal ceremony, my favorite hymns accompanied by a powerful organ, always inspiring. Following the service—traditional, festive—I thought about the deeply rooted, hopeless well-being of the Christian West, maybe even the irreparable bourgeois state of Western Christianity. . . . What God reveals to people is unheard, impossible, and the tragedy consists of this deafness. And this revelation can no longer penetrate Western life without ripping it apart. What is revealed surpasses and therefore tears apart life—the gift of joy "which nobody will take away from you." Genuine Christianity is bound to disturb the heart with this tearing—that is the force of eschatology. But one does not feel it in these smooth ceremonies where everything is neat, right, but without eschatological "other worldliness." This is, maybe, the basic spiritual quality of any bourgeois state of mind. It is closed to the sense of tragedy to which the very existence of God condemns us.[50]

The reader might expect Schmemann's quandary to return to his criticism of Orthodox piety, so tone deaf to the eschatological essence of the Divine Liturgy. He turns instead to Byzantium, in a rather surprising way:

> Maybe it is the absence of the poor and the suffering, but then I realized that this was not the reason. In Byzantium, in St. Sophia, there probably was a thousand times more gold and riches,

---

49. Schmemann, *Journals*, 138.
50. Schmemann, *Journals*, 122.

but Byzantium was not bourgeois. There always should remain
. . . the knowledge that there is but one sadness, which is not be
a saint; it is the hearing of the call, the breath, that cannot be
reduced to "social problems."[51]

Poverty, he continues, may be the crucial issue, but *not* the Western
churches' mistaken call to fight for "economic equality" for the poor. The
Christian call to poverty is significantly different: "Poverty as freedom,
poverty as a sign that the heart has accepted the impossible (hence tragic)
call to the Kingdom of God." With Schillebeeckx, I would encourage
Schmemann not to perceive the call to evangelical poverty and the direct
cry of the poor as discrete, let alone opposed, experiences. Scripture itself
reveals interpersonal (1 John 4:12) and social-ethical (Jer 22:16) engagement as arenas of praxis "essential" for "true knowledge of God."[52] Schmemann, however, concludes: "I don't know. It's so difficult to express it, but
I clearly feel that there is a different perception of life, and the bourgeois
state (religious, theological, spiritual, pious, cultured, etc.) is blind to
something essential in Christianity."[53]

Political theologians—and perhaps most pointedly, Schillebeeckx—
have argued that there is no salvation outside the world. Liberation theologians, such as Sobrino, have sharpened that thesis on the hermeneutical
basis of Scripture, tradition, and history to assert that there is no salvation
outside the poor. Sadly (tragically?), I have searched in vain for the poor in
Schmemann's journals. He never once substantially reflects upon noticing,
and therefore never *remembers*, them in the streets of New York or other
world cities, making just one enigmatic possible allusion to the poor in Mexico City.[54] Despite brief indications not ruling out but rather subordinating
social-ethical praxis to liturgical participation, Schmemann's written corpus
repeatedly insists on the mistaken priority of "bringing [Christ] down into
ordinary life." My concluding (mystical-political) counter-proposal is the
evangelical call (Matt 25:1–13) *to go out to meet him*, the bridegroom an-
nounced in the darkness (one of Schmemann's favorite metaphors for the
world) of midnight. Negative experiences of contrast take a redemptive turn
when believers, confronted by godless situations, enter the struggle with the

51. Schmemann, *Journals*, 122.

52. Schillebeeckx, *Church*, 96.

53. Schmemann, *Journals*, 122.

54. I have pondered uneasily over this short paragraph in Schmemann's Mexico
City entry: "I am worried about Mexican Orthodoxy—so naïve, childish, trustful and
wholesome. Everything is poor and radiant and everywhere these dark-eyed children
who come to you with angelic beauty and light" (Schmemann, *Journals*, 124).

afflicted, and in so doing experience the arrival of God (divine-human presence even in failure!). As Schillebeeckx argues, there is a mystical dimension to Christian ethical living itself.

Participation (*koinonia*) in the mystical-communal work of sacramental worship comprises an essential, irreducible means for the faithful to replenish the oil and trim the wicks of the lamps that are their bodily lives in society.[55] But in turn, solidarity—practical sharing in and with the lives of the suffering and struggling—at times generates experiences that are nothing short of icons of redemption, remembrances the faithful *bring to* the anamnestic transformation the Eucharist catalyzes. Not only in the liturgy but also in the natural, interpersonal, and societal loci of our lives comes the call to meet the bridegroom, so often at a moment or in circumstances unforeseen (Matthew, after all, joins the parable of the sheep and the goats—"Lord, when did we see you?"—with that of the bridesmaids in a single chapter). Not only the beauty but also the "fallenness" of the world thereby have a positive function in the church's life, both in the "spiritual worship" of each member's praxis and in the sacramental worship of Christ's assembled body. In the dialectic of mysticism and politics, liturgy and ethics, come fragmentary moments of evangelical hope and joy, nurturing a peace that a world left to itself cannot give.

55. "Let your light shine before others, so that they may see your good works and give glory to your Father in heaven" (Matt 5:16). Paul identifies believer's bodily, ethical living as "your spiritual worship" (Rom 12:1).

Consent and the Kingdom

Alexander Schmemann and the Roman Rite of Marriage

TIMOTHY P. O'MALLEY

ROMAN CATHOLIC AND ORTHODOX theologies of marriage offer distinctive accounts of the sacramentality of the nuptial union. Whereas the Roman Rite emphasizes the nature of marriage as related to the act of consent and thus the elevation of natural love toward a supernatural end, Orthodox theologians place the stress on the cosmic and universal transformation that unfolds through the performance of the Service of Crowning. Alexander Schmemann's account of liturgical nuptiality in *For the Life of the World* is characteristically Orthodox:

> Indeed, if it is simply a divine *sanction* of marriage, the bestowing of spiritual help to the married couple, a blessing for the procreation of children—all this does not make it radically different from any other act for which we need help and guidance, sanction and blessing. For a "sacrament," as we have seen, necessarily implies the idea of transformation, refers to the ultimate event of Christ's death and resurrection, and is always a sacrament of the Kingdom.[1]

Marriage in Orthodoxy is a transformation of human love, one that transfigures such love, allowing it to participate anew in paradise, in "the nuptial state before the Fall."[2] For this reason, the couple cannot be the ministers of

1. Schmemann, *For the Life of the World*, 81.
2. Evdokimov, *Sacrament of Love*, 126.

201

the Service of Crowning, as they are in the nuptial rites of the West because only the priest can offer the appropriate blessing.[3] The ordained priest facilitates "the entrance of the world into the 'world to come,' the procession of the people of God—in Christ—into the kingdom."[4]

This essay seeks to offer a moment of reconciliation between the positions of the West and the East relative to the sacrament of marriage. In the first part, I present a characteristically Western account of marriage as found in Matthias Joseph Scheeben's *The Mysteries of Christianity*. This position underlines marriage as an exercise of baptismal priesthood, one that is a radical consecration of love, uniting such love to the mystery of divine love. In the second, I then turn to a fuller treatment of Schmemann's sacramentality of human love in *For the Life of the World*. Here, marriage becomes an ecclesial transformation of human love to its destiny through integration into the mystery of Christ through the Church's liturgical action. Lastly, I turn to a reading of *The Order of Celebrating Matrimony* within Mass in Roman Catholicism. Through this reading, I argue that the Nuptial Blessing in the West is that ecclesial act that brings the couple's consent into the Kingdom of God through a proper exercise of baptismal priesthood in the *ekklesia*.

The Mystery of Marriage in Matthias Joseph Scheeben

Matthias Joseph Scheeben's *The Mysteries of Christianity* has contributed to a renewal of the sacramental theology of marriage in Roman Catholicism in the twentieth century.[5] Scheeben's Romantic-era Thomism responds to an over-rationalization of theological discourse, one that reduces Christianity into a system of propositions rather than divine action in human history. Defining mystery within the Christian economy, Scheeben writes, "Christian mystery is a truth communicated to us by Christian revelation, a truth to which we cannot attain by our own unaided reason, and which, even after we have attained to it by faith, we cannot adequately represent with our rational concepts."[6] Human existence is necessarily suffused with a natural sense of the mysterious, one in which the human being lacks perfect knowledge of each and every object of possible contemplation. Christian mystery is broadly congruent with this general account of mystery with the

---

3. Evdokimov, *Sacrament of Love*, 129.

4. Schmemann, *For the Life of the World*, 89.

5. Scola, *Nuptial Mystery*.

6. Scheeben, *Mysteries of Christianity*, 13.

exception of its foundation in divine revelation, and thus its consequent reliance upon analogical rather than rational propositions.

Scheeben situates the sacramental economy of the Church in this sphere of mystery. For Schebeen, the sacraments pertain to mystery in two ways: they reveal to the Christian the hiddenness of divine love manifest in the Trinitarian life of God, as well as lifting up the "natural" and thus sensible sphere of existence into the supernatural.[7] This natural sphere of existence requires the sacramental economy not because divine grace in a fallen world compels God to use bodily mediation as a form of medicine.[8] Instead, "since the generative faculty of human nature depends on the material component of that nature, and is exercised by a material act that is perceptible to the senses, grace also was bound up with the same act."[9] God has fittingly chosen to save human beings through sacraments so that materiality itself, essential to human life, might become the playground for divine life. Such a transformation is possible because of the blessing of the Incarnation whereby "flesh could become, and was made to become, the vehicle of the Holy Spirit."[10] The sacramental economy, as Schebeen describes it, performs a divine pedagogy whereby nature becomes graced.

Marriage is particularly iconic of this general approach to sacramentality. The materiality of natural love is consecrated to God and "henceforth a supernatural tie joins them together for the pursuit of a high and sacred objective."[11] Natural marriage (outside of the sacramental economy), according to Scheeben, has a religious character insofar as the couple offers a vow of permanent fidelity to one another, participating in the kingdom of God through the generation of new life.[12] Scheeben recognizes that the natural act of marriage and child rearing implies a divine sanction:

> With this consecration is intimately connected a divine blessing that directly guarantees the assistance of God to those who are joined in matrimony, inasmuch as the legitimacy of their union

---

7. Scheeben, *Mysteries of Christianity*, 562.

8. Here, a legitimate critique may be made against Louis-Marie Chauvet's diagnosis of metaphysics and thus scholastic theology as seeing mediation as a necessary evil. The bodily quality of the sacraments is built into the very structure of the sacramental economy as gift within Scheeben's description of the sacraments. Thus, bodily mediation is not a necessary evil but intrinsic to divine pedagogy in Scheeben's retrieval of St. Thomas Aquinas. For Chauvet's critique, see Chauvet, *Symbol and Sacrament*, 7–9.

9. Scheeben, *Mysteries of Christianity*, 564.

10. Scheeben, *Mysteries of Christianity*, 566.

11. Scheeben, *Mysteries of Christianity*, 593.

12. Scheeben, *Mysteries of Christianity*, 595.

204 PART 4: SCHMEMANN AND SACRAMENTAL THEOLOGY

confers on them a legitimate claim to the divine concurrence which is necessary for the procreation of their children.[13]

The primordial sacramentality of marriage cannot be discounted in describing the nuptial mystery, even if such an account is not peculiarly Christian.

The Christian sacrament of matrimony is distinct in its ultimate end insofar as it is an act of consent conducted by members of Christ's body. Scheeben writes: "When he contracts marriage with a baptized person, not merely two human beings, or even two persons simply endowed with grace, but two consecrated members of Christ's body enter into the union for the purpose of dedicating themselves to the extension of this union."[14] The baptized couple can extend this union beyond purely natural means because in their act of consent, they become a sign of Christ and the Church. Such a transformation is not reducible to the order of sign, such that in encountering the couple, one is led to think of Christ and the Church. Instead, marriage represents the mystery of Christ and the Church "because the mystery proves active and operative in it."[15] Christian marriage is a sacrament because the very grace that unites Christ to the Church is "intertwined" or "merged" with the nuptial consent of the couple.[16] Christian marriage objectively transforms the couple into a living, efficacious sign of divine love and the couple must conform their wills to this new reality:

> From the nature of Christian marriage . . . husband and wife must love each other not merely with natural love, but with supernatural love, as members of Christ and as representatives of His mystical nuptials with the Church. They must love and honor, educate and rear, their children not only as the fruit of their own bodies, but as the fruit of the mystical nuptials mentioned, that is, as children of God.[17]

Marriage elevates the most mundane aspects of natural love including the education of children, allowing such day-to-day care to become a priestly activity of those baptized into Christ. And the sacrament of matrimony is efficacious not through the blessing of an ordained minister but through the baptismal character of husband and wife.[18]

---

13. Scheeben, *Mysteries of Christianity*, 598.
14. Scheeben, *Mysteries of Christianity*, 599.
15. Scheeben, *Mysteries of Christianity*, 602.
16. Scheeben, *Mysteries of Christianity*, 603.
17. Scheeben, *Mysteries of Christianity*, 605.
18. Scheeben, *Mysteries of Christianity*, 606.

Thus, grace is made available in the sacrament through the act of consent, which is "a holy, mystical union, in which the bridal couple join and are joined in the name of Christ for the extension of His mystical body."[19] The priest's blessing is not intrinsic to the sacrament insofar as the couple's baptismal identity makes possible the nuptial union. Such a perspective is not a rejection of the ecclesial nature of marriage for Scheeben. Instead, marriage functions as an icon of the very identity of the Church:

> Christian marriage is inextricably interwoven with the supernatural fabric of the Church; the greatest danger one can inflict on both is to tear them apart. When such a catastrophe occurs, matrimony completely loses its high mystical character, and the Church loses one of her fairest flowers, wherein her supernatural, all-pervading, transforming power was so splendidly revealed. Nowhere does the mystical life of the Church penetrate more deeply into natural relationships than in matrimony.[20]

In the Church, natural existence becomes the site of supernatural grace. Although Scheeben does not employ the term, there is a dimension of deification in his account of marriage related to the union of human and divine activity in the moment of consent.[21] Marriage is that sacrament that epitomizes the salvific nature of the entire sacramental economy as elevating natural to divine life without erasing humanity.

Marriage in Alexander Schmemann

Alexander Schmemann's account of marriage has resonances with Scheeben's Romantic-era Thomism, particularly the argument that marriage transfigures human love, re-orienting it to its proper destiny in Christ. In his *For the Life of the World*, Schmemann situates the sacramental economy within the orbit of the vocation of the human person toward a cosmic priesthood:

> The first, the basic definition of man is that he is *the priest*. He stands in the center of the world and unifies it in his act of blessing God, of both receiving the world from God and offering it to God—and by filling the world with this eucharist, he transforms his life, the one that he receives from the world, into life in God, into communion with Him. The world was created as "matter,"

19. Scheeben, *Mysteries of Christianity*, 606.
20. Scheeben, *Mysteries of Christianity*, 610.
21. See Spezzano, *Glory of God's Grace*, 15–16.

> the material of one all-embracing eucharist, and man was cre-
> ated as the priest of this cosmic sacrament.[22]

For Schmemann, there is no purely natural dimension of human existence contra Scheeben insofar as all matter was created originally for Eucharistic offering. The sacramental economy of the Church thus restores created matter to its original divine destiny.

Schmemann describes how the Church's celebration of the rite of marriage transforms *eros* into a Eucharistic offering. As described in the introduction, Schmemann emphasizes that marriage cannot be understood as overlaying a natural reality (sex and the family) with a Christian skin. Instead, marriage is "the sacrament of divine love . . . the all-embracing mystery of being itself . . . [that] concerns the whole Church, and—through the Church—the whole world."[23] Marriage reveals the original destiny of human love.

Schmemann's account of the sacrament of marriage begins in a Marian key. Mary is an icon of the Church, revealing that human flourishing unfolds insofar as the creature gives all of his or her existence unto God.[24] Schmemann asserts that this radical openness to God is the fulfillment of "the *womanhood* of creation."[25] Turning to the Scriptures, Schmemann notes that the nuptial mystery pulsating through the biblical narrative reveals the original destiny of the world:

> The world—which finds its restoration and fulfillment in the Church—is the bride of God and . . . in sin this fundamental relationship has been broken, distorted. And it is in Mary—the Woman, the Virgin, the Mother—in her response to God, that the Church has its living and personal beginning.[26]

Creation was to become the Bride of God, totally obedient to her spouse, the Creator. Humanity, in particular, is to become this spouse of God, open to the divine will. In this openness, man and woman alike are transformed through the twin virtues of response and acceptance. Mary's spousal identity as Virgin and Mother is for Schmemann an icon of the transformation of all humanity made possible in the Church.[27]

---

22. Schmemann, *For the Life of the World*, 15.
23. Schmemann, *For the Life of the World*, 82.
24. Schmemann, *For the Life of the World*, 83.
25. Schmemann, *For the Life of the World*, 83.
26. Schmemann, *For the Life of the World*, 84.
27. Schmemann, *For the Life of the World*, 87.

The sacrament of marriage, for Schmemann, is the first fruits of this re-newal of humanity in a Marian key: "it transforms, in fact, not only marriage as such but all human love."[28] He analyzes the two parts of the Orthodox rite of marriage: the betrothal and the crowning.[29] The betrothal is a re-orientation of natural marriage to its ultimate destiny as a sacrament of the kingdom of God. The priest takes the now married couple into the Church in a solemn procession, signifying "the entrance of marriage into the Church, which is the entrance of the world into the 'world to come,' the procession of the people of God—in Christ—into the Kingdom."[30] Marriage is not merely a sacrament for the couple but becomes an icon of creation's *telos*. All that is natural is meant to be eucharistized in the kingdom of God.

The crowning itself, for Schmemann, is a further explication of this eucharistization of an already supernaturally-oriented love. The couple is crowned, signifying their origins as a royal people: "Each family is indeed a kingdom, a little church, and therefore a sacrament of and a way to the Kingdom."[31] This kingdom unfolds in the mundane passage of time in which husband and wife practice the art of self-giving love over the course of a lifetime. The rite of crowning points toward the couple's orientation toward martyrdom. Schmemann writes:

> A marriage which does not constantly crucify its own selfishness and self-sufficiency, which does not "die to itself" that it may point beyond itself, is not a Christian marriage. The real sin of marriage today is not adultery or lack of "adjustment" or "men-tal cruelty." It is the idolization of the family itself, the refusal to understand marriage as directed toward the Kingdom of God.[32]

A purely secular account of marriage focuses upon the family as the *telos* of the nuptial mystery. Yet such an approach treats Christianity as noth-ing more than a cult, which may or may not integrate with the rest of ex-istence.[33] Marriage must become suffused with the cruciform logic of the kingdom of God whereby the couple becomes a divine sacrifice for the world. The drinking of the common cup at the end of the service, remnants

28. Schmemann, *For the Life of the World*, 88.

29. For a full text and commentary on the Orthodox rite of marriage, see Evdoki-mov, *Sacrament of Love*, 105–60.

30. Schmemann, *For the Life of the World*, 89.

31. Schmemann, *For the Life of the World*, 89.

32. Schmemann, *For the Life of the World*, 90.

33. Morrill, *Anamnesis as Dangerous Memory*, 116–18.

of Eucharistic communion, becomes the "ultimate *seal* of the fulfillment of marriage in Christ."[34]

Thus, for Schmemann, the Church enacts a transformation of natural love through marriage in Christ. In fact, the vocation of what is merely "natural marriage" is revealed as supernatural from the beginning. The sacrament of marriage is akin to that of ordination for Schmemann insofar as both pertain to the radicality of kenotic love. He writes:

> Both are manifestations of love. The priest is indeed married to the Church. But just as the human marriage is taken into the mystery of Christ and the Church and becomes the sacrament of the Kingdom, it is this marriage of the priest with the Church that makes him really *priest*, the true minister of that Love which alone transforms the world and reveals the Church as the immaculate bride of Christ.[35]

Marriage and ordination alike are sacraments of vocation that reveal the ultimate destiny of humanity in Christ. Through the celebration of both sacraments, it is revealed that love itself is to become the priestly offering of humanity to God.

Consent and the Kingdom in the Nuptial Blessing

The treatment of consent by a figure like Scheeben reveals that the Western formula for marriage is not reducible simply to a natural contract.[36] Instead, it is an authentic exercise of the baptismal priesthood whereby love is transfigured in light of the mystery of Christ and the Church. Both Western and Eastern accounts of marriage pertain to the deification of love as it is brought into the kingdom of God. Contemporary accounts of nuptial consent by figures like Marc Cardinal Ouellet reveal that the vows shared by the couple are not merely legal but a personal gift of self, made possible through the binding charism of the Spirit. The "yes" of the nuptial consent is itself a priestly act appropriate to the baptized, one that "establishes the *couple* as a permanent sacrament and transforms its history into salvation history—in other words, into a sign that bears the gift of God to his people."[37]

34. Schmemann, *For the Life of the World*, 91.

35. Schmemann, *For the Life of the World*, 94.

36. The reduction of Western consent merely to a legal formula emphasizes the role of consent in canon law in particular. But consent in the West also relates to a theological understanding of the couple as becoming a sign of Christ and the Church through the act of consent. See Reynolds, *How Marriage Became One of the Sacraments*, 389–90.

37. Ouellet, *Marriage and Sacrament of Love*, 70.

Yet, the perils of the West's account of marriage consist of two dimensions. First, there may be a canonical obsession with the validity of the act of consent. Such an obsession risks the possibility that sacramental marriage becomes exclusively concerned with the subjectivity of the man and woman offering consent. Second, the West's account of consent may offer an inadequate account of ecclesial activity in the sacrament of marriage. What is the role of the Church in marriage if the act of the consent is the exclusive space of the sacramentalization of human love?

The Nuptial Blessing in the Roman Catholic rite of marriage provides a way of responding to these two problems. The earliest celebrations of the sacrament of marriage consisted of an act of consent taking place outside of the Church with a blessing offered at a later time.[38] This Nuptial Blessing was originally bestowed exclusively upon the bride in the Roman rite. With the revision of the rite of marriage at the Second Vatican Council, this Nuptial Blessing was then prayed over both the bride and groom alike.[39] As such, the Nuptial Blessing has assumed in the Roman Rite a new importance, one that has not yet been adequately integrated into a sacramental theology of marriage.

In the context of Matrimony celebrated within Mass, the Nuptial Blessing in the Roman Rite takes place immediately after the praying of the Our Father as the rite moves toward Eucharistic communion. In the case of a marriage outside of Mass, between a Catholic and a non-Catholic Christian, the Nuptial Blessing occurs after the Universal Prayer. This blessing is also highly encouraged in a marriage between a Catholic and a non-Christian or catechumen. In light of this essay's focus, I will focus exclusively upon the Nuptial Blessing during Mass.

Ritually, the Nuptial Blessing is to be bestowed either before the altar or in the space where the couple is kneeling. The altar is no mere piece of furniture but is a sign that makes evident the Christocentric and thus ecclesial nature of marriage. As the *General Instruction on the Roman Missal* notes about the altar:

> The altar, on which is effected the Sacrifice of the Cross made present under sacramental signs, is also the table of the Lord to which the People of God is convoked to participate in the Mass, and it is also the center of the thanksgiving that is accomplished through the Eucharist.[40]

38. Stevenson, *Nuptial Blessing*.
39. Turner, *Inseparable Love*, 183–86.
40. Catholic Church, *General Instruction of the Roman Missal*, s.v. 296.

Gathering before the altar, the couple brings their own sacrifice of love made evident in the consent offered to the table of the Lord. Their identity as one convoked by God is evident in this action.

The priest's words preceding the proper blessing establish the act as an offering to God of the couple's act of consent:

> Dear brothers and sisters,
> let us humbly pray to the Lord
> that on these his servants, now married in Christ,
> he may mercifully pour out the blessing of his grace
> and make of one heart in love
> by the Sacrament of Christ's Body and Blood
> those he has joined by a holy covenant.[41]

The consent of husband and wife, an act of the baptismal priesthood, is now celebrated by the whole *ekklesia*. The Church prays for this couple as Christ's Body, as the People of God assembled to offer worship. The Nuptial Blessing becomes a Eucharistic offering of the couple unto God.

There are a variety of texts that may be chosen for the Nuptial Blessing. Yet, the shape of each maintains the Eucharistic dimension of marriage including an epiclesis. The Nuptial Blessing begins with an anamnesis, recalling the origins of marriage in creation, as well as Christ's spousal love. The act of remembering the nuptial mystery at the heart of creation and redemption gives way to an epiclesis whereby the Spirit is called down upon the couple:

> Look now with favor on these your servants,
> joined together in Marriage,
> who ask to be strengthened by your blessing.
> Send down on them the grace of the Holy Spirit
> and pour your love into their hearts,
> that they may remain faithful in the Marriage covenant.[42]

The epiclesis seeks to transform the natural union of husband and wife, the exchange of love shared between the couple, into a living sign of the nuptial mystery of Christ and the Church. Another text for the Nuptial Blessing clearly explicates this theme:

> Grant, O Lord,
> that, as they enter upon this sacramental union,
> they may share with one another the gifts of your love
> and, by being for each other a sign of your presence,

---

41. Catholic Church, *Order of Celebrating Matrimony*, s.v. 73.
42. Catholic Church, *Order of Celebrating Matrimony*, s.v. 74.

become one heart and one mind.[43]

The couple's natural unity, their love for one another, becomes that matter which is transfigured in the sacrament.

The Nuptial Blessing continues after the epiclesis with intercessions related to the Spirit's transformation of the wife and husband. Both are prayed for in their capacity as potential father and mother of children. The Nuptial Blessing concludes with an eschatological request that the couple's love may lead them to enjoy "your great banquet in heaven."[44]

Eucharistic communion follows the Nuptial Blessing. The close proximity of communion to the Blessing reveals a Eucharistic quality to the whole liturgical action. The baptized couple, which pledged their love in Christ, is now brought by the Church before the altar. The unity of husband and wife, made possible through their act of consent, is further sealed by the gift of the Spirit. Such unity becomes a living sign of the Eucharistic vocation of human love whereby husband and wife become one body, one Spirit in Christ. The identity of wife as mother and husband as father brings the mundaneness of family life into the Eucharistic logic of the kingdom of God. Here, all human love discovers in the sign of husband and the wife its final destiny as matter for Eucharistic transformation: "The Christian life, eucharistically lived by the faithful in the reality of marriage and the family, thus becomes a paradigm for every type of human relationship, above all for those which constitute the ecclesial community."[45]

In this sense, the Nuptial Blessing moves beyond a strict concern with consent in the Roman Rite. Instead, one is brought into a comparable account of marriage as found in Schmemann. The love of husband and wife are eucharistized in the kingdom of God as they approach the altar. The freedom of consent, as in Scheeben, still matters. But this consent unfolds as a gift lived Eucharistically in the Church.

Conclusion

Liturgical theologians tend to offer a radical separation between Western and Eastern accounts of sacramental theology. Yet in a close reading of the Romantic-era Thomism of Matthias Scheeben, one discovers a Western account of consent that squares with Schmemann's description of the deification of human love through the ceremonies of the Bethrothal and

43. Catholic Church, *Order of Celebrating Matrimony*, s.v. 207.
44. Catholic Church, *Order of Celebrating Matrimony*, s.v. 207.
45. Scola, *Nuptial Mystery*, 303.

the Crowning. Schmemann's account of marriage encourages the Western reader to look anew at the Roman rite of marriage, to discern the Eucharistic and ecclesial transformation that occurs in the sacrament of marriage. Rather than see a radical divergence between a Western and Eastern approach, the two allow for a personal and ecclesial account of nuptial transformation in the sacrament.

Alexander Schmemann and the Sacramental Imagination[1]

STEVE GUTHRIE

Faith is the touching of a mystery, it is to perceive another dimension to absolutely everything in the world. In faith, the mysterious meaning of life comes alive. Beneath the simple, explicable, one-dimensional surface of things, their genuine content begins to shine. Nature herself begins to speak out and to witness to what is above her, within her, but *separate from her*. To speak in the simplest possible terms: faith sees, knows, senses . . . the presence of God in the world. . . . Truly, for the believer, everything in life and life itself begins to be experienced as *revelation*.[2]

IF ONE'S DESTINATION IS "absolutely everything in the world,"[3] then it might seem that any road would do; no itinerary could fail entirely. If we are looking for God's presence in "everything in life," then it would seem we could look in any direction. Certainly, the trajectory of Alexander Schmemann's sacramental theology encompasses all of created reality. Schmemann did not only think *about* the sacraments but *through* them. His theology is the elaborate expression of a sacramental imagination; a vision of the cosmos brought into focus through the lens of sacrament. His work is informed, from start to finish, by a faith that

---

1. I am grateful to my colleagues Dr. David Dark and Dr. Donovan McAbee for several helpful conversations and many insights I worked on the material in this chapter.

2. Schmemann, *I Believe*, 159–60.

3. Schmemann, *I Believe*, 160.

213

"sees, knows, senses . . . the presence of God in the world."[4] The world, in other words, is sacrament.

Such a universal approach to sacrament might not be obvious to everyone. Jonathan Swift reminds us that there was a time when the province of sacrament was thought—at least in popular discussion—to be far narrower than the cosmos. In fact, Swift parodies sacramental debate as the most fussy and insular of all theological concerns. In his satire of Eucharistic controversies, "Little-endians" and "Big-endians" enter into ferocious and arcane disputes over the proper way to crack an egg, ultimately condemning one another as heretics.[5] Much more recently, the British theologian David Brown could complain that "it is still true that for the most part, the sacraments are treated as the most 'churchy' or ecclesiastical part of a theology course, . . . an issue for the inner circle, as it were."[6] However widespread this perception may be, it is markedly out of step with the actual progression of sacramental theology over the past century. For many, sacrament (or often "sacramentality") became instead a way of describing the relation between God and creation more generally. In this vein, theologians proposed that we recognize the sacramentality of work, visual art, architecture, dance, literature, natural beauty, gardening, interior design, fashion, sport, and jazz improvisation, among other things.[7] William Temple, in his Gifford Lectures, offered a vivid and widely quoted expression of this broadened sacramentality:

> Now if the structure of Reality is such as we described . . . [then] the lower grades [of Reality] . . . only attain to the fullness of their own being so far as they are indwelt and dominated by those above them. They exist then, ultimately, to embody or symbolize what is more than themselves. *The universe is sacramental.*[8]

So again, the cosmic breadth of Schmemann's sacramental vision is not unique, particularly in contemporary theology. Many have commended a sacramentality encompassing "absolutely everything in the world." Still, one might inquire concerning the best route to "absolutely everything." As stated at the outset, if one's destination is the whole cosmos, it might seem that any road would do. But it is precisely a difference of approach that separates Schmemann from other versions of universal sacramentality.

---

4. Schmemann, *I Believe*, 160.

5. Swift, *Gulliver's Travels*, 36.

6. Brown, *God and the Enchantment of Place*, 6.

7. See Spinks, "Sacramentology."

8. Temple, *Christus Veritas*, 16. Emphasis added.

Can we not encounter the world as sacrament *directly*, without passing first of all through the liturgy of the church? This is the implied question behind David Brown's critique of Schmemann. Brown is bothered by those approaches in which:

> the story is told almost entirely from the inside out as it were, that is, with the assumption that such a reading of the world has validity only if it starts with Christ and his church. For example, one can see such an assumption running through what Alexander Schmemann has to say in his influential essay on *The World as Sacrament*.[9]

There is an agreement that the world is sacrament. The question is how we might come to see and experience the world as such. By what means are we to cultivate a sacramental imagination?

Sacrament in Ordinary and An Altar in the World

David Brown is recognized as "one of the pioneers of this broader approach"[10] to sacrament. He urges a "reinvigorated sense of the sacramental;"[11] one that embraces sacrament as "a major and perhaps even the primary way of exploring God's relationship to our world."[12] Brown is eager to move beyond the traditional sacraments of the church, and instead "to reclaim for religious experience great areas of human encounter with the divine that have been either marginalized in contemporary Christianity or almost wholly ignored"[13]:

> Sport, drama, humor, dance, architecture, place, home, and the natural world are all part of a long list of activities and forms of experience that have been relegated to the periphery of religious reflection, but which once made invaluable contributions to a

---

9. Brown, "Sacramental World," 605.

10. "One of the pioneers of this broader approach is D. Brown (1948), who, in a range of interdisciplinary studies, explores the divine disclosure in such things as the body (dance) classical music, pop music, Blues, and opera. Brown's plea is that divine disclosure and divine presence cannot and should not be limited to those rites more traditionally termed sacraments, where human beings are engaged in doing something that carries a promise of divine presence" (Spinks, "Sacramentology").

11. Brown, *God and Enchantment of Place*, 5.

12. Brown, *God and Enchantment of Place*, 6.

13. Brown, *God and Grace of Body*, 1.

human perception that this world is where God can be encountered, and encountered often.[14]

Brown's special interest is "the sacrament in ordinary" (the subtitle of his
2007 volume). The rites of the church do not exhaust the category of the sacramental, and indeed, instances of sacramentality outside the church have
been too often overlooked. "The mistake," he insists (in a critique of the film
Babette's Feast), "is to suppose that only the most explicit forms of religion
are of relevance"; rather, "it is important to acknowledge that the implicit
can be as effective as the explicit, and *sometimes more so*."[15]

The "sometimes more so" in the preceding quotation is significant.
Brown's work displays not only an openness to but also a *preference* for those
"sacramental" experiences that lie outside of the church and avoid any sort
of explicitly Christian reference.

For instance, Brown surveys the musical work of Stravinsky, including a
number of explicitly religious works such as the *Symphony of Psalms*. Brown
believes, however, that these sacred pieces mediate the presence of the Divine much less powerfully and effectively than do those works of Stravinsky
without any clear religious reference: "To my mind, it is not in its surprisingly confident voice that God is to be found but rather in [Stravinsky's]
much earlier *Symphonies of Wind Instruments*."[16] Likewise, in his survey of
opera, Brown declares that "Verdi is surely at his best, not when pulling the
strings of conventional religion, as in *Nabucco*, but rather in an opera like
Don Carlos, where . . . the struggles are so much more real."[17] "It is thus the
openness of plots and the interpretative music that goes with them," he continues and *"not clearly fixed horizons, which generate possibilities*."[18] In the
same way, when considering the work of Bob Dylan, Brown expresses a clear
preference for more recent material, when Dylan's faith is "less explicit"[19] as
opposed to "the arrogant self-certainty"[20] of Dylan's forthrightly Christian
albums. When he turns to rap music, Brown notes that religious themes
are prominent in the music of the rapper KRS-One, but he laments that
these lyrics "move in a more explicitly religious direction," so KRS-One
ends up sounding "rather too much like a lecturing parent."[21] Brown also

14. Brown, *God and Enchantment of Place*, 9.

15. Brown, *God and Grace of Body*, 183. Emphasis added.

16. Brown, *God and Grace of Body*, 286.

17. Brown, *God and Grace of Body*, 382.

18. Brown, *God and Grace of Body*, 383. Emphasis added.

19. Brown, *God and Grace of Body*, 310.

20. Brown, *God and Grace of Body*, 310.

21. Brown, *God and Grace of Body*, 343

has a largely critical assessment of the great country artist Johnny Cash. He notes that only a couple of Cash's songs manage to get beyond "the narrowly conventional."[22] In the main, however, Cash's religious lyrics are dismissed as "trite and commonplace."[23] Brown concludes that in the end, "established conventions were just too strong for him to run counter to them."[24] Brown also gives attention to recording artists who experienced a religious conversion mid-career. In that discussion, Alice Cooper's conversion is contrasted negatively with that of Patti Smith, precisely because Cooper's conversion is too confident, too conventional. His lyrics, Brown complains, present "the implicit threat of a hell at which he once mocked."[25] Brown likewise expresses little interest in contemporary Christian music generally because here "music is acting . . . as a conservator of belief rather than initiating the audience into new experiences of the divine."[26]

In each of the preceding instances then, it would seem that from Brown's perspective, music is most readily experienced as sacramental when it is least closely associated with the church, explicit belief, and the traditional affirmations of the faith community. Perhaps this is understandable. Brown hopes to emphasize that sacrament is outside as well as inside the church. The legitimacy of the church's sacrament is taken as read. Brown's focus, rather, is on those experiences whose sacramental character might less readily be recognized. Nevertheless, precisely because Brown is interested in the sacramental character of the world outside of the church, the confession and the rites of the church are, at best, a distraction and, at worst, an obstacle to his project. He wants to resist, after all, the suggestion that a sacramental imagination "has validity only if it starts with Christ and his church."[27]

In this respect, Brown's project resembles the emphasis in a number of popular Christian authors. In a widely read and artfully written memoir, Barbara Brown Taylor encourages readers to find "an altar in the world."[28] She observes that, "regarded properly, anything can become a sacrament, by which I mean an outward and visible sign of an inward and spiritual connection."[29] She goes on to describe her recent move to "one of the largest

22. Brown, *God and Grace of Body*, 368.
23. Brown, *God and Grace of Body*, 367.
24. Brown, *God and Grace of Body*, 367.
25. Brown, *God and Grace of Body*, 337.
26. Brown, *God and Grace of Body*. Emphasis added.
27. Brown, "Sacramental World," 605.
28. Taylor, *Altar in the World*.
29. Taylor, *Altar in the World*, 30.

chicken-producing areas in the country."[30] As a result, she often "ended up behind loud trucks stacked with wire cages full of those same chickens on their way to be slaughtered."[31] She continues:

> The first time I drove five miles with those feathers glancing off my windshield, the feathers became sacraments for me. I got the connection between them and boneless chicken breasts in a way I had never gotten it before. I saw what dies so that I may live, and while I did not stop eating chicken meat, I began cooking it and eating it with unprecedented reverence.[32]

"Other sacraments take more work," she goes on to say. "But if you are paying attention, even a mail-order catalog can become a sacrament."[33] Like David Brown, in places, Brown Taylor seems to go beyond saying that God can *also be* found outside of ecclesial sacraments. Rather, she writes that (at least for her) the sacramental is *most readily encountered* by "leaving church." She confesses:

> I know plenty of people who find God most reliably in books, in buildings, and even in other people. I have found God in all of these places too, but the most reliable meeting place for me has always been creation. Since I first became aware of the Divine Presence in that lit-up field in Kansas, I have known where to go when my own flame is guttering. To lie with my back flat on the fragrant ground is to receive a transfusion of the same power that makes the green blade rise. To remember that I am dirt and to dirt I shall return is to be given my life back again, if only for one present moment at a time. . . . When I take a breath, God's Holy Spirit enters me. When a cricket speaks to me, I talk back. Like everything else on earth, I am an embodied soul, who leaps to life when I recognize my kin. If this makes me a pagan, then I am a grateful one.[34]

A similar sort of sentiment appears to be behind a widely discussed blog post by the popular Christian author Donald Miller. Miller confesses that he rarely attends church, because (as the title of the post indicates) he is much better able "to connect with [God] elsewhere."[35] Miller explains:

---

30. Taylor, *Altar in the World*, 30.
31. Taylor, *Altar in the World*, 30.
32. Taylor, *Altar in the World*, 30–31.
33. Taylor, *Altar in the World*, 31.
34. Taylor, *Leaving Church*.
35. Miller, "I Don't Worship God by Singing."

> It's just that I don't experience that intimacy [with God] in a
> traditional worship service. In fact, I can count on one hand the
> number of sermons I actually remember. So to be brutally hon-
> est, I don't learn much about God hearing a sermon and I don't
> connect with him by singing songs to him.[36]

There is much in Brown and in Brown Taylor that Schmemann would be
eager to affirm. The world is sacrament. All of creation is intended as a place
of encounter, as the material through which God's presence is mediated to
us. Schmemann likewise laments a parochial and limited view of God's
activity, one which makes the church door the far limit of religious experience.[37] But for Schmemann, the church is no obstacle to be overcome on
the way to a cosmic sacramentality. In fact, Schmemann insists, the church
is a cosmic sacrament: "She is a sacrament in the cosmic sense because she
manifests in 'this world' the genuine world of God, as he first created it."[38]
Brown and Brown Taylor broaden the reach of sacramentality by moving it
away from the church. Schmemann broadens the reach of sacramentality
by moving it through the church. If Barbara Brown Taylor hopes to find an
altar in the world, Schmemann believes that the church brings the world
to the altar in its sacraments. If David Brown affirms the world by moving
beyond the liturgy of the church, Schmemann urges the church to enact
its liturgy "for the life of the world." While the liturgical celebrations of
the church may suggest a certain "separation from the world," nevertheless, Schmemann insists, "we separate ourselves from the world in order to
bring it, in order to lift it up to the kingdom, to make it once again the way
to God and participation in his eternal kingdom."[39]

Brown objects that this conception of sacrament is ultimately world-
denying. Moreover, awarding such a privileged place to the worship of the
church effectively denies the Spirit's freedom to work anywhere and everywhere. Brown complains that in the Orthodox theology of the icon, for
instance:

> it is no longer the world as such that reveals God, but only that
> world when transformed under divine grace . . . [So] it entails
> a world that always needs some further action upon it over and

36. Miller, "I Don't Worship God by Singing."

37. Schmemann deplores "the reduction of the liturgy to 'cultic' categories, its definition as a sacred act of worship, different as such not only from the 'profane' area of
life, but even from all other activities of the Church itself" (Schmemann, *For the Life
of the World*, 25).

38. Schmemann, *Eucharist*, 35.

39. Schmemann, *Eucharist*, 53.

above creation itself, that is to say, some further act of divine grace, in order to point to its creator . . . The whole movement of the icon is seen as decisively in one direction, not towards the world but rather drawing us out of that world and into another.[40]

The Transformed Imagination

Brown is certainly right; Schmemann insists that perceiving the world as sacrament involves a transformation. But this transformation is not "vertical." It is not, in other words, as if earthly realities "below" (in "this world") were made transparent, in order to function as windows into heaven "above" ("some other world"); rather, the transformation is "horizontal." When the church in its liturgy brings this-worldly realities—such as bread and wine, oil and water, marriage and death—into the life of the church, those realities take on the character of the new creation. They are both revealed as their own transformed selves and restored to their authentic character as gifts given to mediate the presence of God: "Christ came not to *replace* 'natural' matter with some 'supernatural' and sacred matter," Schmemann explains, "but to *restore* it and to fulfill it as the means of communion with God. The holy water in Baptism, the bread and wine in the Eucharist, stand for, i.e., *represent*, the whole of creation, but creation as it will be at the *end*, when it will be consummated in God, when he will fill all things with Himself."[41]

Sacrament "is primarily a revelation of the *sacramentality* of creation itself, for the world was created and given to man for conversion of creaturely life into participation in divine life."[42] The world was created to be "the 'matter,' the material of one all-embracing eucharist, and man was created as the priest of this cosmic sacrament."[43] All of the world is gift, offered to humanity as the means for communion with the Giver. The fall, correspondingly, is nothing else but the failure to recognize the world as sacrament. "Sin is itself perceived here as a *falling away* of man, and in him of all creation, from this sacramentality."[44] When we recognize the world as gift of God, then we experience the world as the presence of the Giver. In the act "of both receiving the world from God and offering it to God—and by filling the world with this

40. Brown, *God and Enchantment of Place*, 43.

41. Schmemann, *Of Water and the Spirt*, 49–50

42. Schmemann, *Eucharist*, 33–34.

43. Schmemann, *For the Life of the World*, 15.

44. Schmemann, *Eucharist*, 34. See also Schmemann, *For the Life of the World*, 18.

eucharist, [man] transforms his life, the one that he receives from the world, into life in God, into communion with him."

The "transformation" upon which Schmemann insists—and of which Brown complains—is not then a critique of creation. It does not presume some deficiency; as if the stuff of which the world is made were too poor to reveal God. At least in one respect, the imagination is the locus of the sacramental transformation. We come to see the world differently—as sacrament. The liturgy of the church, then, is not a matter of pointing away from this world, but rather *pointing to* it: *Look! Oil and water, bread and wine! These are the gifts of God, and his presence here among us!* "The essential spiritual act" Schmemann explains, "consists . . . precisely in discerning the essential goodness of all that exists and acts."[45] The sacramental transformation Schmemann describes then is not illustrative, analogical, or one of cause and effect but rather is "epiphanic." "One reality *manifests . . .* and *communicates* the other. It is not that this or that part of 'this world'—space, time, or matter—be made *sacred* but rather that everything in it be seen and comprehended as expectation and thirst for its complete spiritualization: 'that God may be all in all.'"[46] Notice the language of revelation, of discernment, of transformed seeing, and perception remade:

> The Church is the sacrament of the Kingdom—not because she possesses divinely instituted acts called "sacraments," but because first of all she is the possibility given to man to see in and through this world the "world to come," to see and to "live" it in Christ. It is only when in the darkness of *this world* we discern that Christ has *already* "filled all things with Himself" that *these things,* whatever they may be, are revealed and given to us full of meaning and beauty. A Christian is the one who, wherever he looks, finds Christ and rejoices in Him. And this joy *transforms* all his human plans and programs, decisions and actions, making all his mission the sacrament of the world's return to Him who is the life of the world.[47]

It is vitally important to recognize that this "transformed seeing" is not merely a shift in perspective, whereby an alternative interpretive grid is laid overtop a more fundamental reality. Sacrament is precisely how we are intended to experience the world. The sacramental imagination is not some exotic mode of perception by which we translate the world into a religious dialect. Rather, it is the world's own native tongue, as it were; the way in which God intended

45. Schmemann, *Of Water and Spirit*, 84.

46. Schmemann, *Eucharist*, 39.

47. Schmemann, *For the Life of the World*, 113.

the world to address humanity. We do not see the world "*as if*" it were sacrament. Rather, the realities of this world become sacrament when we so receive them. In the words of the medieval dictum, *significando causant*—"they cause by signifying." *By* seeing the world as sacrament, the world comes to exercise its proper sacramental function. The world *is in fact* gift of God. The world *is in fact* created to be the means of communion with God. When we recognize God in and through this-worldly realities, those realities fulfill the role appointed them by God, and so become what they truly are. We do not imagine them to be something other than they are, or recast them in some light generated by our own creative faculties. They are not simply reminders or memorials of grace in a Zwinglian fashion. Rather, we see them as they are, and in so seeing them, they are able to become and function for us as sacraments. Communion with God, the experience of God's presence, is precisely the grace conveyed by a sacramental creation.

Communities of Interpretation

Nevertheless, even if Schmemann's sacramental theology is not "world-denying," still we might ask: *why the insistence upon the mediation of the church?* If Schmemann would have us recognize the world as God's gift and experience God's presence in and through all things, why give such prominence to the church's liturgy? Does not Brown's project end up being a far more thorough-going affirmation of the sacramentality of creation? Is it not a kind of domestication of the Spirit to tie the sacramental efficacy of the created world to the rites of the worshipping community? Does this not amount to a stubborn refusal to acknowledge God's generous presence and activity—not only in the church, but in all the world?

We should in fact prefer Schmemann's vision, but not out of some impulse to protect ecclesial privilege; rather, Schmemann's sacramental theology reflects a more astute account of human knowing.

To perceive objects as sacramental, to experience the natural world or the world of culture as mediating God's presence, is a kind of *seeing-as*. We perceive the world under a particular description, one which makes certain kinds of perception possible, while ruling out others. Philosophers such as John Searle have spoken about "the Background"—the framework within which interpretation takes place: "I see this as a chair, this as a table, that as a glass, indeed, any normal case of perception will be a case of *perceiving as*, where the perceiver assimilates the perceived object to some more or less familiar category. . . . The possibility of perceiving . . . requires a familiarity with the set of categories under which one experiences those aspects. The ability to apply those categories is a Background ability."[48]

Moltmann provides a theological example of this kind of categorical perception when he speaks of perceiving nature *as creation*. "Nature" in the theological tradition came to be understood as the "finite, dependent and contingent reality"[49] of experienceable things. But alongside this reductive understanding of the physical environment remains the possibility of experiencing nature as creation, as gift. In a passage deeply evocative of Schmemann, Moltmann writes:

> In perceiving the world as creation, the human being discerns and enters into a community of creation. This community becomes a dialogue before the common Creator. Knowledge of the world as creation is in its primal form thanksgiving for the gift of creation and for the community found in it, and adoring praise of the Creator. . . . Perceiving the world as creation is not "a matter of opinion"—an intellectual tenet. It implies a particular attitude toward the world and a way of dealing with it which touches the existence of the perceiving person and draws him into a wider fellowship. Perception of the world as creation confers felicity in existence. Offering the world to God in thanksgiving confers freedom in existence.[50]

The world may be experienced *as nature* or *as creation*. One brings a "Background" to one's experience of creaturely reality—"a set of categories under which one experiences" the world. And this Background, and these categories establish "the possibility of perceiving." I can perceive the world as a "dialogue before the common Creator," as occasion for "thanksgiving for the gift," when it is experienced against the Background of "World-As-Creation." The world does not cease to be Creation apart from this Background, but it is only *humanly experienced* as Creation when perceived against this Background. Searle cites the example, not of experiencing the world as Creation, but of falling in love:

> La Rochefoucauld says somewhere that very few people would fall in love if they never read about it; and nowadays, we would have to add if they never saw it on television or in the movies. What they get from television, movies, and reading is, of course,

48. Searle, *Construction of Social Reality*, 133.

49. Moltmann, *God in Creation*, 57.

50. Moltmann, *God in Creation*, 70.

in part a set of beliefs and desires. The point . . . is that beliefs and desires only fix conditions of satisfaction against a Background . . . [against] the dramatic categories that extend over sequences of events.[51]

The preceding quotation highlights an essential point: the imaginative categories within which we interpret experience are not (in the case of mentally healthy people) individual and idiosyncratic constructions. Rather, we *receive* the Background from an interpretive community.

Charles Taylor notes a similarity between the idea of "the Background" and his concept of a "social imaginary:" "That common understanding which makes possible common practices, and a widely shared sense of legitimacy."[52] Taylor draws attention to the reciprocal relationship between this shared understanding and shared practices. "What exactly is involved, when a theory penetrates and transforms the social imaginary?" he asks. "For the most part, people take up, improvise, or are inducted into new practices. These are made sense of by the new outlook, the one first articulated in the theory; this outlook is the context that gives sense to the practices."[53]

A common understanding—whether conceived of as "the Background" or a "social imaginary"—a common understanding makes a certain mode of perception and hence, certain practices, possible. But equally, it is through these practices that one is caught up in and internalizes the social imaginary: "In this process, what is originally just an idealization grows to a complex imaginary through being taken up and associated with social practices, in part traditional ones, but often transformed by the contact."[54] So,"if the understanding makes the practice possible, it is also true that it is the practice which largely carries the understanding."[55]

The clearest route to "absolutely everything in the world" is one that passes through the life of the church. Again, this is not a chauvinistic demand for special ecclesial prerogatives. It is the recognition that a social imaginary emerges from the life and practices of a community. It is the interpretive community of the church, then, which provides the Background against which the world can be perceived as gift, as God's presence. And it is the liturgy of the church through which we internalize this imaginative vision. It seems reasonable to suggest, in fact, that it is precisely their immersion in the community of the church that allowed Brown, Brown Taylor, and

51. Searle, *Construction of Social Reality*, 135.
52. Taylor, *Secular Age*, 172.
53. Taylor, *Secular Age*, 175.
54. Taylor, *Secular Age*, 175.
55. Taylor, *Secular Age*, 173.

Miller to so clearly recognize God's presence outside of it. This, Schmemann argues, is precisely what is meant to happen through the life and liturgy of the church. *Leitourgia*, he reminds us, originally meant:

> a function or "ministry" of a man or of a group on behalf of and in the interest of the whole community. . . .Thus, the Church itself is a *leitourgia*, a ministry, a calling to act in this world after the fashion of Christ, to bear testimony to Him and His kingdom.[56]

> The Liturgy is not to be treated as an aesthetic experience or a therapeutic exercise. Its unique function is to reveal to us the Kingdom of God.[57]

> The Church as *institution* exists in order to reveal—in "this world"—the "world to come," the Kingdom of God.[58]

There is much to affirm and appreciate in the Romantic image of a solitary figure wandering through the woods, perceiving God here and there. Of course, individuals do have such experiences, often profound and personally transformative. Blake discerns "heaven in a wild flower";[59] Elizabeth Barrett Browning recognizes "every common bush afire with God";[60] Wordsworth has glimpses "of Proteus rising from the sea";[61] and Gerard Manley Hopkins declares that "the world's charged with the grandeur of God."[62] This is all to the good. But if the "sacramental imagination" is to be a transformative vision for a society—for a culture, rather than simply the occasion for private and individual spiritual experience—then that imagination must be the common possession of a community, embedded in its practices and shared life. It is precisely for the "life of the world" in this sense, then, that the liturgy of the church matters so profoundly. Brown speaks often of "experiences of transcendence" and "encounters with mystery." But what if the sacramental imagination could generate more than individual moments of wonder? What if the sacramental imagination meant a different "social imaginary"—one that made a particular conception of the world available to a community; a conception which, in turn, might transform that

56. Schmemann, *For the Life of the World*, 25.
57. Schmemann, *Liturgy and Tradition*, 100.
58. Schmemann, *Liturgy and Tradition*, 77.
59. Blake, "Auguries of Innocence," 493.
60. Browning, *Aurora Leigh*.
61. Wordsworth, "World is Too Much With Us," 113.
62. Hopkins, "God's Grandeur," 15.

community's way of being in the world?[63] What if the sacramental imagination might lead to a more just, peaceful, and joyful world? One example of this is in the sacramental transformation of suffering and death.

The Sacraments of Suffering and Death

As we've already seen, Schmemann extends "sacrament" well beyond bread and wine—oil and water may also be sacramental. But he likewise extends "sacrament" well beyond the good and beautiful things of this created world. Suffering and death are to be made sacraments as well. "In Christ," he says, "*everything* in this world, and this means health *and* disease, joy *and* suffering, has become an ascension to, and entrance into this new life, its expectation and anticipation."[64] Suffering is also drawn down the transformational path of sacrament.[65]

> Here is a man suffering on his bed in pain and the Church comes to him to perform the sacrament of healing. For this man, as for every man in the whole world, suffering can be defeat, the way of complete surrender to darkness, despair, and solitude. It can be *dying* in the very real sense of the word. And yet, it can be also the

63. Brown does in fact argue for the importance of social setting and communities of interpretation in his two volumes, Brown, *Tradition and Imagination*, and Brown, *Discipleship and Imagination*. Brown urges that Christians should more whole-heartedly embrace tradition as a source of revelation; not only the conciliar and ecclesial traditions of the church but traditions outside the church as well, including the critical traditions of scholarship that have challenged orthodox teachings and philosophical and religious traditions outside of the Christian faith. God's thoroughgoing activity in human history and generous presence in all of creation means that culture, too, is one site where God reveals himself. So, Brown might respond that one can acknowledge the importance of social imaginaries for interpretation, without recourse to the church. God is at work through other communities and other interpretive visions. This response, however, still would not allay the concerns articulated here. One might acknowledge that God is at work in the imaginative vision of rural Buddhist farmers, for instance, and that Christians can and should appropriate some of the insights available through that community. The point is that even so adopted, those insights would only shape the life and the imaginative vision of the members of the community to the extent that they are fully integrated into the life and activities of the community. Similarly, in *God and Enchantment of Place* and *God and Grace of Body*, Brown explores various instances of architecture, sport, dance, song, and so on through which one might experience the presence of God. The possibility and reality of such experiences can be acknowledged. But the formation of a *sacramental imagination*—a comprehensive description under which we perceive reality—does not arise from particular experiences but rather from inhabiting an interpretive community.

64. Schmemann, *O, Death*, 106. Emphasis added.

65. Schmemann, *O, Death*, 107, 108, 109.

ultimate victory of Man and of life in him. The Church does not
come to restore health in this man. . . . [It] comes to take this man
into the Love, the Light and the Light of Christ. . . .

Through [Christ's] own suffering, not only has all suffering
acquired a meaning but it has been given the power to become
itself the sign, the sacrament, the proclamation, the "coming"
of that victory; the defeat of man, his very *dying* has become a
way of Life.

If suffering and dying can be sacrament, then even more audaciously, Christianity insists that death itself, the last enemy, can be experienced as sacrament. The character of a sacrament is that it manifests God's presence. The ugliness and horror of death correspondingly, is "not in its being the 'end' and not in physical destruction" but rather "by being separation from the world and life, it is separation from God. The dead cannot glorify God."[66] The character of death is anti-sacramental; it is that event which excludes all possibility of the communion with God. But what then if *death* has become the means by which God is revealed in our midst? What if death has manifested the presence of God with us? Then truly, Death has been trampled down by death; its horror and separation transformed into sacrament. This is indeed what has happened:

In [Christ], death itself has become an act of life, for he has filled
it with himself, with his love and light. . . . And if I make this new
life mine, mine this hunger and thirst for the Kingdom, mine
this expectation of Christ, mine the certitude that Christ is Life,
then my very death will be an act of communion with Life.[67]

The Slavery of Death

This transfiguration of suffering and death certainly brings hope, comfort, and peace to individuals. But transforming the meaning of death might have carried a more far-reaching impact than providing individual comfort. The fear of death reaches into and then out through the structures and institutions of society with malignant and menacing power. In Orthodox perspective, it is not simply that human sin has brought death into the world. It is also the case that death brings sin into the world. "Unnourished by the divine energy, our existence fades into subjection to corruption and death. In such a state, our mortality becomes a source

66. Schmemann, *O, Death*, 101.

67. Schmemann, *For the Life of the World*, 106.

of anxiety. Futile attempts to defend ourselves from it lead us into active sin and estrange us from trust in God. Now sinfulness is more a result of mortality than morality of sinfulness."[68]

Richard Beck, drawing on the existential psychology of Ernest Becker, demonstrates the ways in which this fear of death controls us—binding us to destructive behaviors; generating an idolatrous attachment to institutions and ideologies.[69] We learn and love and work and grow and create, and yet, always on the horizon, we see the all-annihilating approach of death. All we do and achieve will be laid low by death; we and all those we love will be whisked away and forgotten. The grave makes a mockery of all our attempts at significance, and so we are left crying, along with the Preacher of Ecclesiastes, "Vanity! All is vanity!" Becker argues that in response to this crushing burden of human mortality and finitude, cultures create "hero systems," "in which people serve in order to earn a feeling of primary value, of cosmic specialness, of ultimate usefulness to creation, of unshakeable meaning."[70] These hero systems promise a pseudo-immortality by connecting our lives to ideals, structures, and institutions that will outlive us. Cultural hero systems, Beck writes:

> step in to provide paths toward death transcendence—a means toward a symbolic (or literal) immortality. Life achieves significance and meaning when we participate in these "greater goods" that can transcend our finite existence. For example, my life is deemed meaningful because my children outlive me, or I wrote a book, or I helped the company have its best quarter of the year. Child, book, and company are all forms of "immortality," ways to continue living into the future in an effort to "defeat" death.[71]

But these institutions and ends exact a high price for the immortality they promise. They function as gods, promising deliverance from death and the hope of immortal life, and as deities, they demand absolute obedience. Driven by fear of death, we become enslaved to these hero systems. However much we would like to, we feel unable to offer our lives, time, and resources to others with open-handed abandon because these are claimed by work, community, career, or a particular vision of family. We compete with others at work, pursue a particular vision of success with single-minded devotion, and sacrifice time, health, and relationships in order to achieve the lasting significance we are promised. Rather than putting

68. Heim, *Depth of Riches*, 68.
69. Beck, *Slavery of Death*.
70. Ernest Becker, quoted in Beck, *Slavery of Death*, 35–36.
71. Beck, *Slavery of Death*, 37.

others' interests ahead of our own, rather than laying down our life for others, we pour our lives into our culture's hero-making systems in the hope of attaining the eternal life they offer.

Most troubling of all Beck argues, our fear of death breeds violence. The hero-making structures which promise us immortality are regularly placed under threat. We may have staked our immortality on the investment we have made in our nation, our family legacy, a particular political party, a denomination, or a church fellowship. How, then, will we react when the existence of that organism is threatened, or when its absolute claims are challenged by another country or political system or competing group? We will defend the institutions to which we are committed, certainly, but not out of simple loyalty or devotion. Rather, our very hope of immortality is tied to the investment we have made. If (say) one has sacrificed oneself in the cause of democracy, then any system that challenges the superiority of the democratic system challenges the god that has provided a way to overcome death:

> Those who are different from us implicitly or explicitly call into question the things we hold most dear, the cultural values that ground and shape the contours of our identity and self-esteem in the face of death. In this, out-group members become a source of anxiety, an existential threat. To cope with the anxiety, we rush to defend our worldview and become dogmatic, fundamentalist, and ideological in regard to our values, culture, and way of life. We embrace our worldview as unique and exceptional, as superior to other worldviews, which we deem inferior, mistaken, and even dangerous.[72]

The Community Freed from Death

A concrete example might help. A 2012 study indicates that "becoming famous is the major aspiration of children from ten to twelve years of age."[73] According to a 2009 British survey, "the top three career aspirations for five to eleven-year-olds in Britain were sports star, pop star, and actor, compared with teacher, banker, and doctor twenty-five years ago."[74]

These and similar studies are a striking and poignant manifestation of just one of the "hero systems" of contemporary society and the way those hero

72. Beck, *Slavery of Death*, 64.
73. Uhls and Greenfield, "Value of Fame."
74. Brockes, "I Want to Be Famous."

systems fund the imagination of a whole culture. I am not suggesting that all of the ten-year-olds aspiring to pop stardom are driven by a fear of death. The example is poignant precisely because such a connection with mortality may never have occurred to them. Instead, through the liturgies of popular culture they have become acolytes of the various false immortalities worshipped by that culture. Sacred rites like the Grammys, Oscars, and Emmys, episodes of *The Voice, American Idol,* and *America's Got Talent* model for disciples the kinds of lives and achievements that are worthy of celebration. A pop song from a generation ago is a hymn to the eternal life promised:

> Fame!
> I'm gonna live forever . . .
> People will see me and cry—
>
> Fame!
> I'm gonna make it to heaven.
> Light up the sky like a flame—
>
> Fame!
> I'm gonna live forever!
> Baby, remember my name.[75]

If the aspiration to fame were nothing more than adolescent daydreaming about TV success or YouTube followers, then it might not be cause for concern. But the desire for immortality through the hero system of fame, reputation, and recognition manifests itself in all forms of ambition: the drive for academic and scholarly achievement, business success, political power, or a large and thriving ministry; the aspiration to lead a large and influential church, to write a blog with thousands of followers, or even to exercise influence in the local community or school district. In each instance, the hero system of fame nurtures an ethic and an approach to life that is profoundly antithetical to the gospel—one that seeks to advance oneself rather than serve others. The point is not to single out celebrity culture as the chief evil. Altruism, self-sacrifice, family legacy, or religious heritage can be death-denying, "hero-making" systems as well. The point, rather, is to suggest how one prominent strand in the narrative of our culture might be a hero-making system connected to the fear of death. It is to show how a generation might be initiated into that hero-making system through the practices, institutions, and media of a culture. It is to show how the decisions and life trajectory of that generation might be shaped by having been

---

75. Gore and Pitchford, "Fame." The song won the 1980 Academy Award for Best Original Song.

so initiated—the imagined vision of immortality that will guide their investment of time, passion, energy, and resources.

It is to suggest, too, how such a hero-making system might be over-
turned and undone by a sacramental imagination. If I carry my death into the
life of the church and make of it a sacrament, it is no longer a lord, controlling
me through fear. Instead it becomes a thing offered to God, to be filled with
his presence. Just so, suffering, dying, and death are "carried into" the worship
of the church—by the rites of Christian burial, prayer for, and anointing of
the sick; through the testimony of those who suffer and through the experience of worshipping alongside them; and supremely, through the Eucharist,
where we celebrate Jesus' unmaking of death through his death. In these acts,
suffering and death are sacramentally transformed. They are no longer malig-
nent threats that hold us enslaved but the means by which we experience the
presence of God. The Background or social imaginary of the gathered community is fashioned through these practices, and so the gathered community
is initiated into a different way of perceiving suffering and death. I know that
Jesus, having been obedient "to the point of death, even death on a cross"
(Phil 2:8), "therefore," received from God "the name that is above every other
name" (Phil 2:9). So I no longer need to be one of those who say, "Come, let
us make a name for ourselves" (Gen 11:4).

Moreover, this is worship "for the life of the world." From the worship
of the Church, the sacramental community goes out into the wider community, no longer enslaved by the fear of Death. No longer impelled to pursue immortality through success, they go to their places of work happy to
advance other's interests; happy to lay aside competitiveness, posturing, and
turf wars. No longer committed to the structures and systems that promise
significance, they go out into their community, free to engage in those costly
acts of service that are not rewarded by the hero-making systems of their
culture. No longer bound to the pseudo-immortality offered by institutions
and ideologies, they are no longer threatened by those who are "other" than
them. Instead, they are liberated to welcome and love those who are outsiders; strangers who are unlike themselves and who look at the world in
radically different ways. This is a sacramental imagination that does more
than produce meaningful individual experiences but which has the power
to transform communities and cultures.

And perhaps this is the point at which we can return to our opening
question—if one's destination is "absolutely everything in the world," will
not any route do? If one is attending to all of creation, cannot one look in
any direction? Certainly, the Christian should affirm that one may journey
out to meet God everywhere and in everything. Jürgen Moltmann observes
that because God's Spirit fills creation, "it is . . . possible to experience God

in, with, and beneath each everyday experience of the world."[76] Indeed, "in everything, God is waiting for us."[77] Athanasius insists that "no part of creation [has] ever been without [the Logos of God], Who, while ever abiding in union with the Father, yet fills all things that are."[78] These theologians stand alongside Romantics like Elizabeth Barrett Browning and theologians like David Brown, who insist that:

> Earth's crammed with heaven,
> and every common bush afire with God.[79]

And yet, Browning continues:

> But only he who sees, takes off his shoes,
> The rest sit round it and pluck blackberries,
> and daub their natural faces unaware.[80]

The question, then, is not whether God is present in the world. *In him we live and move and have our being!* (Acts 17:28) The question is how we—who, with heavy boots and hooded eyes trample over holy ground, wholly unsuspecting—might be made aware of that presence. Schmemann, like Browning, suggests that this happens not when we leave liturgy behind, but when we "take off our shoes," and enter into worship.

76. Moltmann, *Spirit of Life*, 34.

77. Moltmann, *Spirit of Life*, 36

78. Athanasius, *On the Incarnation of the Word*, 2.2.8.

79. Browning, *Aurora Leigh*.

80. Browning, *Aurora Leigh*.

Bibliography

Anderson, Paul B. *No East or West.* New York: YMCA, 1985.

Athanasius. *On the Incarnation of the Word.* New York: Macmillan, 1946.

Aune, Michael B. "The Current State of Liturgical Theology: A Plurality of Particularities." *St. Vladimir's Theological Quarterly* 53 (2009) 209–29.

———. "Liturgy and Theology: Rethinking the Relationship: Part 1: Setting the Stage." *Worship* 81 (2007) 46–68.

———. "Liturgy and Theology: Rethinking the Relationship: Part 2: A Different Starting Place." *Worship* 81 (2007) 141–69.

Ayres, Lewis. *Nicaea and Its Legacy: An Approach to Fourth-Century Trinitarian Theology.* Oxford: Oxford University Press, 2004.

Barnes, Michel René. "Augustine in Contemporary Trinitarian Theology." *Theological Studies* 56 (1995) 237–50.

———. "De Régnon Reconsidered." *Augustinian Studies* 26 (1995) 51–79.

Bartholomew, Craig. *Contours of the Kuyperian Tradition: A Systematic Introduction.* Grand Rapids: Eerdmans, 2017.

———. *Where Mortals Dwell: A Christian View of Place Today.* Grand Rapids: Baker Academic, 2008.

Bavinck, Herman. *Sin and Salvation in Christ.* Vol. 3 of *Reformed Dogmatics.* Edited by John Bolt. Translated by John Vriend. Grand Rapids: Baker Academic, 2006.

Beck, Richard. *The Slavery of Death.* Eugene, OR: Cascade, 2014.

Bernanos, George. *The Diary of a Country Priest.* London: Bodiswood, 1937.

Billings, Todd. *Remembrance, Communion, and Hope: Redisovering the Gospel at the Lord's Table.* Grand Rapids: Eerdmans, 2018.

Blake, William. "Auguries of Innocence." In *The Complete Poetry and Prose of William Blake,* edited by David V. Erdman, 490–96. Berkeley: University of California Press, 1982.

Boersma, Hans. *Heavenly Participation: The Weaving of a Sacramental Tapestry.* Grand Rapids: Eerdmans, 2011.

Bonhoeffer, Dietrich. *The Cost of Discipleship.* New York: Macmillan, 1961.

Bradshaw, Paul F. "Difficulties in Doing Liturgical Theology." *Pacifica* 11 (1998) 181–94.

———. *The Search for the Origins of Christian Worship: Sources and Methods for the Study of Early Liturgy.* Oxford: Oxford University Press, 2002.

———. *Two Ways of Praying.* Nashville: Abingdon Press, 1995.

Bratt, James. *Abraham Kuyper: Modern Calvinist, Christian Democrat*. Grand Rapids: Eerdmans, 1998.

———. *Dutch Calvinism in Modern America*. Grand Rapids: Eerdmans, 1984.

Brockes, Emma. "I Want to Be Famous." *The Guardian*, April 17, 2010. https://www.theguardian.com/lifeandstyle/2010/apr/17/i-want-to-be-famous.

Brown, David. *Discipleship and Imagination: Christian Tradition and Truth*. New York: Oxford University Press, 2000.

———. *God and Enchantment of Place: Reclaiming Human Experience*. New York: Oxford University Press, 2004.

———. *God and Grace of Body: Sacrament in Ordinary*. New York: Oxford University Press, 2007.

———. "A Sacramental World: Why It Matters." In *The Oxford Handbook of Sacramental Theology*, edited by Hans Boersma and Matthew Levering, 605. New York: Oxford University Press, 2015.

———. *Tradition and Imagination: Revelation and Change*. New York: Oxford University Press, 2000.

Browning, Elizabeth Barrett. *Aurora Leigh*. Reprint. Chicago: Academy Chicago Printers, 1979.

Bulgakov, Sergei. "Meditations on the Joy of the Resurrection." In *Ultimate Questions: An Anthology of Modern Russian Religious Thought*, edited by Alexander Schmemann, 299–304. New York: Holt, Rinehart, and Winston, 1965.

Caroll, Lewis. *Through the Looking Glass*. London: Macmillan, 1872.

Catholic Church. *General Instruction of the Roman Missal*. Washington DC: United States Catholic Conference, 2003.

Catholic Church. *The Order of Celebrating Matrimony*. Collegeville, MN: Liturgical, 2016.

Catholic Church. *Rite of Christian Initiation of Adults*. Washington DC: United States Catholic Conference, 1988.

Chan, Simon. *Liturgical Theology: The Church as Worshipping Community*. Downers Grove, IL: InterVarsity, 2006.

Chauvet, Louise-Marie. *Symbol and Sacrament: A Sacramental Reinterpretation of Christian Existence*. Translated by Patrick Madigan and Madeleine Beaumont. Collegeville, MN: Liturgical, 1995.

Cherry, Constance. *The Worship Architect*. Grand Rapids: Baker, 2010.

Chilton, Bruce. *A Feast of Meanings: Eucharistic Theologies from Jesus through Johannine Circles*. Leiden: Brill, 1994.

Chryssavgis, John. "The World as Sacrament: Insights into an Orthodox Worldview." *Pacifica* 10 (1997) 1–24.

Clerk, Paul De. "'Lex orandi, lex credendi': The Original Sense and Historical Avatars of an Equivocal Adage." *Studia Litugica* 24.2 (1994) 178–200.

Clough, Leonard. "Reflections on the 19th Quadrennial Conference." Unpublished Personal Report. February 2, 1964.

Congar, Yves. *Yves Congar: My Journal of the Council*. Collegeville, MN: Liturgical, 2012.

Counelis, James Steve. "Relevance and the Orthodox Christian Theological Enterprise: A Symbolic Paradigm on *Weltanschauung*." *Greek Orthodox Theological Review* 18 (1973) 35–46.

Crouch, Andy. "Abraham Kuyper Goes Pop." *Christianity Today* 58.8 (2014) 72.

Cuneo, Terence. *Ritualized Faith: Essays on the Philosophy of Liturgy*. Oxford: Oxford University Press, 2016.

Daniélou, Jean. "Les orientations présentes de la pensée religieuse." *Études* 249 (1946) 5–21.

de Lubac, Henri. *At the Service of the Church: Henri de Lubac Reflects on the Circumstances That Occasioned His Writings*. Translated by Ann Elizabeth Englund. San Francisco: Ignatius, 1993.

———. *Surnaturel: études historiques*. Paris: Desclée de Brouwer, 1991.

———. *Vatican Council Notebooks*. Translated by Andrew Sefanelli and Anne Englund Nash. Vol. 1. San Francisco: Ignatius, 2015.

Denysenko, Nicholas E. *Liturgical Reform after Vatican II: The Impact on Eastern Orthodoxy*. Minneapolis: Fortress, 2015.

Dix, Gregory. *The Shape of the Liturgy*. Westminster: Dacre, 1949.

Dunlap, David W. "An Episcopal Vicar Who Loved Avant-Garde Russian Art." *The New York Times*, November 14, 2012. http://www.cityroom.blogs.nytimes.com/2012/11/14/an-episcopal-vicar-who-loved-avant-garde-russian-art.

Eldridge, Michael. "The Mega-Church and Its Micro-Liturgy." Paper presented at Fuller Theological Seminary, Pasadena, CA, September 14, 2007.

Eliot, T. S. *Four Quartets*. Orlando: Harcourt, 1971.

Ellis, Christopher. *Gathering: A Theology and Spirituality of Worship in Free Church Tradition*. London: SCM, 2004.

Enquist, Roy. "We Have Been Given a Gift." *Communique: National Student Christian Movement Newsletter* 20.2 (1963) 1.

Evans, Sara M. *Journeys that Opened Up the World: Women, Student Christian Movements and Social Justice, 1955–1975*. New Brunswick, NJ: Rutgers University Press, 2003.

Evdokimov, Paul. *The Sacrament of Love: The Nuptial Mystery in the Light of the Orthodox Tradition*. Translated by Anthony P. Gythiel and Victoria Steadman. Crestwood, NY: St. Vladimir's Seminary, 1995.

Fagerberg, David W. "The Cost of Understanding Schmemann in the West." *St. Vladimir's Theological Quarterly* 53.2/3 (2009) 179–207.

———. *Theologia Prima: What Is Liturgical Theology?* Chicago: Hillenbrand, 2004.

———. "What is the Subject Matter of Liturgical Theology?" *Roczniki Liturgiczno-Homiletyczne* 57 (2010) 42.

Feckanin, Anna Marie. "Stand Up and Take Note." *The Russian Orthodox Journal* 36.1 (1964) 15–16.

Fisch, Thomas. "Schmemann's Theological Contribution to the Liturgical Renewal of the Churches." In *Liturgy and Tradition*, edited by Thomas Fisch, 4–6. Crestwood, NY: St. Vladimir's Seminary, 1990.

Flynn, Gabriel. "Introduction: The Twentieth-Century Renaissance in Catholic Theology." In *Ressourcement: A Movement for Renewal in Twentieth-Century Catholic Theology*, edited by Gabriel Flynn and Paul D. Murray, 1–19. New York: Oxford University Press, 2012.

For the Life of the World. Directed by Eric Johnson and David Michael Phelps. Monument, CO: Exploration Films, 2015.

Frank Herbert's Dune. Directed by John Harrison. TV Mini-Series. Sci-Fi Channel, 2000.

Galazda, Peter. "Schmemann Between Fagerberg and Reality: Towards an Agenda for Byzantine Christian Pastoral Liturgy." *Bollettino della Badia Greca di Grottaferrata, terza serie* 4 (2007) 7–32.

———. "Twentieth-Century and Contemporary Orthodox Sacramental Theology." In *The Oxford Handbook of Sacramental Theology*, edited by Hans Boersma and Matthew Levering, 441. Oxford: Oxford University Press, 2015.

Garklavs, Alexander. "In Memoriam: Fr. George Timko." *Jacob's Well.* 2001. http://jacwell.org/Spring_2001/fr_timko.htm.

Garrigou-Lagrange, Reginald. "La nouvelle théologie où va-telle?" *Angelicum* 23 (1946) 126–45.

Geertz, Clifford. "Thick Description: Toward an Interpretive Theory of Culture." In *The Interpretation of Cultures: Selected Essays*, by Clifford Geertz, 3–30. New York: Basic, 1973.

Gillquist, Peter E. *Becoming Orthodox: A Journey to the Ancient Christian Faith.* Ben Lomond, CA: Conciliar, 2010.

———. *Coming Home: Why Protestant Clergy are Becoming Orthodox.* Ben Lomond, CA: Ancient Faith, 2006.

Goheen, Michael W., and Craig Bartholomew. *Living at the Crossroads: An Introduction to Christian Worldview.* Grand Rapids: Baker Academic, 2008.

Gore, Michael, and Dean Pitchford. "Fame." Performed by Irene Cara. *Fame.* London: RSO Records, 1980.

Greeban, Ted, and Annette Milkovich. "St. Vladimir's Becomes a Permanent Home." *The Russian Orthodox Journal* 35.7 (1962) 8–11.

Green, Frederica Mathewes. *Facing East: A Pilgrim's Journey into the Mysteries of Orthodoxy.* San Francisco: HarperOne, 2006.

Guardini, Romano. *The Church and the Catholic, The Spirit of the Liturgy.* New York: Sheed and Ward, 1935.

Gutiérrez, Gustavo. *A Theology of Liberation: History, Politics, and Salvation.* Maryknoll, NY: Orbis Books, 1973.

Handler, M. S. "Students Heart Churches Chided on Inactivity in Changing World." New York Times, December 29, 1963.

Heckman, Theodore. "On the Silent Prayers of the Liturgy: A Conversation, Part Two." *Alive in Christ* 18.2 (2002) 24–36.

Heim, Mark S. *The Depth of Riches: A Trinitarian Theology of Religious Ends.* Grand Rapids: Eerdmans, 2001.

Hoffman, Lawrence A. *Beyond the Text: A Holistic Approach to Liturgy, Jewish Literature, and Culture.* Bloomington: Indiana University Press, 1987.

———, ed. *My People's Prayer Book: Traditional Prayers, Modern Commentaries.* 10 vols. Woodstock, VT: Jewish Lights, 1997.

"The Holy Spirit at the 19th Quadrennial." *The Christian Century*, March 18, 1964.

Hopkins, Gerard Manley. "God's Grandeur." In *"God's Grandeur" and Other Poems*, edited by Thomas Crofts, 15. New York: Dover Thrift Editions, 1995.

Humphrey, Edith M. *Grand Entrance: Worship on Earth as in Heaven.* Grand Rapids: Brazos, 2011.

Hütter, Reinhard. "Desiderium Naturale Visionis Dei—Est Autem Duplex Hominis Beatitudo Sive Felicitas: Some Observations about Lawrence Feingold's and John Milbank's Recent Interventions in the Debate over the Natural Desire to See God." *Nova et Vetera* 5 (2007) 81–183.

Irwin, Kevin. *Liturgical Theology: A Primer.* Collegeville, MN: Liturgical, 1990.

Jillions, John A. "Connecting Liturgy and Spirituality: Notes from Eastern Christian Experience." *Logos: A Journal of Eastern Christian Studies* 49 (2008) 91–108.

Johnson, Maxwell E. "Can We Avoid Relativism in Worship?: Liturgical Norms in the Light of Contemporary Liturgical Scholarship." *Worship* 74 (2000) 135–55.

———."Liturgy and Theology." In *Liturgy in Dialogue: Essays in Memory of Ronald Jasper,* edited by Paul Bradshaw and Bryan Spinks, 202–25. London: SPCK, 1993.

———. *The Rites of Christian Initiation: Their Evolution and Interpretation.* Collegeville, MN: Liturgical, 1999.

Johnson, Todd E. "Video: Monstrance for a New Millennium." *Prism* 9 (2002) 17–19.

Jungmann, J. A. *Pastoral Liturgy.* New York: Herder and Herder, 1962.

Kaethler, Andrew T. J. "Eucharistic Anthropology: Alexander Schmemann's Conception of Beings in Time." In *The Resounding Soul: Reflections on the Metaphysics and Vivacity of the Human Person,* edited by Eric Austin Lee and Samuel Kimbriel, 60–77. Eugene, OR: Cascade, 2015.

Kallaur, Constantine, and Arlene Kallaur. "How it Happened in Athens." *The Russian Orthodox Journal* 26.1 (1964) 9.

Kavanagh, Aidan. *On Liturgical Theology: The Hale Memorial Lectures of Seabury-Western Theological Seminary, 1981.* New York: Pueblo, 1984.

Kemper, Jeffrey M. "Liturgy Notes." *Liturgical Ministry* 8 (1999) 46–51.

Kerr, Fergus. *Twentieth-Century Catholic Theologians: From Neoscholasticism to Nuptial Mysticism.* Malden: Blackwell, 2007.

Kilmartin, Edward J. *Christian Liturgy: Theology and Practice.* Kansas, MO: Sheed and Ward, 1988.

———. *The Eucharist in the West: History and Theology.* Edited by Robert J. Daly. Collegeville, MN: Liturgical, 1998.

Klinghardt, Matthias. *Gemeinschaftsmahl und Mahlgemeinschaft: Soziologie und Liturgie früchristlicher Mahlfeiern.* Tübingen: Francke, 1996.

———. "'Nehmt und eßt, das ist mein Leib!' Mahl und Mahldeutung im frühen Christentum." In *Die Religionen und das Essen: Das Heilige im Alltag,* edited by P. Schmidt-Leukel, 37–69. n.p. München, 2000.

———, and Hal Taussig, eds. *Mahl und religiöse Identität im frühen Christentum.* Tübingen: Francke, 2012.

Kolb, Robert. "Luther on the Theology of the Cross." *Lutheran Quarterly* 16 (2002) 443–66.

Kuyper, Abraham. "Sphere Sovereignty (1880)." In *Abraham Kuyper: Centennial Reader,* edited by James D. Bratt, 461. Grand Rapids: Eerdmans, 1998.

———. *Be Near Unto God.* 2nd ed. Grand Rapids: Eerdmans, 1925.

———. *Lectures on Calvinism.* Reprint. Grand Rapids: Eerdmans, 1987.

———. *Our Worship.* Grand Rapids: Eerdmans, 2009.

———. "The Worship of the Reformed Church and the Creation of Its Service Book." *Calvin Theological Journal* 50 (2015) 59–61.

LaCugna, Catherine Mowry. *God for Us: The Trinity and Christian Life.* San Francisco: Harper, 1991.

Lamb, Matthew L. "Political Theology." In *The New Dictionary of Theology,* edited by Joseph A. Komoncak, et al., 772–73. Collegeville, MN: Liturgical, 1987.

Larin, Vassa. "Fr. Alexander Schmemann and Monasticism." *St. Vladimir's Theological Quarterly* 53.2–3 (2009) 301–18.

Lathrop, Gordon W. *Holy Ground: A Liturgical Cosmology*. Minneapolis: Fortress, 2003.

———. *Holy People: A Liturigcal Ecclesiology*. Minneapolis: Fortress, 1999.

———. *Holy Things: A Liturgical Theology*. Minneapolis: Fortress, 1998.

———. "New Pentecost or Joseph's Britches? Reflections on the History and Meaning of the Worship Ordo in Megachurches." *Worship* 72 (1998) 521–38.

Lazor, Paul. "Father Alexander Schmemann—A Personal Memoir." Presented at the 23rd Annual Fr. Alexander Schmemann Memorial Lecture, St. Vladimir's Seminary, Yonkers, NY, January 28, 2007. https://www.svots.edu/content/father-alexander-schmemann-personal-memoir.

Letham, Robert. *Through Western Eyes: Orthodoxy in Reformed Perspective*. Scotland: Mentor, 2010.

Lim, Swee Hong, and Lester Ruth. *Lovin' on Jesus: A Concise History of Contemporary Worship*. New York: Abingdon, 2017.

Lonergan, Bernard J. F. *Insight: A Study of Human Understanding*. Edited by Frederick E. Crowe and Robert M. Doran. Collected Works of Bernard Lonergan 3. Toronto: University of Toronto Press, 1992.

———. *Method in Theology*. Toronto: University of Toronto Press, 1971.

Louth, Andrew. "French Ressourcement Theology and Orthodoxy: A Living Mutual Relationship?" In *Ressourcement: A Movement for Renewal in Twentieth-Century Catholic Theology*, edited by Gabriel Flynn and Paul D. Murray, 495–507. New York: Oxford University Press, 2012.

———. *Modern Orthodox Thinkers: From the Philokalia to the Present*. Downers Grove, IL: InterVarsity, 2015.

McGowan, Andrew. *Ancient Christian Worship: Early Church Practices in Social, Historical, and Theological Perspective*. Grand Rapids: Baker, 2014.

———. *Ascetic Eucharists: Food and Drink in Early Christian Ritual Meals*. Oxford: Clarendon, 1999.

———. "'First Regarding The Cup . . .': Papias and the Diversity of Early Eucharistic Practice." *JTS* 46 (1995) 551–55.

———. "Naming the Feast: The Agape and the Diversity of Early Christian Meals." *Studia Patristica* 30 (1997) 314–18.

———. "Rethinking Eucharistic Origins." *Pacifica* 23 (2010) 173–91.

McGrail, Peter. *The Rite of Christian Initiation: Adult Rituals and Roman Catholic Ecclesiology*. Burlington: Ashgate, 2013.

Merton, Thomas. "Orthodoxy and the World." *Monastic Studies* 4 (1966) 107.

———. *Seven Storey Mountain*. New York: Harcourt and Brace, 1948.

Mettepenningen, Jürgen. "Nouvelle Théologie: Four Historical Stages of Theological Reform Towards Ressourcement (1935–1965)." In *Ressourcement: A Movement for Renewal in Twentieth-Century Catholic Theology*, edited by Gabriel Flynn and Paul D. Murray, 172–84. New York: Oxford University Press, 2012.

Metz, Johann Baptist. *Faith in History and Society: Toward a Practical Fundamental Theology*. Translated and edited by J. Matthew Ashley. New York: Crossroad, 2007.

———. *A Passion for God: The Mystical-Political Dimension of Christianity*. New York: Paulist, 1998.

Meyendorff, Paul. "Alexander Schmemann: Theologian of the Orthodox Liturgy." In *How Firm a Foundation: Leaders of the Liturgical Movement*, edited by Robert L. Tuzik, 300–6. Chicago: Liturgy Training, 1990.

———. "A Life Worth Living." *St. Vladimir's Theological Quarterly* 28.1 (1984) 4–6.

———. "The Liturgical Path of Orthodoxy in America in the 20th Century: Past, Present, and Future." *St. Vladimir's Theological Quarterly* 40 (1996) 43–64.

———. "Postscript: A Life Worth Living." In *Liturgy and Tradition*, edited by Thomas Fisch, 145–48. Crestwood, NY: St. Vladimir's Seminary, 1990.

Miller, Donald. "I Don't Worship God by Singing. I Connect With Him Elsewhere." *Storyline*, February 3, 2013. http://storylineblog.com/2014/02/03/i-dont-worship-god-by-singing-i-connect-with-him-elsewhere.

Miller, Matthew Lee. *American YMCA: Russian Culture: The Preservation and Expansion of Orthodox Christianity 1910–1940.* New York: Rowan and Littlefield, 2013.

Mills, William C. "Alexander Schmemann's *For the Life of the World*: A Retrospective." *Logos: A Journal of Eastern Christian Studies* 54.3/4 (2013) 199–228.

Moltmann, Jürgen. *God in Creation: A New Theology of Creation and the Spirit of God.* Translated by Margaret Kohl. Minneapolis: Fortress, 1993.

———. *The Spirit of Life: A Universal Affirmation.* Translated by Margaret Kohl. Minneapolis: Fortress, 1992.

Morrill, Bruce T. *Anamnesis as Dangerous Memory: Political and Liturgical Theology in Dialogue.* Collegeville, MN: Liturgical, 2000.

———. "Morrill, "Review of *Journals of Father Alexander Schmemann, 1973–1983.*" *Worship* 76.2 (2002) 187–89.

———. "Sacramental-Liturgical Theology Since Vatican II: The Dialectic Of Meaning And Performance." *Proceedings of the Catholic Theological Society of America* 67 (2012) 1–13. https://ejournals.bc.edu/ojs/index.php/ctsa/article/view/2173/2044.

———, and Don E. Saliers. "Alexander Schmemann: Liturgy as Life for the World." In *Primary Sources of Liturgical Theology: A Reader*, edited by Dwight W. Vogel, 52–54. Collegeville, MN: Liturgical, 2000.

Mudd, Joseph C. *Eucharist as Meaning: Critical Metaphysics and Contemporary Sacramental Theology.* Collegeville, MN: Liturgical, 2014.

Mulcahy, Bernard. *Aquinas's Notion of Pure Nature and the Christian Integralism of Henri de Lubac: Not Everything Is Grace.* New York: Peter Lang, 2011.

Myers, Fred. "National Council of Churches." Press Release. January 3, 1964.

Naugle, David. *An Introduction to Christian Worldview.* Downers Grove, IL: InterVarsity, 2017.

———. *Worldview: History of the Concept.* Grand Rapids: Eerdmans, 1982.

Niehbur, H. Richard. *Christ in Culture.* New York: Harper and Row, 1956.

Novak, Joseph. "Revaluing Prosper of Aquitaine in Contemporary Liturgical Theology." *Studia Liturgica* 44.1/2 (2014) 211–33.

O'Donnell, Emma. *Remembering the Future: The Experience of Time in Jewish and Christian Liturgy.* Collegeville, MN: Liturgical, 2015.

Ouellet, Marc. *Marriage and Sacrament of Love: A Theology of Marriage and the Family for the New Evangelization.* Grand Rapids: Eerdmans, 2015.

Papathansiou, Athanasius. "The Church as Mission: Fr. Alexander Schmemann's Liturgy Theology Revisited." *Proche-Orient Chretien* 60 (2010) 6–41.

Payton, James R., Jr. *Light from the Christian East.* Downers Grove, IL: InterVarsity, 2007.

Pilz, Sonja K. "The Earth Is the Eternal's and the Fullness Thereof: Jewish Food Culture and the Blessings before Eating." *Liturgy* 32.2 (2017) 18–20.

Pius XII, Pope. "*Humani generis.*" Encyclical delivered at St. Peter's, Rome, Italy, August 12, 1950. http://w2.vatican.va/content/pius-xii/en/encyclicals/documents/hf_p-xii_enc_12081950_humani-generis.html.

Plantinga, Cornelius, Jr. *Engaging God's World.* Grand Rapids: Eerdmans, 2002.

Plekon, Michael. "The Church, the Eucharist, and the Kingdom: Towards an Assessment of Alexander Schmemann's Theological Legacy." *St. Vladimir's Theological Quarterly* 40 (1996) 119–43.

———. "The Liturgy of Life: Alexander Schmemann." *Religions* 7 (2016) 127.

Possi, Janna. "History and Significance of Syndesmos." MDiv Thesis, St. Vladimir's Seminary, 1995.

Presbyterian Church. *Book of Common Worship.* Louisville: Westminster John Knox, 1993.

Reynolds, Philip L. *How Marriage Became One of the Sacraments: The Sacramental Theology of Marriage from Its Medieval Origins to the Council of Trent.* New York: Cambridge University Press, 2016.

Richardson, Mary N. S. "Guide to the National Christian Federation Archives." Yale Divinity School Library (January 2013). Unpublished.

Robertson, C. Alton. "*For the Life of the World*—But Why?" *The Methodist Woman.* Undated.

Rosenzweig, Franz. *The Star of Redemption.* Translated by William W. Hallo. Notre Dame: University of Notre Dame Press, 1985.

Ross, Melanie. "Joseph's Britches Revisited: Reflections on Method in Liturgical Theology." *Worship* 80.6 (2006) 528–50.

Ruth, Lester. "A Rose By Any Other Name." In *The Convictions of Things Not Seen,* edited by Todd E. Johnson, 33–52. Grand Rapids: Brazos, 2002.

———. "Lex Agendi, Lex Orandi: Toward and Understanding of Seeker Services as a New Kind of Liturgy." *Worship* 70 (1996) 386–405.

———. "Lex Amandi, Lex Orandi: The Trinity in the Most-Used Contemporary Christian Worship Songs." In *The Place of Christ in Liturgical Prayer: Trinity, Christology, and Liturgical Theology,* edited by Bryan Spinks, 342–59. Collegeville, MN: Pueblo, 2008.

"*Sacrosanctum Concilium.*" In *The Conciliar and Post Conciliar Documents,* edited by Austin Flannery, 1–36. Vol. 1 of *Vatican Council II.* New rev. ed. Northport, NY: Costello, 1998.

Saliers, Don E. "Theological Foundations of Liturgical Reform." *Studia Liturgica* 14.1/2 (2014) 112.

———. *Worship As Theology: Foretaste of Glory Divine.* New York: Abingdon, 1994.

Scheeben, Matthias Joseph. *The Mysteries of Christianity.* Translated by Cyril Vollert. New York: Crossroad, 2006.

Schillebeeckx, Edward. *Christ: The Christian Experience in the Modern World.* Translated by John Bowden. The Collected Works of Edward Schillebeeckx 7. London: Bloomsbury T&T Clark, 2014.

———. *Church: The Human Story of God.* Translated by John Bowden. The Collected Works of Edward Schillebeeckx 10. London: Bloomsbury T&T Clark, 2014.

———. *God the Future of Man.* Translated by N.D. Smith. The Collected Works of Edward Schillebeeckx 3. London: Bloomsbury T&T Clark, 2014.

Schmemann, Alexander. "Between Utopia and Escape." Lecture delivered in Greenville, DE, March 22, 1981. Transcribed from tape by Martha Ruth Hoffmaster. http://www.schmemann.org/byhim/betweenutopiaandescape.html.

———. *Church, World, Mission: Reflections on Orthodoxy in the West.* Crestwood, NY: St. Vladimir's Seminary, 1979.

———. *The Church Year: Sermons.* Vol. 2 of *Celebration of Faith.* Translated by John Jillions. Crestwood, NY: St. Vladimir's Seminary, 1997.

———. *Confession and Communion: Report to the Holy Synod of Bishops of the Orthodox Church in America.* Syosset, NY: Orthodox Church in America, 1972.

———. "Divine Worship and Time." In *Third Hour: In Memory of Helen Iswolsky.* New York: Third Hour Foundation, 1976.

———. "The East and West May Yet Meet." In *Against the World For the World: The Hartford Appeal on the Future of American Religion,* edited by Peter L. Berger and Richard John Neuhaus, 126–137. New York: Seabury, 1976.

———. "Ecclesiological Notes." *St. Vladimir's Seminary Quarterly* 11.1 (1967) 36.

———. *The Eucharist: Sacrament of the Kingdom of God.* Translated by Paul Kachur. Crestwood, NY: St. Vladimir's Seminary, 1987.

———. *For the Life of the World: Sacraments and Orthodoxy.* Rev. ed. Crestwood, NY: St. Vladimir's Seminary, 1973.

———. *Great Lent: Journey to Pascha.* Crestwood, NY: St. Vladimir's Seminary, 1974.

———. *I Believe: Celebration of Faith.* Vol. 1. Crestwood, NY: St. Vladimir's Seminary, 2003.

———. *Introduction to Liturgical Theology.* Crestwood, NY: St. Vladimir's Seminary, 1966.

———. *The Journals of Father Alexander Schmemann, 1973–1983.* Translated by Juliana Schmemann. Crestwood, NY: St. Vladimir's Seminary, 2000.

———. *Liturgy and Life: Christian Development through Liturgical Experience.* New York: Department of Religious Education of the Orthodox Church in America, 1993.

———. "Liturgy and Theology." *Greek Orthodox Theological Review* 17.1 (1972) 86–100.

———. *Liturgy and Tradition: Theological Reflections of Alexander Schmemann.* Edited by Thomas Fisch. Crestwood, NY: St. Vladimir's Seminary, 1990.

———. "The Mission of Orthodox Youth." *Concern: Orthodox Concern for the Life of the World* 3.4 (1968) 5–9.

———. "Missionary Imperative in the Orthodox Tradition." In *The Theology of the Christian Mission,* edited by Gerald H. Anderson, 250–57. New York: McGraw Hill, 1961.

———. *O, Death, Where is Thy Sting?* Translated by Alexis Vinogradov. Crestwood, NY: St. Vladimir's Seminary, 2003.

———. *Of Water and the Spirit: A Liturgical Study of Baptism.* Crestwood, NY: St. Vladimir's Seminary, 1974.

———. "Orthodoxy and Mission." *St. Vladimir's Seminary Quarterly* 3.4 (1959) 41–42.

———. "Pasternak" *Volnaia Mysl* 3 (1961) 18–25.

———. "Prayer, Liturgy, and Renewal." *Greek Orthodox Theological Review* 14.1 (1969) 7–16.

———. "Problems of Orthodoxy in America: II. The Liturgical Problem." *St. Vladimir's Seminary Quarterly* 8.4 (1964) 164–85.

———. "Problems of Orthodoxy in America: III. The Spiritual Problem." *St. Vladimir's Seminary Quarterly* 9.4 (1965) 171–93.

———. "Worship in a Secular Age." *St. Vladimir's Theological Quarterly* 16.1 (1972) 6–7.

Schmemann, Juliana. *My Journey with Father Alexander.* Montreal: Alexander, 2006.

Schmidt, Leigh Eric. *Holy Fairs: Scotland and the Making of American Revivalism.* 2nd ed. Grand Rapids: Eerdmans, 2001.

Scola, Angelo. *The Nuptial Mystery.* Translated by Michelle K. Borras. Grand Rapids: Eerdmans, 2005.

Searle, John R. *The Construction of Social Reality.* London: Penguin, 1995.

Segundo, Juan Luis. *The Sacraments Today.* Translated by John Drury. A Theology for Artisans of a New Theology 4. Maryknoll, NY: Orbis, 1974.

Senn, Frank. *The Witness of the Worshipping Community.* Mahwah, NJ: Paulist, 1993.

———. "Worship Alive: An Analysis and Critique of 'Alternative Worship.'" *Worship* 69 (1995) 194–224.

Sitton, Claude. "Birmingham Bomb Kills 4 Negro Girls In Church; Riots Flare; 2 Boys Slain." *The New York Times,* September 15, 1963. http://www.nytimes.com/learning/general/onthisday/big/0915.html.

Smith, James K. *Awaiting the King: Reforming Public Theology.* Grand Rapids: Baker Academic, 2017.

———. *Desiring the Kingdom: Worship, Worldview, and Cultural Formation.* Grand Rapids: Baker Academic, 2009.

———. *Imagining the Kingdom: How Worship Works.* Grand Rapids: Baker Academic, 2013.

———. *Letters to a Young Calvinist.* Grand Rapids: Brazos, 2010.

———. *You Are What You Love.* Grand Rapids: Baker Academic, 2015.

Sobrino, Jon. *No Salvation Outside the Poor: Prophetic-Utopian Essays.* Maryknoll, NY: Orbis, 2008.

Soelle, Dorothee. *Suffering.* Translated by Everett R. Kalin. Philadelphia: Fortress, 1975.

Spearin, Carole. "For the Life of the World: Ecumenical Conference." *Ecumenical Notes* 3.4 (1964) 8.

Spezzano, Daria. *The Glory of God's Grace: Deification According to Saint Thomas.* Ave Maria, FL: Sapientia, 2015.

Spinks, Bryan D. "From Liturgical Theology to Liturgical Theologies: Schmemann's Legacy in Western Churches." *St. Vladimir's Theological Quarterly* 53.2/3 (2009) 231–49.

———. "Sacramentology." In *The Cambridge Dictionary of Christian Theology,* edited by Ian A McFarlane, et al. Kindle edition. Cambridge: Cambridge University Press, 2011.

St. Vladimir's Orthodox Theological Seminary. *A Legacy of Excellence 1938–1988.* Crestwood, NY: St. Vladimir's Seminary, 1988.

Standing, Guy. *The Precariat.* New York: Bloomsbury Academic, 2011.

Stanford University. "National Conference on Religion and Race." Martin Luther King, Jr. Encyclopedia. https://kinginstitute.stanford.edu/encyclopedia/national-conference-religion-and-race.

Stevenson, Kenneth. *Nuptial Blessing: A Study of Christian Marriage Rites.* London: SPCK, 1982.

Stout, Harry. *The Divine Dramatist: George Whitefield and the Rise of Modern Evangelicalism.* Grand Rapids: Eerdmans, 1991.

Swift, Jonathan. *Gulliver's Travels.* Oxford: Oxford University Press, 1989.

Taft, Robert F. "The Liturgical Enterprise Twenty-Five Years After Alexander Schmemann (1921–1983): The Man and His Heritage." *St. Vladimir's Theological Quarterly* 53.2/3 (2009) 163–64.

———. "Mrs. Murphy Goes to Moscow: Kavanagh, Schmemann, and the 'Byzantine Synthesis.'" *Worship* 85.5 (2011) 386–407.

Tanner, Norman P. *Decrees of the Ecumenical Councils.* Washington, DC: Georgetown University Press, 1990.

Tarasar, Constance J., ed. *Orthodox America 1794–1976: Development of the Orthodox Church in America.* Syosset, NY: The Orthodox Church in America, 1975.

Taylor, Barbara Brown. *An Altar in the World: Finding the Sacred Beneath our Feet.* London: Canterbury Norwich, 2009.

———. *Leaving Church: A Memoir of Faith.* San Francisco: HarperSanFrancisco, 2006.

Taylor, Charles. *A Secular Age.* Cambridge, MA: Belknap, 2007.

Temple, William. *Christus Veritas.* London: Macmillan, 1924.

Torrance, Thomas F., ed. *Theological Dialogue Between Orthodox and Reformed Churches.* 2 vols. Edinburgh: Scottish Academic Press, 1985.

Turner, Paul. *Inseparable Love: A Commentary on The Order of Celebrating Matrimony in the Catholic Church.* Collegeville, MN: Liturgical, 2017.

Uhls, Y. T., and P. M. Greenfield. "The Value of Fame: Preadolescent Perceptions of Popular Media and Their Relationship to Future Aspirations." *Developmental Psychology* 48.2 (2012) 315–26.

Unamuno, Miguel de. *The Tragic Sense of Life.* Translated by J. E. Crawford Flitch. New York: Dover, 1954.

Vagaggini, Cipriano. "Lex Orandi Lex Credendi: Reciprocal Influences between Faith and Liturgy." In *Liturgical Dimension of the Liturgy: A General Treatise on the Liturgy,* 529–41. Translated by Leonard Doyle and W. A. Jurgens. Collegeville, MN: Liturgical, 1976.

Vander Zee, Leonard J. *Christ, Baptism, and the Lord's Supper: Recovering the Sacraments for Evangelical Worship.* Downers Grove, IL: InterVarsity, 2004.

Veenhof, Jan. *Nature and Grace in Herman Bavinck.* Translated by Albert M. Wolters. Sioux Center, IA: Dordt College Press, 2006.

Vincie, Catherine. *Celebrating Divine Mystery: A Primer in Liturgical Theology.* Collegeville, MN: Liturgical, 2009.

Vogel, Dwight W. *A Lukan Book of Feasts.* Nashville: OSL, 2018.

———, ed. *Primary Sources of Liturgical Theology: A Reader.* Collegeville, MN: Pueblo, 2000.

Ward, Graham. *Reformed Sacramentality.* Collegeville, MN: Liturgical, 2018.

Webber, Robert. *Ancient-Future Worship: Proclaiming and Enacting God's Narrative.* Grand Rapids: Baker, 2008.

———. *Worship Old and New.* Grand Rapids, MI: Zondervan, 1982.

———, and Donald Bloesch. *The Orthodox Evangelicals.* Nashville: Thomas Nelson, 1978.

White, James. "How Do We Know It Is Us?" In *Liturgy and the Moral Self: Humanity at Full Stretch Before God,* edited by Bruce T. Morrill and E. Byron Anderson, 55–65. Collegeville, MN: Liturgical, 1998.

———. *Protestant Worship: Traditions in Transition.* Louisville: Westminster John Knox, 1989.

Willson, Cory. "The Heart of Worship: Learning to Inhabit the Liturgy for the Life of the World." *Reformed Worship* 123. 2017. https://www.reformedworship.org/article/march-2017/heart-worship.

Witvliet, John D. "The Institutional Church and the Mission of Calvin College: Some Redemptive Possibilities for the Way Forward." *Calvin College Spark* (2007) 18–21.

Wolterstorff, Nicholas. *The God We Worship: An Exploration of Liturgical Theology.* Grand Rapids: Eerdmans, 2015.

———. *Hearing the Call: Liturgy, Justice, Church, and World.* Grand Rapids: Eerdmans, 2011.

———. *Until Justice and Peace Embrace.* Grand Rapids: Eerdmans, 1983.

Wood, John Halsey. *Going Dutch in the Modern Age: Abraham Kuyper's Struggle for a Free Church in the Nineteenth-Century Netherlands.* Oxford: Oxford University Press, 2013.

Wordsworth, William. "The World is Too Much With Us." In *The Classic Hundred Poems: All Time Favorites,* edited by William Harmon, 113. 2nd ed. New York: Columbia University Press, 1998.

Zimmerman, Joyce Ann. *Liturgy and Hermeneutics.* Collegeville, MN: Liturgical, 1999.

———. *Liturgy as Language of Faith: A Liturgical Methodology in the Mode of Paul Ricoeur's Textual Hermeneutics.* Lanham, MD: University Press of America, 1988.

———. *Liturgy as Living Faith: A Liturgical Spirituality.* Scranton, PA: University of Scranton Press, 1993.

———. "Liturgy Notes." *Liturgical Ministry* 8 (1999) 107.

———. "Paschal Mystery—Whose Mystery? A Post-Critical Methodological Reinterpretation." In *Primary Sources of Liturgical Theology: A Reader,* edited by Dwight W. Vogel. Collegeville, MN: Liturgical, 2000.

Made in the USA
Columbia, SC
29 January 2022

54990929R00150